Baseball and the Music of Charles Ives

A Proving Ground

Timothy A. Johnson

The Scarecrow Press, Inc.
Lanham, Maryland • Toronto • Oxford
2004

SCARECROW PRESS, INC.

Published in the United States of America
by Scarecrow Press, Inc.
A wholly owned subsidary of The Rowman & Littlefield Publishing Group, Inc.
4501 Forbes Boulevard, Suite 200
Lanham, Maryland 20706
www.scarecrowpress.com

PO Box 317
Oxford
OX2 9RU, UK

British Cataloging in Publication Information Available

Library of Congress Cataloging-in-Publication Data

Johnson, Timothy A., 1961–
  Baseball and the music of Charles Ives : a proving ground /
Timothy A. Johnson
    p.   cm.
  Includes bibliographical references and index.
  ISBN 0-8108-4999-2 (pbk. : alk. paper)
    1. Ives, Charles, 1874–1954—Themes, motives.   2. Music and
baseball.   3. Baseball—United States—History.   I. Title.
ML410.I94J64 2004
780'.92—dc   2004000189

Printed in the United States of America

$\otimes$[TM] The paper used in this publication meets the minimum requirements
of American National Standard for Information Sciences—Permanence of
Paper for Printed Library Materials, ANSI/NISO Z39.48-1992.
Manufactured in the United States of America.

To my family

Contents

Musical Examples and Illustrations

MUSICAL EXAMPLES

vii

ILLUSTRATIONS

Preface

I first became aware of the music of Charles Ives when I was a junior in high school, at Pinkerton Academy in Derry, New Hampshire. I decided to do a music-related project for my U.S. history class, and in researching music in the United States, naturally, I found numerous references to Charles Ives. The nearby city library had a few recordings of his music, which I immediately borrowed, and my first experience with the music of Charles Ives totally changed my sound world. Ives was the most radical composer that I had experienced, and I could not understand the string quartet I heard, with its mixture of extremely dissonant and purely traditional styles. However, instead of being turned off by my lack of comprehension, I decided that I wanted to be able to understand this music that was so highly regarded in the literature I had read, yet was impenetrable to me. As I continued to listen to as many Ives recordings as I could find, I became enamored with everything I heard, but especially the chromatically altered melodies and new harmonic contexts Ives invented for the hymn tunes I learned on my mother's knee.

My interest in Ives continued through college and graduate school, and I thought I might like to do my dissertation on Ives. But my advisor dissuaded me, saying, "Ives is a tough nut to crack!" Instead I focused my attention on John Adams's music and wrote the first dissertation on this highly regarded contemporary composer's work. A few years after graduation, after some further work with minimalism, I returned my attention to my first love, the music of Charles Ives.

Like my interest in Ives, my interest in baseball began early; I have been fascinated with baseball for as long as I can remember. As a youth I avidly played Wiffle Ball with my brothers in our yard, played hardball in the "Grasshopper" and Minor Little Leagues since age seven, and happily warmed the bench on the school team. I now attend baseball games as often as I can in various minor league ballparks in central New York—Syracuse (Triple-A International League), Binghamton (Double-A Eastern League), Auburn (Single-A New York–Penn League), Elmira (independent Northeast League), and Ithaca (New York Collegiate Baseball League), and I stand up and cheer in my living room whenever my Boston Red Sox beat the New York Yankees on television. Given my long-standing admiration for the music of Charles Ives and enthusiasm for the game of baseball, it is a pleasure to be able to combine both of these lifelong passions in this book.

I would like to thank Ithaca College for its generous support for the writing of this book, in the form of a Summer Grant for Faculty Research, an Academic Project Grant, and released time granted by the Center for Faculty Research and Development. I also thank my colleagues for their encouragement and friendship. I would like to thank my former student Adam Ramsey, who helped set the musical examples. Excerpts from the unpublished writings of Charles Ives, held at the Charles Ives Papers at the Yale University Music Library, are reprinted by kind permission of the American Academy of Arts and Letters, the copyright owner.

Portions of some of the material in this book were presented first at the Fifteenth Cooperstown Symposium on Baseball and American Culture (Cooperstown, New York, June 11–13, 2003), at the Twenty-Sixth Annual Meeting of the Society for Music Theory (Madison, Wisconsin, November 5–9, 2003), at the Fourteenth Annual Conference of Music Theory Midwest (Bloomington, Indiana, May 16–17, 2003), at the special meetings of the Society for American Music at *Toronto 2000: Musical Intersections* (Toronto, Ontario, November 1–5, 2000), and at several informal presentations at Ithaca College. I am grateful for the suggestions and encouragement I received from conference attendees at these meetings. I especially appreciate being made to feel welcome in the community of baseball scholars and the community of Ives scholars. In this regard, I especially would like to thank Timothy Wiles, who went out of his way to assist me and make me feel comfortable at the Hall of Fame Library and at the symposium, and H. Wiley Hitchcock, who treated me like a seasoned Ives scholar instead of the rookie that I was, and who offered a number of very useful comments. I would like to thank James Sinclair, who helped me locate some essential sources and offered his encouragement. Special thanks go to J. Peter Burkholder for his invaluable advice and his continual support of this project.

Baseball is about fathers and sons. And Doris Kearns Goodwin has shown that this special connection extends also to fathers and daughters as well as to mothers and sons in her delightful book, *Wait Till Next Year*

(Simon & Schuster, 1997). Unfortunately, as the present book will show, Ives and his father did not share this common bond through baseball. In contrast, I am very pleased to say that I have been privileged to enjoy sharing an interest in baseball with my whole family.

I dedicate this book to my wife, Anne Marie, who scores the games she attends with me, and I thank her for curtailing birding expeditions when I needed to work, for giving me a boost when I needed one, and for her timely advice and suggestions; to my niece, Abby, a hard-hitting softball player and budding clarinetist; to my nephew, Russell, who is keeping the family hope alive with his four-seam fastball and whom I was privileged to accompany on his first trip to the Hall of Fame (though I spent the whole time in the library while he and my brothers toured the museum); to my sister-in-law, Lynda, who plays Rotisserie baseball and knows the value of a five-tool player; to my brother, Corey, a baseball simulation fanatic who can keep track of multiple leagues at a time, both real and imaginary; to my brother, Nyles, a physical education teacher and coach who, along with Corey, reminds me almost every day how much I love baseball; to my dad, who still plays on the church softball team at seventy-two years of age and tells me his remarkably high batting average whenever he gets the chance; to the memory of my mom, who took her cuts in the batting cage on a family outing, even after her terminal cancer diagnosis in the last year of her life; and to the memory of my grandfather, Ralph, who marked a triple for me in his scorebook (which he kept at every one of my games when I was a youngster), and who stood by his judgment when questioned later. Inwardly, we both knew it was a three-base error through the first baseman's legs, but he gave this eleven-year old ballplayer the thrill of an extra-base hit, duly recorded, and a lasting memory!

Introduction

Charles Ives saw baseball as a fondly remembered childhood game, a competitive prep-school sport, and the national pastime; however, he also considered baseball to be an art form that was an essential component of his life, rather than merely an unconnected amusement. In the postface to his private publication of his *114 Songs*, he observed "that an interest in any art-activity from poetry to baseball is better, broadly speaking, if held as a part of life, or of a life, than if it sets itself up as a whole."[1] Thus, to understand Ives's life as an artist fully, the *art* of baseball must be included as a part of the examination, and baseball must be viewed as a serious component of his life rather than merely as a game. Ives's love for baseball permeated his entire life and was an inseparable component of his character and of his music. Baseball was a place where Ives felt he could prove himself as a man, and baseball provided a framework within which he could build new musical ideas.

This book will discuss the significance of baseball in Ives's life and music. From playing the game as a boy to his use of baseball analogies in his later writings, baseball remained a lifelong fascination. In order to better understand this attraction, this book explores Ives's interest in baseball as a player, as a fan, and as a composer.

Chapter 1 outlines some pertinent aspects of Ives's life and music in an attempt to familiarize readers generally with the primary subject of this book. The chapter shows that Ives's life and music were distinctly American in numerous ways, and therefore his interest in baseball, "the American pastime," was simply another manifestation of his Americanism. The chapter discusses Ives's reputation as an eccentric individualist, his career as a professional insurance executive in New York City, and his role as an experimental composer. The chapter describes his music as being in an American idiom, but at the same time with a heavy European influence, and it discusses his habit of borrowing from the music of other composers (as well as his own) in his compositions. The chapter concludes with an assessment of the reception and impact of his music.

Chapter 2 presents a chronology of the history of baseball over the course of Charles Ives's life. Significant events, prominent players, team development, and important rule changes show how the game of baseball changed dramatically between 1874 and 1954. Ives was born almost contemporaneously with the birth of major league baseball, and he died before New York–area teams began to relocate to the west coast, changing both the scope and appearance of the national pastime significantly.

Chapter 3 examines the role of baseball in Ives's hometown of Danbury, Connecticut, to show how Ives grew up along with the sport in late nineteenth-century small-town life. Whereas chapter 2 focuses on the national game, this chapter explores baseball on a more local and specifically small-town level. This exploration includes an investigation of Ives's attitude, and nineteenth-century society's collective attitude, toward baseball as a source for masculine identity—an important aspect of Ives's view of himself and a topic that constantly appears in his writings. In addition to discussing Ives's boyhood involvement in baseball, this chapter examines the role of baseball during the remainder of Ives's life—including his participation in baseball at Hopkins Grammar School, his exclusion from sports at Yale University, and his continued fascination with the game as revealed especially by his baseball analogies in his writings and by the memorabilia with which he surrounded himself in his studio at home as he aged.

After this discussion of baseball in Ives's life, the next two chapters present detailed analytical and contextual treatments of Ives's musical compositions pertaining to baseball. Chapter 4 examines his completed baseball-related pieces. Each of the five pieces for various instruments and ensembles pertains more to Ives's memories of baseball, played as a boy, than to major league baseball. On the other hand, chapter 5 focuses on his unfinished sketches—material he intended for two orchestral works and a chamber work. In both of these chapters, the baseball references in these compositions are described in relation to contemporary accounts of the game, and the ballplayers that Ives immortalizes, in order to come to a better understanding of the musical techniques he developed to depict these baseball references. In addition, detailed analyses of these pieces will shed further light on the baseball references in these works.

Finally, in the last chapter of this book, chapter 6, the compositional techniques employed in Ives's baseball-related music are isolated, and their use in his later music is described, in an effort to show how Ives took these picturesque musical ideas and adopted them into his own musical language. His pieces and unfinished sketches about baseball, among other works, provided a vehicle for him to invent new musical ideas in reference to specific baseball situations that he could use as part of his basic musical language in later pieces. The chapter isolates certain compositional techniques found in the baseball sketches and shows how these techniques reappear in some of Ives's later pieces. The chapter also describes precisely how the musical material found in a single baseball-related sketch relates directly to several derivative works.

Nearly every major biographical source on Ives mentions his participation in baseball and other sports. Of only two photographs included in the "Ives" article in the *New Grove Dictionary of American Music*, one of these shows Ives in his Hopkins Grammar School baseball uniform.[2] Henry and Sidney Cowell, Ives's first biographers, note his participation in football and baseball and recount that "when people fussed over his music and asked what he played, he liked to reply gruffly: 'Short-stop!'"[3] Frank Rossiter discusses Ives's participation in baseball in connection with issues of gender identity—issues to be explored further in this book, as mentioned earlier.[4] Jan Swafford describes Ives's own participation in sports in some detail.[5] However, he mentions only one of Ives's baseball sketches (*Rube Trying to Walk 2 to 3!!*) in the context of his late-night compositional habits, and Swafford misidentifies the reference to Rube by repeating an attribution made by John Bowman and Joel Zoss—which I will dispute later in this book.[6] Stuart Feder, on the other hand, whose "psychoanalytic biography" delves deep into the developing persona of Charles and his relationship with his father, seems to recognize the importance of baseball and other sports in the development of Ives's character. He discusses the apparent dichotomy between baseball and music that "became a source of open friction between father and son," and Feder also explores the connection between sports and Ives's gender identity.[7]

The only thorough discussion of Ives's music about sports that I have encountered appears in Thomas Giebisch's *Take-off als Kompositionsprinzip bei Charles Ives*.[8] This book provides detailed commentary on all of Ives's "take-offs," including the baseball pieces and sketches that are explored in this book. However, although Giebisch discusses the nature and significance of Ives's involvement and interest in sports, he does not attempt to explain the baseball references cited by Ives in these works.

A brief treatment of Ives's sporting interests and his music about sports appears in a *Sports Illustrated* article by Jay Feldman.[9] This article summarizes the musical activity in four of Ives's baseball-related pieces and provides a more detailed treatment of the most frequently cited sports piece in the literature, the *Yale-Princeton Football Game*. This earliest sports piece by Ives, and the only one devoted to football, was composed in 1899, shortly after he completed his studies at Yale, based on a game he attended with his future brother-in-law, David Twichell.[10] It includes many sonic aspects of a football game, including fight songs and cheers, and it musically depicts several football plays and formations—such as the wedge, where the notes on the page depict the wedge-shaped formation of the football team to protect the ball carrier as he runs down the field behind them; and the quarterback scramble, represented by a twisting and rambling trumpet line.[11] Football was certainly one of Ives's favorite sports, especially during his youth. However, baseball, which rose dramatically in popularity around the turn of the twentieth century, remained Ives's best-loved sport and continued to engage him throughout his life.

The New England poet Donald Hall said: "Baseball, because of its continuity over the space of America and the time of America, is a place where memory gathers."[12] In many ways Ives's involvement in baseball reflects this sentiment. Ives's interest in baseball spans the space of America: Although his baseball experiences cover only seventy miles and two states in terms of distance, his experiences ranged from amateur and semiprofessional ball in his hometown of Danbury to the professional level in the country's largest and most baseball-active major league city. The poet's idea of baseball's "continuity over the space of America" primarily suggests this union of disparate locales through their common, though distinct, relationship to the sport. Baseball's "continuity over the time of America" is also represented by Ives's life, which paralleled the growth of the game in a number of ways. Finally, baseball gathered in the mind of Ives as manifested by his music, writings, and memorabilia. As Charles Ward noted, "The importance of memories and visual reflections on the past cannot be underestimated in Ives' music."[13] Thus, these baseball memories and visual representations of the sport are important tokens of Ives's interest in baseball and, as this book claims, are intertwined with his music. As a composer, Ives evoked memories of his American upbringing through his incorporation of old American tunes and his depiction of American subjects, including baseball; moreover, nearly all of his music is about *memories* of his own or his father's boyhood. Therefore, both baseball and Charles Ives's music, indeed, are places "where memory gathers."

Chapter 1

An American Sport—An American Composer

THE AMERICAN PASTIME

Walt Whitman, the world-renowned nineteenth-century American poet, remarked that "base-ball is our game: the American game: I connect it with our national character."[1] About a century later, television news anchor Tom Brokaw saw similarly strong associations between baseball and America:

> Baseball has an enduring connection to the idea of America because it is really an extension of democracy. It is played in all of the levels of our national life, from small town to big city, from the reservation to the barrio, from manicured suburban fields to rocky pastures.[2]

For both of these commentators, baseball is uniquely associated with America—an essential part of our national character and a reflection of the widespread diversity of American life.

Charles Ives was emphatically an American composer. His music has a recognizably American flair, and he was a distinctly American character. His attraction to baseball surely was influenced by its role in American society as well as his own American ideals. To illustrate this aspect of Ives's life, this chapter begins with a brief overview of his position in American culture. Although Ives is hailed widely as the father of American music, this recognition came slowly for a number of reasons.[3] His approach to composition was influenced strongly by his individuality as well as his American character. An eccentric businessman who composed on the side, Ives's unconventional musical experiments, though important and fascinating in their own right, prepared him for his eventual success as a composer. The first part of this chapter presents some distinctive aspects of his eccentric and individualistic personality, provides a summary of his career as a businessman, and describes some of his experimental music. Each of these areas of his life reflect important aspects of his attitude toward baseball. The final section of this chapter presents an outline of Ives as a composer, and specifically as an American composer, in order to provide some context for the extended discussions of Ives's music about baseball that appear later in this book. This overview of Ives as a composer includes a discussion of his cultivation of a truly American musical idiom, a description of the influence of European music and ideas upon his music, and an account of the reception of his music, historically and by his peers, as well as his impact on later composers.

Ives's pieces that involve baseball cannot be appreciated fully without at least some understanding of the sort of music for which Ives is well known. In general, this chapter aims to provide sufficient background material about Ives's life and music so that his involvement in baseball and his music about baseball may be viewed as integral parts of his life and work, rather than merely as isolated events and experiments.

AN AMERICAN CHARACTER

Eccentric Individualism

The nature of Charles Ives's character is paradoxical and difficult to pin down. His life was wonderfully diverse: He excelled in both his vocation, insurance, and in his avocation, music. He was an accomplished musician and an excellent ballplayer; he was a loner as a composer, yet at the same time a devoted family man; and he held individualistic and unyielding views on a variety of subjects, ranging from the circumstances under which America should enter into war to the position his nephew should play on the baseball team. He composed in his spare time, yet he created music that later would be hailed as innovative masterpieces of the twentieth century. Finally, he was an affluent businessman who rallied for a direct, voter-oriented system of government and a more even distribution of personal resources.[4] Thus, in more ways than one, Ives may be perceived as an idiosyncratic eccentric, one who shaped his own approach to life and to music as circumstances warranted. And for the most part, his music may be viewed in the same light—as "willfully eccentric."[5]

While his music remained of primary importance to him, he pursued business, rather than music, following in the footsteps of the distinguished Ives family of Danbury, Connecticut, rather than in the footsteps of his father, the Danbury bandmaster. Jan Swafford claimed that when Ives was born,

> all over Danbury the question was doubtless raised in one form or another: Would this new Ives follow that musical quirk of his father's, or would he be a real Danburian and a real Ives? Which is to say: business, both feet.[6]

In a sense he would follow both paths. As he began to prepare for a career in business at Yale, he also pursued music studies with the composer Horatio Parker. It appears that he would have relished an opportunity to gain recognition as a composer and to devote his entire life to music, but only if he could do so without compromising his creative independence. However, when Ives experienced what he perceived as a major setback as a composer, he decided to abandon any hopes of a career in music, instead devoting himself to his budding business career.

Ives gave up the idea of being a professional musician and composer in 1902, just a few years after leaving Yale and arriving in New York. His cantata, *The Celestial Country*, was performed and his own reaction to the mixed success of the event was swift and severe. Stuart Feder recounted the chain of events that led to Ives's abandonment of music:

> Ives could scarcely suppress an enthusiasm that harbored the hope that the première might direct the course of his professional life. . . . It was a serious and professional effort which merited critical reviews in the press. Both *The New York Times* and the *Musical Courier* noted Ives's apprenticeship as Parker's student, and the reviews, while hardly effusive, were politely complimentary. . . . Their reviews, while critical, were honorable but Ives seemed inordinately discouraged by the response. It was not simply the post-performance let-down which left the ever-moody Ives vulnerable to depression. It seems likely that his fantasied expectation went far beyond what could reasonably be expected from a performance of a neophyte's non-secular work.
>
> In any event, Ives's response seemed radically disproportionate to the outcome. Within the week following the performance, Ives gave notice of his resignation from the Central Presbyterian [as church organist] and six weeks later played his last Sunday service. He never again held any professional position related to music, nor did he earn any money from his music during his lifetime. In addition, there was not a single public performance of any of his music during the next fourteen years.[7]

To say that Ives overreacted to the reviews would be an immense understatement. The review in the *Musical Courier* closed by noting that "an audience completely filling the church listened with expressions of pleasure, and at the close the composer was overwhelmed with congratulations, which he accepted in modest fashion."[8] It seems certain that the event was hardly a failure. But Ives turned inward as a composer, though fortunately he continued to compose avidly. He simply ceased to seek public attention for his work, until much later in his life when the stakes were lower— when his livelihood and the financial security of his family would not depend upon his success. Ironically, his decision to resign as organist seemed to open up new opportunities for his development as a composer.[9] Because he no longer sought an audience, he was free to explore radically experimental works as he composed in his spare time, including some pieces that depict baseball situations and players to be discussed in this book. He no longer held the expectation that his music would be performed in a public setting—neither church nor concert hall.

His response to this public performance of his music both reflects and contributed to his eccentricity. Many composers would have been pleased with the reviews (some might have been thrilled to have been reviewed by the *New York Times* in the first place). However, even composers who thought that the performance and the critics' reactions fell short of their ideals likely would have redoubled their efforts and continued to pursue their compositional goals, fueled by their ambition to improve upon this first endeavor. But Charles Ives's choice to abandon music, just as it began to garner public attention, reveals aspects of his idiosyncratic character. At the same time as this abandonment of professional musicianship, Ives was able to create highly personal music that needed to appeal to no one except himself and his own eccentric tastes. On the other hand, while he no longer sought *public* performance opportunities, he still maintained a need for approval from his peers, and he tried out many of his most experimental compositions informally for his personal friends and associates.

When Ives's music finally began to be recognized in the musical community at large, in the second quarter of the twentieth century, his reputation as an individualist and as an eccentric grew rapidly. At that time the appeal of his music rested simultaneously on both the highly original and complex musical constructions and on the very childlike nature of his borrowings from hymns and popular nineteenth-century tunes. In this sense, he was both an extreme modernist and a pure nostalgist. Even today he is viewed in these contradictory terms, as Leon Botstein concluded:

Charles Ives—despite significant recent contributions to the analytic and biographical literature—has lost little of his aura as an anomalous, enigmatic, and paradoxical figure in the history of music. He remains hard to place in a larger historical narrative and explanatory framework. His music has been judged to be ahead of its time and uniquely innovative, rebellious, and modernist. At the same time, Ives's personal history, writings, and use of vernacular materials in his music—the sources and strategy of quotation and borrowing—reveal an allegiance to a past remembered, a pre-modern, nineteenth-century America.

Cultural nostalgia and aesthetic innovation seem inextricably but counterintuitively linked in Ives's music.[10]

These features also are related directly to Ives's interest in baseball. Ives's "cultural nostalgia" is reflected in his nostalgia for baseball that he maintained throughout his life, as will be discussed in chapter 3, and his "aesthetic innovation" contributed to his development as a composer by means of his attempts to invent ways to depict baseball through music, as will be discussed in chapters 4, 5, and 6.

Professional Businessman

Ives's rejection of a musical career in 1902 paved the way for him to continue to develop what would become an overwhelmingly successful business career. Feder referred to the premiere of Ives's *Celestial Country* as "a magical shot in the dark to provide fate with the opportunity to favor him richly."[11] Beginning in 1898, after graduation from Yale, Ives commenced his business career, near the bottom of the ladder, as a clerk with a large New York insurance firm, Mutual Life.[12] Eventually, Ives and his business partner, Julian Myrick, formed their own insurance agency, initially called Ives & Co. and later Ives & Myrick, and rose dramatically in the industry.[13] Ives and Myrick prospered in part because of their business savvy and their complementary skills, but mostly because they were in the right place at the right time and because they created business opportunities for themselves concurrently with a continuous upswing in the economy. Along with this new prosperity, many citizens began to see insurance as a necessity to secure their financial independence regardless of their income level. The main challenge for insurers was to document the level of need for each potential insured, and Ives proved to be very adept in rising to this challenge. He was responsible for creating the materials that would be used to document the appropriate amount of insurance for any individual, and he was responsible for helping to train the sales agents who would convince these individuals of their insurance needs.[14]

Moreover, Ives's approach to insurance advertising and his invention of the concept of estate planning were extremely innovative for the time.[15] He was a kind of surrogate salesman, knowledgeable and skilled in the art of selling insurance and able to communicate his expertise to the agency's representatives, but lacking the capacity to sell insurance himself.[16] Although this combination of abilities may seem ironic, as an executive and co-owner of his own agency, he certainly would not have been expected to sell insurance door to door in any case. In addition, the more public responsibilities of managing the agency could be handled with aplomb by his partner. The pair of young businessmen complemented

each other and formed a ideal partnership, where each had his own responsibilities that matched his own strengths.[17]

The partnership flourished, and the pair became wealthy. Ives &
Myrick grossed over $450 million in a span of twenty-one years, and Ives
netted approximately $1.8 million himself in the first twelve years alone.[18]
This sum is equivalent to roughly $30 million in 2002 dollars, and Swaf-
ford claimed that Ives made even more money in the second half of his career. The success of Ives's business pursuits created a comfortable life for
him and his family and afforded him the luxury of setting aside time for
composing, and eventually for promoting his compositions through self-
financed publication.

On the surface it may appear that Ives's pursuit of business over music
was a sacrifice intended to free his music from outside influences. However, some authors, such as Rossiter, have observed other objectives:

> It was by no means a clear-cut case of his defending his artistic integrity
> against the commercial "lily pads"; there were positions in the music profes-
> sion that would not have required him to compose for money, positions that
> would have given him more time for his private experimentation than the
> business world ever did. The real choice lay between barely eking out a liv-
> ing at music or taking his chances on the business world, with all the advan-
> tages that his Yale associations would give him in business. Ives chose the
> second alternative and became a wealthy man. It would be perverse to call
> his action a sacrifice.[19]

His success as a businessman also afforded him ample time for baseball.
With the absence of lighted stadiums, baseball was a game played before
primarily white-collar fans. While he and his friends were trying to establish themselves in business during the first decade of the twentieth
century, they also pursued a spectator sport designed for businessmen of
a stature to which they aspired. Baseball was a fitting entertainment for a
young urban businessman like Charles Ives, and he recorded his attendance at baseball games in a unique and surprising way—by means of
musical compositions, to be described in chapter 5. These and other experimental pieces had a profound effect on his development as a composer, as suggested in the following section and as discussed in detail in
chapter 6.

Musical Experiments

Ives's independence as a composer, unconnected with a community of
peers and unaffected by a need to respond to an audience's desires, had a
profound influence on his experimentalism. Certainly, his father's own
musical experiments conducted when Charles was a boy were a primary

influence upon his later predilection to create his own experimental music. But the lack of public audiences with whom to share his musical compositions also influenced his experimental attempts. Much of Ives's music may seem tame compared to the music of other composers of the first part of the twentieth century, yet his experimental music is what most distinguishes him from his peers. He continued to experiment compositionally throughout his career, and many of his experiments featured new or unusual techniques and devices—such as polytonality, whole-tone scales, clusters, wedge-shaped counterpoint, planing, nontertian harmony, palindromes, serialism, atonality, and quarter tones.[20]

Many of these experiments bear descriptive titles and sometimes include programmatic commentary within the music to identify the location or incident being depicted.[21] The importance of programs for Ives's music cannot be overstated. Ives once asked, "Is not all music program music?"[22] With their clearcut references to true-life events, or even fictional situations, real people, and actual places, these pieces offer a familiar point of entry into Ives's music for many listeners and serve as autobiographical entries in a musical scrapbook of Ives's life.[23] From Feder's viewpoint these programmatic pieces provide "a knothole in the fence through which one may observe what is happening within . . . that permits us to relate his private life to the notes on the page in a manner that few, if any, other composers have allowed."[24] (The incidental "knothole" reference to baseball only enhances the picturesque nature of Feder's point.)

In creating these pictorial and autobiographical pieces, Ives's experimental music also reveals a connection with Americanism. Ives was mainly reflecting the average American experience in his experimental music, including his baseball pieces, and in this way he connected his musical depictions of events from the common life with his strong American democratic ideals.[25]

But his experimental pieces alone would be insufficient to cement his reputation as a great American composer of the twentieth century. Only the synthesis of his disparate ideas in some of his later works would establish his reputation as an outstanding composer. However, late in the first decade of the twentieth century and in the second decade, he began harnessing some of the ideas from his experimental music and began to create fully worked-out pieces of more lasting significance. Thus, his experimental pieces hold the threads that helped to sew up his reputation as a composer.

The highly influential experimental music that resulted from his isolation as a composer was not the only result of this isolation. Rossiter noted several implications of Ives's musical seclusion:

Ives was deeply affected by the widespread feeling in his culture that high art and the artists who made it were somehow unmanly, undemocratic, and

un-American. His inner acceptance of this value judgment about art and
artists made it difficult for him even to reach the point where he could accept
himself as an artist. . . . Ives's artistic isolation, then, arose not only from his
desire to write experimental music, but also from his desire to be a good
American; this is perhaps the central paradox of his career as a composer.[26]

The following section addresses this paradox by discussing Ives's status
as a composer of distinctively *American* music.

AN AMERICAN MUSIC

American Idiom

While Ives's American character is evident in his individualism, his direct involvement in capitalism through his career in business, and his musical experimentalism, as discussed earlier in this chapter, Ives established
himself as an American *composer* by following a path that was completely
contrary to that of his American contemporaries. Other American composers of his time did not stray far from their European models. Although
Ives's music certainly was crafted from European molds, he depicted
American ideals and scenes, used American music as source tunes upon
which to base his music, and created innovative musical resources
through which to explore these American ideas in his music. Thus, his activities as an experimental composer—where he invented new compositional strategies and techniques, in part, in order to represent American
subjects—are directly tied to his status as an American composer.[27]

The connection between his Americanism and his experimentism is
commutative. His Americanism stems from his strong individualistic feelings of his music as distinct from its European forerunners. Therefore, his
experimentism reflects his American separatist ideals. At the same time
his experimentism largely took the form of creating images, through music, of American scenes, characters, and beliefs. Among these images are
musical depictions of baseball, the national pastime.

The association of Ives's music with American ideals was purely inten-
tional on Ives's part; Ives was very aware of his distinct role as an American composer. He deliberately set out to create music that truly could be
called *American*—not just music by an American composer, but American
music, distinct from its European precedents, because it represents the
American human experience.[28] Thus, in basing some of his music on the
manifestly American experience of playing baseball, Ives was reaching for
a more lofty goal than merely attempting to depict certain baseball situations and ballplayers through music. These pieces, though many are incomplete, are at the very core of his philosophical approach to music,

whereby he attempted to create truly American music in part by depictions of what he saw as American activities.

For many listeners Ives's identity as an American is deeply embodied in the music itself. For example, upon hearing Ives's *Concord Sonata* at its premiere performance, noted music critic Lawrence Gilman heard a distinctly American composer, as reflected in his review of the first performance of this piece:

> This sonata is exceptionally great music—it is, indeed, the greatest music composed by an American, and the most deeply and essentially American in impulse and implication. It is wide-ranging and capacious. It has passion, tenderness, humor, simplicity, homeliness. It has imaginative and spiritual vastness. It has wisdom and beauty and profoundity, and a sense of the encompassing terror and splendor of human life and human destiny—a sense of those mysteries that are both human and divine.[29]

Although the program of this work is conspicuously American—through its portrayal of four prominent and distinctive figures from American literature—Gilman found that its American qualities went beyond its programmatic aspects.

Burkholder, likewise, found Ives's voice to be specifically American, particularly in his borrowings of American vernacular tunes:

> His music was American because he sought to communicate the experience of Americans like himself, especially their experience of and emotional involvement with the music of their everyday life. He wrote art music because it was the only type of music that could serve as a framework for conveying such experiences, the only type of music that could coordinate such a breadth of styles and materials within a unified discourse, the only type of music one listened to with rapt attention, so that the composer could talk in the music itself about his experience with music. But the music he talked about was the music of his own people, the people of small-town and urban America in the northeast in the late nineteenth century. Through his music, Ives celebrates what American music means to Americans.[30]

Thus, Ives established himself not only as a composer of American music in the classical tradition but also as a classically trained and classically oriented composer whose work might connect with American citizens through allusion to music that would be familiar and meaningful to them.

Ives's aspirations to be a distinctly American composer began quite early in his career; however, he reached his greatest synthesis of his American ideals, his experimental creativity, and his understanding of traditional musical discourse in his more mature works. This compositional maturity was nurtured by his wife, Harmony, who became a lifelong companion, muse, inspiration, and personal champion. (*Harmony*—what name could be more perfect for a composer's spouse, especially for a composer who is notorious for loving *dissonance*?) She admired him as a composer when no one else did, and she believed in what he was trying to accomplish through music. She also influenced his work greatly, though she always seems to have remained in the background. Burkholder claimed that

> the question of an American music had been one of long-standing concern for Ives. . . . Ives had written compositions incorporating American tunes all along. . . . But Harmony had a sense of idealism about what it meant to be an American that seemed to hit a responsive chord in Charles Ives, and his music from the period of his engagement to the end of his career as a composer is both more directly about American life and literature and more idealistic at its core. . . . Harmony's faith in the idealism underlying her country deepened and intensified Ives's similar feelings and led him to represent instances of that idealism and events from American life in his music.[31]

Harmony's encouragement of music that depicted American events also suggests that she would have supported Charles's attempts to depict baseball through music.

Ives's paradox, between being an American composer and being a composer like other Americans, was especially complex because he, like other American composers of the time, worked within a style that drew primarily from earlier Europeans. Despite all of the factors that distinguish his music, both from his peers and from his European predecessors and contemporaries, he still wrote music in the classical tradition, adopting its melodic tendencies, harmonic vocabulary, rhythmic devices, textural framework, and formal designs. Ives took European traditions and transformed them into an American sound by incorporating experimental elements along with his use of American vernacular music, in many cases combined to depict scenes and ideas from Americana.[32] With a few exceptions he did not undertake to write in the style of the popular music of his day, though he certainly derived many ideas and often used material from these sources. However, despite these clear American allusions, the music of the European masters had a profound effect on Ives's music.

European Influence

Just as Ives as an American composer was heavily influenced by European music, baseball, which grew to become the American pastime, developed from European models. Although a popular myth of the origin of baseball is that it was invented, outright, by Abner Doubleday in Cooperstown, New York—the present home of the Baseball Hall of Fame for that reason—the sport actually developed from earlier European games, such as an English game called rounders, which is still played in England by school children of all ages.[33] The Abner Doubleday myth was perpetuated by a special commission assembled in 1908 in order to document the origin of baseball. However, the commission was tainted by the special interests of several individuals, and the commission erroneously concluded that baseball derived from "One old cat," an American children's game played with a ball and a bat (which figures prominently in one of Ives's pieces, as discussed in chapter 4), rather than from earlier games involving a ball and a bat.[34] However, in establishing a fabricated American birthplace and birthright for baseball, what the commission failed to see is that baseball was truly and purely an American game because of its own course of development, to be outlined in chapter 2, regardless of its origins. A simple game with a ball and a bat, rounders or any number of other potential forerunners, was transformed by Americans into a national obsession, completely superceding its rudimentary models. Creating a myth to cement its reputation as an American sport was unnecessary.

A similar myth surrounds Charles Ives's status as an American composer. However, Burkholder attempted to rectify this erroneous viewpoint by documenting Ives's debt to his European predecessors:

> Charles Ives is widely regarded as a uniquely American composer, one who turned his back on the European tradition of art music and struck out in a new direction. He is seen as a forerunner of the avant-garde whose music anticipated most of the important developments of the century. . . . Yet this picture of Ives is incomplete and misleading. . . . Ives was as much a part of the European tradition of art music as were Mahler, Debussy, Schoenberg, Bartók, Stravinsky, Berg, and the other progressive composers of his time. Like them, Ives sought to write music that would find a place in the permanent repertoire beside the masterpieces of the eighteenth and nineteenth centuries.[35]

Thus, the importance of Ives's music lies not only in his experimental ideas and his borrowing of American vernacular sources but also in the classical molds into which he poured his musical ideas. Similar to baseball, Ives's status as an American composer is not diminished by his use of European idioms, but it is established by his own unique American approach to those same idioms.

In some ways even Ives's attempts to recreate local scenes, sights, and sounds (including those of baseball) through music was a manifestation of nineteenth-century European Romantic ideals.[36] Ives embraced the Romantic conception of the composer as the supreme creator of a sound world into which to draw the listener as a story is told through music. To Ives, musical works were not generic constructions crafted out of common musical materials, as for instance in the time of J. S. Bach. Instead, Ives adopted a more personal approach to the compositional experience, probably derived mainly from his composition teacher at Yale, Horatio Parker, an American composer whose music was primarily in the European Romantic style.[37] At the same time, Ives's personal approach to composition included an extensive use of borrowed musical materials, and although the use of borrowed materials likewise was derived from his European Romantic forebearers, Ives borrowed and alluded to more tunes, more often, and to a larger variety of sources than perhaps any composer in the history of music.[38] His habit of borrowing is a distinctive feature of his style, despite its origin as a common feature of the music of his time. And his borrowings, by and large, had a definitively American impact.

Borrowing

Ives's use of borrowing is one of the most distinctive features of his music. These borrowings of music that is for the most part relatively simple and diatonic appear paradoxically in a highly developed and intricate musical style. It would be easy to misunderstand these borrowings as foreign elements that intrude upon his music, distracting from his personal compositional style. As suggested by Henry and Sidney Cowell,

> Ives, however, uses musical reminiscence as a kind of stream-of-consciousness device that brings up old tunes with their burden of nostalgic emotion. These snatches of hymns, minstrel songs, college songs, fiddle tunes, and so on, sewn through the fabric of his music, are never left as quotations only; certain fragments soon develop a life of their own, and some aspect of their musical structure is always made the basis of the piece's subsequent behavior.[39]

Thus, the borrowed tunes are actually an integral part of his compositional style and often serve as the foundation upon which his music is built.[40] Ives's use of borrowing in his baseball music is integral both musically and extramusically, as will be discussed in chapters 4 and 5. In these pieces, as well as many of his other works, Ives exploited nostalgic references represented by the tunes he borrowed, and he also created new associations for these references by means of the new contexts into which he placed these tunes.[41] And these associations became as much a part of Ives's music as the tunes themselves; Ives viewed the tunes he borrowed as treasures from which he could draw to enrich his musical palette.[42]

More often than not, the borrowings Ives used in his music seem to evoke the sentiments of an earlier time—Ives's boyhood or the imagined boyhood of his father.[43] Ives's music in general harbors a yearning for the past—or nostalgia, perhaps the single most important affect in Ives's work.[44] As Ives looked back to the baseball experiences of his youth in some of his pieces to be discussed in chapter 4, he was reexperiencing what were some of the most affirming experiences of his life—when he could prove himself as a man on the ballfield. In many cases Ives's borrowings of earlier music helped serve as a vehicle to transport the listener, and (perhaps more importantly) Ives himself, into an earlier time.

Reception and Impact

Ives's biographical background, experimental leanings, American aspirations, and penchant for borrowing combined to produce some pieces that are now widely regarded as masterpieces of twentieth-century music. Henry and Sidney Cowell claimed that Ives was one of the four great composers of the first half of the twentieth century (along with Schoenberg, Stravinsky, and Bartók).[45] Yet, or perhaps consequently, his music fails to conform to a single compositional style.[46] While Ives's music is diverse in style and draws from the work of other composers, it is at the same time unique.

Ives's music was slow in gaining recognition, but both its reception and its impact have been substantial, though late. Until he published the *Concord Sonata* at his own expense and distributed copies personally to musicians, composers, critics, libraries, and publishers, his music was virtually unknown. At first only a few enthusiasts, mainly avant-garde composers who sensed Ives as a similar spirit, began to recognize Ives's talent. For example, Henry Cowell, a well-known composer himself, actively promoted Ives's music by publishing some of his music in the periodical Cowell founded, *New Music*; by arranging performances and recordings of Ives's music (all of which was underwritten financially by Ives); and by coauthoring Ives's first biography. Soon other more mainstream musicians, rather than just the experimentalists who were first attracted to Ives's music, began to see the value and importance of his music, not just as bizarre experiments but as true masterpieces worthy of serious consideration.[47] For example, Aaron Copland, one of the foremost American composers of the twentieth century, fostered much interest in Ives's music by presenting seven songs at Yaddo, an influential contemporary music colony near Albany, New York, during a festival in 1932.[48]

Most important among Ives's champions was "Lawrence Gilman, music critic for the *New York Herald Tribune*, whose review of Kirkpatrick's [*Concord Sonata*] recital . . . brought Ives to national prominence almost overnight."[49] Eventually, well-established and highly placed conductors, including Leonard Bernstein and Leopold Stokowski, began to premiere some of Ives's symphonic works. Significant awards, feature articles in magazines, enthusiastic reviews, and other prominent performances soon followed.[50]

Sidney Cowell claimed in 1969: "Today the music of Charles Ives has a much wider audience in the United States than that of the other three major composers of the first half of the twentieth century. Just why, it is not easy to say."[51] Swafford, extending the comparison even further historically, declared that "if Ives is not the peer of his musical heroes Bach, Beethoven, and Brahms, he belongs in their company."[52]

Clearly, Ives continued the Romantic tradition of earlier European composers, but at the same time his version of Romanticism included a new American sound ideal and a new approach to beauty. According to Henry and Sidney Cowell:

> To achieve beauty in accordance with accepted standards does not interest Ives, because he believes that people's notions of beauty depend upon what they are used to, or whatever will bother them least. . . . Ives prefers to put his hearers' ears to work, and he points out that the ear can take in much more than it is used to if it must. To concern one's self with beauty . . . diverts one from the search for spiritual strength and integrity. Besides, "dissonances," [Ives] says, "are becoming beautiful."[53]

Embracing dissonance, not as a novel and abstract compositional device to explore but as a way of creating fresh new beauties, and "obsessed by the past, he wrote a music of the future."54

Chapter 2

Constant Change—The Growth of Major League Baseball

THE NATIONAL GAME

A chronology of major league baseball aligned with significant events in Ives's life, to be presented in this chapter, will reveal how drastically the game changed over the course of Ives's life and even in short periods of time during Ives's lifetime. This account will provide some historical context for the remainder of the book, where more specific relationships between Ives's life and baseball are drawn. Finally, the chapter will suggest that, in many ways, the growth of major league baseball paralleled Ives's own growth as an individual.

This chronology is very selective: Some important events in the history of baseball are included while others are overlooked. No attempt has been made to give a complete history; instead, this chronological treatment strives to show major events and changes in the game during Ives's life. This historical overview highlights the individual achievements of certain players and the collective efforts of outstanding teams. It tracks the successes and failures of major league baseball in certain cities and the successes and failures of the leagues into which these teams were organized. Although your favorite team may appear only briefly, if at all, the teams to which Ives primarily was exposed figure prominently in this account. This chronology provides insights on specific changes to rules, to ballparks, or simply to the way major league baseball was played over the years, and it shows how certain events affected the development of the game.

While all of these changes were occurring, as major league baseball developed, Charles Ives experienced similar growth. When the game was young, major league baseball teams came and went annually, and the rules were changing constantly: Baseball was in its childhood, and Charles Ives was likewise a child during this time. As baseball began to move through periods of turmoil toward stability, Ives similarly grew into adolescence. And as baseball developed into the national pastime, Ives similarly developed into a mature individual, seeking to establish himself in the insurance industry and at the same time to compose meaningful music. Finally, as baseball aged into its "golden years" and achieved unprecedented popularity, Ives retired from the insurance business, began organizing and publishing his music, and finally came to be recognized and acclaimed as an extraordinarily gifted composer. Ives lived long enough to see the racial integration of the game, and he died just as teams began to scatter from their concentration in the established urban centers of the northeastern quadrant of the country to the Midwest, and soon California, thus altering the reach and impact of game—but making the national pastime truly *national* in scope.

CHRONOLOGY

1870s

In 1874, the year of Charles Ives's birth, major league baseball was a very different game than it is now in the twenty-first century.[1] Professional baseball had begun only three years earlier, and both the rules of the game and the performance of the players on the field varied significantly from when baseball later achieved its more familiar status as the national pastime. Noted baseball historian Bill James described this early version of the game:

> Baseball in 1870 resembled fast-pitch softball more than any other, including modern baseball. The pitch was delivered underhand from a distance of 45 feet [rather than 60 feet, 6 inches, as in the modern game]. The rules required a stiff arm so as to limit velocity, but the rules were not tightly enforced, and pitchers could move the ball in there pretty good with a flick of the wrist. The ball was not wound as tight as it would be later; it was a handmade ball of yarn with a cover on it, not terribly standard in size or shape, and to hit the thing 400 feet would probably have been impossible.[2]

One of the most significant differences between baseball at the turn of the twenty-first century and baseball in the 1870s was the large number of errors in the earlier version of the game, especially due to the lack of the fielder's glove, which did not become commonplace equipment until the mid-1880s.

> But it was baseball; you wouldn't have any trouble recognizing it. The games were a little long and the scores were a little high, but it was baseball. The

skills in demand were the same, the personalities were the same, the arguments were the same.[3]

The winningest pitcher, Al Spalding, won 52 games in 1874.[4] His team—the Boston Red Stockings, which later became the Boston Braves and eventually the Atlanta Braves—likewise won a season-best 52 games. Spalding won *all* of the games for his first-place team. His 65 complete games in 617 innings pitched with a 1.92 earned run average would be the envy of the entire pitching staff of every major league team at the turn of the twenty-first century. In 2000, to provide some perspective, no major league *team* had more than 16 complete games by all of its pitchers combined, and the Boston Red Stockings in 1874 played less than half (71) of the number of games played by present-day major league teams (162). The winningest pitcher in 2000—Tom Glavine of the Atlanta Braves, the same franchise for which Spalding earlier pitched—had 21 wins in 241 innings, a far cry from Spalding's 52 wins in 617 innings. On the other hand, Spalding in 1874 was not afraid to let the hitters put the ball into play: He struck out only 31 opposing batters and walked only 19. However, at the time, it took nine balls to record a walk, rather than the present-day four.[5] Of course, throwing underhand at a lower rate of speed obviously took a lesser toll on the arm, so his complete game and win totals reflect very different standards. Nevertheless, he was a remarkably successful pitcher and was in high demand. Spalding soon changed his "hosiery" from red to white by signing with the Chicago White Stockings (which later became the Cubs, rather than their present-day namesakes, a newer team called the White Sox), and he later founded a sporting goods company that bears his name and continues to be a premier enterprise in the marketplace today.

When Ives was born, there was only one professional major league—the National Association of Professional Baseball Players. Eight teams competed in the association that year, and the number of games played by each club was by no means regular. Major cities of the eastern United States were well represented, but some smaller communities supported teams as well. The total list of teams in order by number of wins in 1874 included the Boston Red Stockings, Mutual of New York, Athletic of Philadelphia, Philadelphia Pearls, Chicago White Stockings, Atlantic of Brooklyn, Hartford Dark Blues, and Lord Baltimores. Of these eight teams, only two still play in the major leagues—Boston (Braves) and Chicago (Cubs)—however, major league teams currently reside in each of these cities except Brooklyn and Hartford.[6] If Ives had been born earlier, he might have been able to attend his first major league baseball game as a child in Hartford, Connecticut, only sixty miles or so from his hometown of Danbury. But major league baseball only lasted three years in Hartford, and Ives would have to wait until he arrived in New York as a recent college graduate before he could see a major league game in person.

A year later, while Ives was still just a baby, the National Association saw its demise at the end of the 1875 season. The Lord Baltimores, who finished last the previous year, had disbanded a few games before the end of that season. Although they were replaced by six new teams in a newly formed league, only one of these newcomers finished the season (the St. Louis Brown Stockings, unrelated to the later St. Louis Browns). Unfortunately, the New Haven Elm Citys, where Ives would attend Yale University about twenty years later, failed miserably and folded in the middle of the season with a 7–40 record. A total of 17,500 seats were sold in New Haven that year—just under the *average* attendance *per game* in Milwaukee in 2000, and apparently not enough to sustain a major league baseball team even in 1875.

Pitching continued to be strong in the league: Joe Borden (of the Philadelphia Phillies, previously known as the Pearls and unrelated to their present-day namesakes) pitched the first no-hitter in professional baseball history in July 1875. The long ball still was not a factor at this time, which is not a surprise given the inferior construction of the ball by today's standards. Jim O'Rourke, a Boston outfielder, led the league with six home runs that year, one more than he socked in the previous season. By contrast, the turn of the twenty-first century seems to have found no limit for home runs, with decades-old records being broken practically every year.

Although the National Association had been short-lived (lasting only five years), the league that replaced it in 1876 became immortal. The National League of Professional Baseball Clubs (known today simply as the National League) was founded in the year of Ives's second birthday. Although he was too young to realize it, some of the players who would later play in this league would have a profound impact on Ives's life and on his development as a composer (as will be detailed in chapter 5). This league—often referred to as the "senior circuit," due to its early formation—has enjoyed longevity in a constantly changing sport. It opened with six teams retained from the National Association along with two additional independent teams that already had been strongly established, the Cincinnati Red Stockings and the Louisville Grays. Along with the birth of this new league, the number of games played by each team stabilized, and all teams played out their seasons.

1880s

By 1880, when Ives would turn six years old, the National League was in full swing, but teams still came and went with remarkable frequency.

For example, the Cincinnati Red Stockings, for rejecting a league rule that outlawed alcohol and Sunday ballgames, were removed from the league after five successful seasons. In addition, the Providence Grays, who finished no lower than third place for seven seasons in a row, had to disband later when they fell to fourth place in 1885 and attendance declined as a result by about 25 percent. Only Boston and Chicago were able to continue operation through the entire decade.

Cap Anson—the hard-hitting Chicago first baseman, who ultimately was elected to the Hall of Fame on the very first ballot—began to excel offensively in 1880. He led the league in runs batted in (RBI) for three consecutive years and for seven of the next ten years. A major blight on his record, however, occurred in the mid-1880s when he refused to play against black ballplayers; as a strong influence in the game and as the player-manager of the White Stockings, his unyielding stance had the inauspicious outcome of delaying the integration of major league baseball for almost seventy years.[7]

Major league baseball became a much rougher sport in the 1880s, during the time that Ives began playing ball as a local amateur himself. Insults and obscenities directed at the opposition were commonplace, and fights between players, between fans, and between players and fans erupted from time to time. However, baseball mainly was played in a reasonable and responsible manner. Bill James claimed that "the average man in the 1880s, while rougher than today, was not a thug, nor was the average ballplayer helpless to defend himself. Many games were marked by the best sportsmanship on all sides."[8]

The New York Gothams began play in the National League in 1883. This would become the primary ballclub that Ives would watch when he arrived in New York around the turn of the twentieth century. Ives would know the team as the New York Giants, and this is the same team that continues today as the San Francisco Giants.

In 1884 the number of home runs hit by the league-leading hitters increased dramatically over previous years. Four Chicago players each hit more than twenty home runs—Ned Williamson (27), Fred Pfeffer (25), Abner Dalrymple (22), and Cap Anson (21)—while the next highest total was only 14 by Dan Brouthers of the Buffalo Bisons. The previous high mark for home runs in the league barely had reached double digits (10 by Buck Ewing of New York in 1883). This seemingly remarkable turnaround in power hitting was actually the result of a rule change and a short fence in Chicago. These home runs would have counted as doubles in previous seasons, because balls hit over the unusually short fences in Chicago were counted as doubles until 1884, when the same hits were counted as homers. Moving to a new field the following year brought the numbers back down somewhat, but the fence distances were still comparatively short, and Chicago led the league in home runs for eight consecutive seasons. The importance of the home field advantage in this case is best summed up by the career of Williamson, who hit fifty-seven of his career sixty-four home runs at home—and only seven on the road.[9]

In 1887, the year of Ives's thirteenth birthday, an earlier baseball rule that allowed a batter to request a high or low pitch was eliminated. Although the number of strikes required for a strikeout changed for a single year to four strikes in 1887, "three strikes and you're out" was otherwise a fixture of the sport nearly from its beginnings. An important and lasting change in equipment occurred during this year as well. Instead of a stone, iron, or wooden home plate, the invention of a two-part rubber home plate, a white piece fastened atop a slightly larger black piece so that the black edges show around the upper white portion, standardized the form of the plate that remains in use today.[10]

The rules changed every year during the 1880s as the two leagues attempted to find the proper balance between hitting and pitching. The number of balls required for a walk was reduced gradually from nine in the 1870s to eight in 1880, seven in 1881, six (in the recently formed American Association) in 1886, five (in both leagues) in 1887, and finally four (the number that has endured to this day) in 1889.

1890s

Bill James vividly described the primary changes to baseball in this decade:

> Dirty. Very, very dirty. The tactics of the eighties were aggressive; the tactics of the nineties were violent. The game of the eighties was crude; the game of the nineties was criminal. The baseball of the eighties had ugly elements; the game of the nineties was just ugly.[11]

Spiking, grabbing, tripping, fighting, shoving, spitting, and punching were conventional elements of the game on the ballfield. This kind of aggression likely would only have made the game appeal to Ives more, given his generally combative nature and his perceived need to establish his own masculinity through the sport, as will be discussed in chapter 3.

In 1892 the National League increased from eight to twelve teams after absorbing some of the better teams from the American Association, which folded the previous year, leaving only one league again. Although attendance had remained strong overall in the American Association, the instability of individual teams, a few of which folded each year, made continuation of the league impractical.

In 1893 when Charles Ives enrolled at Hopkins Grammar School in order to prepare himself academically for college and began pitching for the school team, the pitcher's rubber in the major leagues was moved back to the present distance of 60 feet, 6 inches. Before this time, the pitching distance changed almost constantly as major league baseball continually tried to achieve a proper balance between pitching and hitting. This rule change was intended to promote offense, since the greater distance required to pitch the ball also would make it easier to hit. The batters responded as expected, and the league batting average increased—from .245 in 1892 to .280 in 1893 and to a highpoint of .310 in 1894. Batting averages remained generally at this higher level for the remainder of the decade.

In 1898, when Ives completed his studies at Yale University and moved to New York City, Wee Willie Keeler, who later would figure prominently in one of Ives's musical sketches, led the league in batting average and hits for the second consecutive season, batting at the unthinkably high percentage of .424 with 239 hits in 1897 and batting .385 with 216 hits in 1898. At that time, Keeler played for the Baltimore Orioles of the National League (unrelated to the present-day team of the same name) before he moved to the New York area, where this remarkably gifted hitter caught Ives's attention, as will be discussed in chapter 5.

1900s

In 1900 the National League returned to its pre-1892 format of eight teams. Four of the twelve teams were dropped: the Washington Senators, Louisville Colonels, Baltimore Orioles, and Cleveland Spiders—each of which had been founded originally in the defunct American Association. The following year a new professional baseball league—which would endure, unlike the earlier counterparts to the National League—was formed when the American League (formerly a minor league called the Western League) unilaterally declared itself a major league. Founded twenty-five years after the National League, this newer league is still referred to as the "junior circuit." Despite some initial disputes with the senior circuit over territorial rights and the reserve clause (which limited player movement between teams), this new league proved to become even more stable than the National League had been. For the next fifty years, the American League's teams and cities remained unchanged.

A major rule change, beginning in 1901, restored the dominance of pitching that was lost when the pitching distance increased to 60 feet, 6 inches, eight years earlier. Foul balls began to be counted as strikes; before this time, a batter could foul off pitches at will without a consequence. This rule change, according to Bill James, "was probably the defining force of the decade."[12] Batting averages, power hitting, and even stolen bases plummeted, while strikeouts increased dramatically. Ives would have witnessed these changes to baseball firsthand for the first time, as he began to build his career in the insurance industry in New York, as outlined in chapter 1.

It took two years after the American League began play in 1901 before the first World Series occurred, pitting the champion of each league against each other. The Boston Pilgrims (later to become "my" Boston Red Sox) beat the Pittsburgh Pirates in a best-of-nine-game series.

A newly formed team in the American League called the Baltimore Orioles (not to be confused with the Baltimore Orioles of the National League that folded three years earlier, nor even with the unrelated present-day team of the same name) moved to New York in 1903 and began play as the Highlanders (the team that later would become the Yankees). American League officials had wanted a team in New York and were able to execute this relocation over the objection of the New York Giants of the National League, who wanted to retain control of the local market. This second New York team would give local fans, like Charles Ives, a chance to see teams of the junior circuit in action, in addition to teams from the long-established league.

In the 1905 World Series, the New York Giants's ace pitcher, Christy Mathewson, achieved the nearly impossible feat of three shutouts:

> New York and Philadelphia, the two largest cities and the country's main commercial centers, squared off in the first official World Series. . . . And from it emerged the first true superstar of the American sports scene.
>
> October 9 at Philadelphia, Mathewson faced Plank and won 3-0. The next day, [Philadelphia's] McGinnity faced [New York's] Bender and lost 3-0. There was no game on October 11, so Mathewson started with two days' rest at the Polo Grounds [in New York] on the 12th, pitched another four-hit shutout, and won 9-0. . . . Then, on Saturday, October 14, Mathewson went out again with *one* day's rest and pitched his third shutout, this time a five-hitter. . . . His All-America persona—tall, handsome, college trained, forthrightly Christian, clean-living sportsman yet fierce competitor—combined with his achievements to give professional baseball a degree of respectability much higher than it had [ever] enjoyed. A case can be made that 1905 marks the real beginning of "baseball as we know it."[13]

Ives's interest in major league baseball seems to have blossomed in this year, but he was not drawn to Christy Mathewson's immaculate image: Other ballplayers who excelled in 1905, but who played a little "dirtier," would catch the eye (and ears) of the composer, as will be discussed in chapter 5.

The Chicago Cubs began to dominate the National League in 1906 when they won a record 116 games that stood unequaled for almost a century. (The Seattle Mariners tied that record in the 2001 season with a record of 116–46, though the Mariners had to play ten additional games to match it.) In each subsequent year through the remainder of the decade, the Cubs added to that total until they became the winningest team in the history of baseball in any span of one to five years between 1906 and 1910.[14] The dominant Chicago Cubs would be an important rival to the New York Giants in the National League and would figure prominently in one of Charles Ives's sketches, as will be described in detail in chapter 5.

In 1907, when Charles Ives and Julian Myrick established their own insurance agency, the Detroit Tigers won the first of three consecutive American League pennants, led by the hitting and hard-nosed baserunning of Ty Cobb, who finished his career in 1928 with a remarkable lifetime .366 batting average, 892 stolen bases, and 4,189 hits (a record that stood until Pete Rose broke it in 1985).

Although 1908 was a momentous year in the life of Charles Ives, the year of his wedding to Harmony Twichell, baseball suffered one of its most humiliating moments of all time. One of the biggest baseball blunders in history occurred late in the season, and *baserunning*, or the lack thereof, cost the New York Giants the pennant against their chief rivals:

> Fred Merkle's boner, as it has come to be known, occurred in a Cubs-Giants game at New York's Polo Grounds on September 23, 1908. In the bottom of the ninth, with the score tied 1-1 and two out, the nineteen-year-old Merkle singled, advancing a teammate to third and putting himself on first base. The next batter, Giant shortstop Al Bridwell, followed with a sharp single to center field. Merkle, seeing the man on third cross the plate with the apparent winning run, assumed the game was over—so instead of continuing all the way to touch second base he turned and ran for the clubhouse, to avoid the jubilant crowd surging onto the field.
>
> But Johnny Evers, the quick-thinking Cub second baseman [and later a subject of Ives's music, in a different context], shouted to center fielder Solly Hofman to throw him the ball. What happened thereafter is not clear, but evidently Hofman threw the ball in to Evers at second. The Giants' Iron Man Joe McGinnity, however, realizing what was about to happen, rushed on to the field, got to the ball ahead of Evers, and threw it as far as he could into the stands. Evers, not to be outmaneuvered, got another ball from somewhere, touched second base, and ran to the umpires screaming that Merkle was out, the inning was over, and the run didn't count.
>
> After much confusion—pandemonium would be a better word—it was finally ruled that Johnny Evers was right. Since the crowd was all over the field by now, and it was getting dark anyway, the game was declared a 1-1 tie.[15]

The game was repeated at the end of the season to settle the tie between the Giants and Cubs, and the Cubs consequently won the pennant due in part to Merkle's boner.

1910s

The American League won the World Series eight times in the next decade, failing only in 1914, when the Boston Braves won, and in 1919, when certain players of the Chicago White Sox (known thereafter as the "Black Sox") intentionally lost the series to Cincinnati, as discussed later in this section. The domination of the junior circuit over the senior circuit during the 1910s helped create the long odds against the National League pennant winners in 1919 that contributed to that scandal.

In 1911 a change in equipment had a profound effect on the game:

> A cork-center baseball was invented by Ben Shibe in 1909 and marketed by the Reach company, which supplied baseballs for the American League. Spalding followed, developing a cork-center ball for the National League. This caused battings levels to jump in 1911 and 1912. Runs scored per game in the American League in 1911 went from 3.6 to 4.6. Ty Cobb hit .420 in 1911 and .410 in 1912, and Joe Jackson hit .408 in 1911. Those are the only .400 seasons between 1901 and 1920.[16]

For two seasons the new cork-centered baseball resulted in higher batting averages and better power numbers, but two years later in 1913 pitchers found a way to return to dominance. By accident, a pitcher named Russ Ford learned that scuffing a baseball would cause it to drop as it reached the plate, making it very difficult to hit. Balls defaced in this way were not removed from the game at that time, and eventually every pitcher was using scratched or scuffed balls, resulting in a steep decline in offensive numbers for the remainder of the decade.[17]

Another upstart league, the Federal League, entered the major league scene in 1914. But after only two years, the league folded mainly due to low attendance. The league built eight ballparks for its teams, one of which remains—Wrigley Field, the magnificent present home of the Chicago Cubs, who in 1916 moved into the vacated new stadium. However, the broader, and lasting, results from the introduction of this ephemeral league into the marketplace of baseball were a destabilization of salaries and ultimately baseball's biggest scandal. The new league caused salaries to spike, as teams bid against each other for baseball talent. Some successful teams like the Philadelphia Athletics sold their quality players to their wealthier counterparts, like Boston and Chicago. Minor leaguers, including a teenaged pitcher named Babe Ruth, were sold to major league teams looking to fill out their rosters with talented, if raw, players. Then when the Federal League suddenly folded, the market crashed, and the contracts of even veteran ballplayers were renegotiated at much lower salaries. Some of these players, bitter about their treatment by management and strapped for cash, began to look elsewhere for funds.[18]

The 1919 World Series between the heavily favored Chicago White Sox and the Cincinnati Reds was tainted by the influence, and money, of gamblers. The Reds won the nine-game series 5–3, but several of the White Sox players conspired to throw the series in order to collect a substantial promised payoff. In the end, eight players were banished from baseball for life for fixing the World Series—including the White Sox's most outstanding player, "Shoeless" Joe Jackson—who hit .375 in the series, despite his own admission that he was mixed up in the scheme. Despite many who have argued for clemency, Jackson and the other players involved remain ineligible for the Hall of Fame due to this significant blight on their records.

Baseball was relatively unaffected by the onslaught of World War I and the beginning of American involvement in the war during this decade. However,

> Ives was much affected. A creative marker for what was to come can be seen and heard in *From Hanover Square North, At The End of a Tragic Day, The Voice of the People Again Arose* (eventually part of the . . . *Second Orchestral Set*). It commemorates in music the grim years of World War I as represented by the day a German submarine torpedoed the *Lusitania*, May 7, 1915.[19]

Only the 1918 season was significantly disrupted by the war. A number of players were drafted or enlisted before the start of the season, and the season later was shortened to 140 games so that all of the players could join the war effort by September 1 as required by the United States Selective Service. The players involved in the World Series, between the Chicago Cubs and the Boston Red Sox, held earlier than usual at the beginning of September, received an extension to this mandate. It appeared that the war would necessitate the cancellation of the 1919 season, but the war ended on November 11, and the following season, though reduced to 140 games, took place without interruption.[20]

1920s

The Black Sox scandal became public in the latter part of the 1920 season. After several seasons of low attendance, this scandal threatened the integrity of the game and had the potential to devastate public support. However, this new knowledge of the scandal came at the same time that Babe Ruth arrived in New York, after being sold to the Yankees by the Boston Red Sox for $100,000 plus a $300,000 mortgage on Fenway Park. Ruth had hit an *unthinkable* twenty-nine home runs the previous season, a major league record at the time. Frank Baker, whose power-hitting abilities prompted the nickname "Home Run Baker," was tied for second in the American League with ten, only about a third of Ruth's total.

But in 1920 Ruth followed up this remarkable performance by shatter-
ing his own record with fifty-four home runs. Ruth's success and flashy
style helped mitigate the effect of the Black Sox scandal in the eyes of the
public, and, as Bill James observed, the owners as well as the fans embraced the new surge in offensive production:

> The fans were galvanized by the Ruth phenomenon; his explosion on the New
> York scene in 1920 was the biggest news story that baseball has ever had.
> When the Black Sox scandal broke late in the 1920 season, major league mag-
> nates were faced with sudden prosperity on the one hand, and doom and dis-
> aster on the other. Under those unique circumstances, the owners did not do
> what they would have done at almost any other time, which would have been
> to take some action to prevent Ruth, as they would see it, from making a
> mockery of the game [through total domination]. Instead they gave Ruth
> room to operate, allowed him to pull the game wherever it wanted to go.[21]

Thus, the owners instituted no change in equipment, no dramatic rule
changes, no increase in the size of stadiums, and no reduction of the pitching distance—in order to swing the advantage back to the pitchers—as
they had always done by constantly tinkering with the rulebook in the
nineteenth century.

Amazingly, unlike the .400 hitters from 1911 to 1912 who benefited from
a change to a more lively ball, Ruth achieved this remarkable total with
the same baseball design that had been used in previous seasons. The sec-
ond-place home run total was nineteen by George Sisler of the St. Louis
Browns, and it took only fifteen home runs for Cy Williams of the
Philadelphia Phillies to lead the National League. Pitchers tried to pitch
around Ruth: He walked 150 times—fifty-three more times than his near-
est competitor, Sisler—but Ruth still managed to shatter the single-season
home run record, almost doubling his previously unthinkable total.

As baseball gained recognition through the achievements of Ruth, Ives
began to gain recognition as a composer. His self-publication of the *Concord Sonata* brought a few letters of thanks from musicians as well a review of the work by Henry Bellamann, who would become one of Ives's
primary champions. Although Ruth garnered immediate support by his
unprecedented exploits on the field, Ives's recognition took much longer
to achieve fully, as mentioned in chapter 1.

In 1923, Ives's insurance company, by now called Ives & Myrick, en-
joyed a remarkable increase in profits, probably resulting from a revised
business plan drawn up by Ives.[22] The success in the company paralleled
the success of the nearby New York American League team—whose triumphs resulted from a revised approach to baseball, featuring the power
hitting of Ruth and his teammates. In 1923 the Yankees moved into Yankee Stadium, dubbed "the house that Ruth built" due to its unprecident-

edly large capacity needed to accommodate the many fans who wanted to see Ruth blast a homer or two. The Yankees had been sharing the Polo Grounds with the New York Giants for twenty years. If Ives attended any games in the new stadium—which seems at least possible, given his continued interest in baseball and the phenomenal draw of both the park and the Yankees—he unfortunately did not save a program or a ticket stub.

Many baseball historians and fans name the 1927 Yankees as the best team ever. The lineup was phenomenal:

> They called it Murderer's Row. The Yankees won 110 games. Ruth hit 60 home runs [a record that would stand for over thirty years], breaking his 1921 record, [Lou] Gehrig 47, [Tony] Lazzeri 18—and they were 1–2–3 in the league. Gehrig hit .373 and knocked in 175 runs. Ruth and [Earle] Combs hit .356 each, Ruth driving in 164. [Bob] Meusel at .337 was overshadowed despite 47 doubles (Gehrig had 52), and Combs had 23 triples. The team batting average was .307. But all that went with terrific pitching. . . . There was, naturally, no pennant race. The final margin was 19 games.[23]

The Yankees went on to sweep the World Series. "America was told that Yankee batting practice in [Pittsburgh's] Forbes Field the day before the Series opened so intimidated the Pirates that they were beaten then and there."[24]

Ives also had a great year in 1927. Parts of his Fourth Symphony were performed for the first time in public, at Town Hall in New York; an influential article on his music by Henry Bellamann appeared in the journal, *Pro Musica Quarterly*; and a very important supporter of Ives's music, fellow composer Henry Cowell, wrote his first letter to the composer. With the sudden appearance of this new enthusiasm for his work, Ives too may have felt like he (finally) had "swept the World Series."

1930s

On January 1, 1930, Ives officially retired as a businessman. Myrick later wrote a moving tribute to Ives's achievements in the insurance industry, "What the Business Owes to Charles E. Ives," in which Myrick celebrated Ives's creation of visionary literature and analysis of insurance and finance. Myrick closed with the words: "The passing years will demonstrate that his philosophy will ever hold good."[25]

In baseball in 1930, a player achieved a record that the passing years also has shown to "hold good." Hack Wilson of the Chicago Cubs set the all-time record for runs batted in (RBI) for a single season, a mark that still stands over seventy years later. Wilson drove in 191 runs, aided by a .356 batting average and a league-best fifty-six home runs. Clearly, his hitting skills in this season alone proved that he was anything *but* his moniker.

The first All Star Game was held in 1933. This recognition of the game's top players, placing the best of the two leagues in opposition, was immediately popular with the fans and has been repeated ever since. When Ives was born, almost sixty years earlier, such a contest would have been unthinkable, because of the lack of league continuity and the lack of public recognition of baseball's star players. But over time as the leagues stabilized, the fans became acutely aware of the most prominent ballplayers in each league.

The first night baseball game in the major leagues was played in Cincinnati on May 24, 1935, between the Reds and the Philadelphia Phillies.[26] The game began at 8:30 P.M., and a remote "switch," pressed by President Franklin Roosevelt from the White House, turned on the light standards that lit the field. By shifting some games into the evening, baseball created an opportunity for more fans, and specifically more working-class or blue-collar fans, to enjoy the sport. If night baseball had been available sooner, perhaps Ives would not have felt as compellingly drawn to major league baseball as a fitting amusement for a budding insurance executive, who had the luxury of a flexible schedule that allowed him to attend games with his friends and colleagues in the daytime earlier in the century.

In 1939 Ives's *Concord Sonata*, hailed as "deeply and essentially American in impulse and implication," premiered at Town Hall in New York by John Kirkpatrick.[27] The primary news of the baseball season that year was not nearly as positive, but the lasting impact of one event, for many fans, also has come to represent baseball as "deeply and essentially American in impulse and implication." Lou Gehrig's streak for consecutive games played came to an end in 1939. This record would stand for over fifty years, until it was topped by Cal Ripken of the Baltimore Orioles in 1995.

> Gehrig's string ran out at 2,130 games when he told [his manager Joe] Mc-Carthy he couldn't play as the team was to start a western trip in Detroit on May 2. . . . Lou [later] went to the Mayo clinic and learned that he had ALS, amyotrophic lateral sclerosis, unheard of then by the public, now called Lou Gehrig's disease. He announced his retirement June 21 but stayed with the club to act as captain and take the lineup to the umpires. On July 4 . . . he made his famous speech ("[Today,] I consider myself the luckiest man on the face of the earth") before a gathering of old teammates in a packed Yankee Stadium.[28]

For many baseball fans, this speech was a defining moment for an American hero. Just two years after playing 2,130 consecutive baseball games, spanning fourteen years, Lou Gehrig died.

1940s

In 1941 Joe DiMaggio had a fifty-six-game hitting streak, hitting safely in every New York Yankee game from May 15 through July 16. In the same year Ted Williams of the Boston Red Sox became the last player to hit over .400 to date, by hitting .406 along with a league-leading thirty-seven home runs. Despite missing the triple crown (the leader in batting average, home runs, and runs batted in) by just five RBI, Williams was not named the most valuable player. Joe DiMaggio received the American League award primarily on the strength of his unparalleled streak and the fact that his Yankees outpaced Williams's Red Sox by seventeen games in the final standings.

On January 15, 1942, about a month after the Japanese attack on Pearl Harbor, President Franklin Delano Roosevelt wrote a letter to Major League Baseball Commissioner, Judge Kenesaw Mountain Landis, to answer the commissioner's inquiry on whether or not professional baseball should be played during the war. President Roosevelt's reply shows the importance that the country seems to have placed on baseball at this time and also foreshadows how the sport would change over the next several years. Roosevelt wrote,

> I honestly feel that it would be best for the country to keep baseball going. There will be fewer people unemployed and everybody will work long hours and harder than ever before. And that means that they ought to have a chance for recreation and for taking their minds off their work even more than before. . . . As to the players themselves, I know you agree with me that individual players who are of active military or naval age should go, without question, into the services. Even if the actual quality of the teams is lowered by the greater use of older players, this will not dampen the popularity of the sport.[29]

Between 1943 and 1945, many baseball stars—including two of the finest hitters of all time, DiMaggio and Williams—left their teams to join the service during World War II. The game that was left behind was in many ways second-rate, but the ballplayers' willingness (including the superstars) to serve their country made them first-rate in the eyes of most fans of the national pastime, and interest in major league baseball did not suffer a significant decline. Bill James portrayed the caliber of play during those years as substandard, yet ironically still captivating:

> During wartime the quality of the baseballs used was inferior, as there was something in regular baseballs that was needed to make explosives or O.D. green paint or something, and the balls manufactured were rather lifeless. The quality of the play wasn't too lively, either. With most of the good players in the service, a collection of old men and children and men with one arm [Pete Gray] and seven dependents gathered regularly and batted around a dull spheroid, and this was called "major league baseball" for three years.[30]

Ives's interests, too, were focused upon the war during these years. He privately recorded his revised song, retitled "They Are There," written in honor of American soldiers fighting in Europe; he hoped his song "could help win the war, change the world."[31]

In 1947 Jackie Robinson of the Brooklyn Dodgers changed the world by becoming the first African American major league baseball player since the nineteenth century, when attempts to integrate the sport had failed, due in part to the efforts of Cap Anson, as reported earlier. Robinson won the Rookie of the Year award, the first year that the award was given on a national basis, hitting .297 and stealing a league-leading twenty-nine bases. Robinson's appearance in major league baseball, which eventually led to the full integration of the sport, likely would have pleased Ives greatly. There were "several important abolitionist works" in the family library, and "members of the Ives family practiced their faith and witnessed to their convictions in their actions as well."[32] His grandfather and grandmother "both campaigned for the abolition of slavery. Charles Ives would endlessly retell the family story of his grandmother leading a group of women to rescue a fugitive slave caught in New Fairfield."[33] His father continued the "strong family tradition of tolerance and concern for social justice . . . and passed on [this tradition] to his two sons."[34] Finally, Ives commemorated the "54th Massachusetts Volunteer Infantry: the Civil War's legendary black regiment" in a very moving slow march for orchestra, "The 'Saint-Gaudens' in Boston Common (Col. Shaw and His Colored Regiment)," one of Ives's *Three Places in New England*.[35]

1947 also was the year that Ives was awarded the Pulitzer Prize in music for his Third Symphony. According to legendary accounts, Ives replied to the committee, "Prizes are for boys. I'm grown up." Moreover, he claimed that "prizes are the badges of mediocrity."[36] But this public reaction perhaps has been overplayed. As Jan Swafford noted, "In private he hung the certificate proudly on the wall."[37]

Babe Ruth, who almost singlehandedly was responsible for the remarkable growth of baseball since the 1920s, died in 1948. The *New York Sun* summed up the news:

> Game called by darkness—let the curtain fall. No more remembered thunder. . . . The greatest figure the world of sport has ever known has passed from the field. Game called on account of darkness. Babe Ruth is dead.[38]

1950s

Baseball teams relocated rapidly during the 1950s, compared with the previous half century of baseball during which teams remained in their own cities. Baseball players, on the other hand, stayed put: Almost all players stayed with their teams for their entire careers, and baserunners stayed on their bases. Strategy was deemphasized in favor of the three-run homer. Speed was not viewed as an important baseball attribute; power attracted the large salaries, even if the home runs were only sporadic. Fittingly, as strategies decreased during the early 1950s, attendance decreased correspondingly.[39]

In 1951 Bobby Thompson hit a home run to end the third game of a three-game playoff between the New York Giants and the Brooklyn Dodgers, thus clinching the pennant for the Giants and capping an exciting finish to their long comeback during the latter part of the season.[40]

> The dramatic impact of this climax to a two-month comeback cannot be overemphasized. It was telecast nationally, and [radio announcer] Russ Hodges screaming "The Giants win the pennant, the Giants win the pennant!" in a radio broadcast became folklore. . . . It was the ultimate fictional situation actualized in real life, a championship *reversed*—not simply won—by one swing of the bat. It had never happened before and has happened only once since (in 1992). . . . They called it "the shot heard around the world."[41]

During the latter years of his life, we can only hope that Charles Ives listened to the team he used to watch in his younger days and heard the breathtaking account of this historic event himself.

In 1953 the Boston Braves moved to Milwaukee, where they remained for thirteen years before moving back east to their present location in Atlanta. The following year a rookie hitter named Hank Aaron joined the Milwaukee club and eventually went on to supercede Babe Ruth's astonishing record of 714 career home runs: Aaron finished his long and distinguished career with 755 home runs.

In 1954 the St. Louis Browns moved east to become the Baltimore Orioles. The Athletics played their last season in Philadelphia before moving halfway across the country to Kansas City and finally (in 1968) the rest of the way to Oakland. Before the end of the decade (in 1958), both the New York Giants and the Brooklyn Dodgers would desert their Eastern fans and head West to California. But Ives did not survive to feel these demoralizing losses of beloved local teams. The New York Giants that he saw in the first decade of the twentieth century was the same ballclub in the same location from when he was eight years old until he died of a stroke on May 19, 1954, in a hospital in New York.

CORRESPONDING TURNING POINTS

As revealed in this chronology, the major turning points in Ives's life and in the development of baseball occurred almost in tandem. Ives's birth in 1874 occurred just two years before the birth of the National League, the oldest league of professional baseball still in existence. Likewise, Ives arrived in

New York City in 1899 to begin building his business career two years before the American League joined the older National League, when major
league baseball stabilized and began to build itself into a highly successful
business venture. As baseball exploded in popularity due primarily to the
appearance of the incomparable Babe Ruth in the early 1920s, Ives's public
standing as a composer started to rise after he began to attract notice from
the self-publication of his *Concord Sonata*. Finally, just a few years after Ives
passed away in 1954, baseball passed into a new era—now spanning coast
to coast, but at the same time deserting and disappointing countless faith-
ful fans through the relocation of several longstanding ballclubs to new
cities spread across the nation.

Ives was born along with major league baseball, grew up with baseball,
reached maturity simultaneously with baseball, and—at least for fans of
the Boston Braves, Philadelphia Athletics, Brooklyn Dodgers, and Ives's
own New York Giants—died with baseball. To be sure, major league baseball continues to thrive. But Charles Ives continues to prosper as well, because his music as well as his life seem to attract more and more interest
with each passing year. While this chronology has given a glimpse of the
correspondence between the development of baseball and the life of Ives,
the following chapter will provide a more detailed look at the significance
of baseball in the life of Ives by examining his own participation as a
player and the sustained prominence of baseball in his life as he aged.

Chapter 3

A Life of Baseball—
A "Manly" Game

BASEBALL IN DANBURY

Noted historian and scholar Jacques Barzun wrote:

> Whoever wants to know the heart and mind of America had better learn
> baseball, the rules and realities of the game—and do it by watching first
> some high school or small town teams. The big league games are too fast for
> the beginner and the newspapers don't help.[1]

Charles Ives learned the game in this same way—by watching and participating in small-town baseball—and through his appreciation of the
game, we can see glimpses of the heart and mind of an American. He
learned the thrills and virtues of the game in the same way that he learned
his most innovative musical techniques: through experience.

> Accuracy and speed, the practiced eye and hefty arm, the mind to take in and
> readjust to the unexpected, the possession of more than one talent and the
> willingness to work in harness without special orders—these are the Ameri-
> can virtues that shine in baseball. . . . Baseball is a kind of collective chess
> with arms and legs in full play under sunlight.[2]

Sports News

Although the local newspapers included some coverage of the major
leagues, Danbury baseball fans seemed to focus mainly on local activities.
However, interest in the professional sport on a national level increased
over time in the local press as well as in Ives's own life as both he and major league baseball grew up. For example, in 1883, when Ives was nine

years old, the *Danbury Evening News* included baseball scores only if space was available (or perhaps *when* scores were available), rather than on a daily basis. Standings were supplied periodically with some very brief notes on the development of the pennant races. By 1885, line scores (showing the number of runs scored in each inning) appeared almost daily, though sometimes just the final scores were published. By 1890, when Ives was sixteen, the scores often were expanded to include the batteries (pitchers and catchers), the number of hits and errors produced by each team, and the attendance. Nevertheless, professional baseball news almost always occupied the front or back page, suggesting its relative importance to local readers, despite the paucity of detailed information.

Almost entirely lacking from the newspaper coverage of professional baseball during this period of time, however, was any news about the exploits of individual players. The only exceptions were occasional mentions of local players who were playing professional baseball:

> Timmy Sullivan is playing short field for the Wilmington (Del.,) club this season. . . . Grant Briggs, who is well-known to Danbury, is catching for the Syracuse club of the American Association. He is a star catcher this season.[3]

The rare stories of games that did appear offered minimal details:

> The postponed Albany-Troy game was played at Pleasure Island and Albany was not in it. Casey, the "phenom" went in the box for the Albanys, but in three innings he was hammered for eight hits, one three-bagger and seven runs were tallied. He was taken out and Sprogel put in with not much better results. The fielders were cut off from the game by the crowd filling in around all the bases. Brahan pitched a good game for Troy. About 4,000 attended the game.[4]

In general, instead of detailed accounts of the games played and descriptions of the achievements of star ballplayers, the newspapers usually recounted controversial plays or described organizational aspects of the professional leagues (such as conflicts between the National League and the Players League, an upstart rival to the older National League) or other oddities of common interest. For example, a loss of equipment, rather than home runs or hitting streaks, prompted a news story:

> The Brooklyn-Columbus game Sunday was awarded to the Columbus team, by a score of 9 to 0, because the Brooklyns were unable to furnish a new ball, when in the eighth inning, the old one was batted out of the grounds.[5]

Likewise, an argument always seemed to attract the attention of journalists:

> Owing to the large attendance at the game between Columbus and Toledo Sunday a ground rule allowing only two bases on a hit into the crowd was

adopted. In the fourth inning with two men on bases, Lehane, Columbus first baseman, made a three bagger into left center, which was clear of people. Umpire O'Day, however, ordered him back to second base, as well as one of the runners, who had scored. After ten minutes spent in wrangling Columbus finished the game under protest.[6]

These stories seemed to be geared toward a wider audience, rather than any avid young baseball fan who may have been eager for news of distant baseball heroes. At best, baseball coverage in the Danbury newspapers was uneven. It might be possible to follow professional baseball closely, but the inning-by-inning line scores for each game revealed only who was ahead at any given time, who held leads, and who came from behind. No celebrities emerged from the newspaper reports, and details on how the runs scored were not offered. Professional baseball could be seen strictly as a team game in Danbury. One could know the outcomes of the games, but, for the most part, not even sketchy accounts of the games were provided. It would have been next to impossible for professional baseball idols to develop for a young fan in Danbury, Connecticut, from the newspaper accounts.

A few annual guides were published that listed, for example, the current rules of baseball, brief notes on the development of the game, information on scoring techniques, and the names and statistics of the professional baseball players from the previous year.[7] Some of the descriptive or historical parts of these annual guides remained the same from year to year, to provide an introduction to the game, while the professional-league statistics and list of rules were updated in each edition. *The Sporting Life* (a widely distributed newspaper published weekly from Philadelphia) contained box scores, stories about players, some detailed accounts of games, and information about all levels of the professional leagues. However, such specialized publications may not have been available in small towns like Danbury. Furthermore, although a fan could obtain some very specific, though dated, summary information about professional baseball from these sources, it would be difficult to follow the sport closely and develop a long-distance love of professional baseball from these guides and periodicals. With the lack of professional baseball coverage available locally, Charles Ives's interest in major league baseball did not develop early. His childhood attraction to the sport, on the other hand, naturally and almost necessarily focused on local amateur and semiprofessional baseball.

Local baseball seems to have been very popular among Danbury citizens. The newspaper account of the crowd for opening day in 1895 suggests that attendance at baseball games in Danbury was customarily large, particularly when no admission was charged:

The base ball season was opened in a blaze of glory Saturday. The crowd of spectators was immense and its enthusiasm unbounded. Nothing was lacking to make the opening a successful one, even to the victory by the home team. The attendance was fully as large as in the days when base ball was free, and a half hour before the game was called the grand stand was filled and the sale of seats stopped. Free seats had been provided along the east and west sides of the diamond, but these were taken early and standing room within view of the field was at a premium. The knolls outside the grounds, and even the tree tops within sight of the grounds were black with people.[8]

This widespread enthusiasm for baseball in Danbury likely fueled Ives's own interest in the sport.

In general, the local baseball newspaper stories were almost always on a different page than the professional reports, suggesting that local baseball was seen as an entirely different activity than its professional counterpart, not just different tiers of the same sport. The newspapers printed detailed box scores of many local games, while in the same issue provided only line scores for the professional games. For example, the box score for opening day 1895, mentioned above, contained at bats, runs, hits, put outs, assists, and errors for each player. It also had the time of the game (2 hours and 20 minutes), earned runs, two-base hits, stolen bases, and double plays, as well as the number of bases on balls and strikeouts recorded by each pitcher and the number of passed balls by each catcher.[9] On the other hand, many of the newspaper accounts, similarly to the coverage of the professionals, focused on broader aspects of the game, rather than the actual performances of players and outcomes of the games:

> Base ball is not as lively, as exciting a game as polo, but what it lacks in these particulars it more than makes up in its rows and riots. In the Connecticut league this is particularly noticeable. Scores of games have been played, and the chief feature of many of them has been dissension.[10]

In addition to reporting the results of local games, the Danbury newspapers also ran descriptive stories about the teams in the area:

> The Young Men's T. and L. [Temperance and Literacy] society base ball club is showing up strong this year. . . . The West Danburys will go to Croton Falls, Decoration Day, to play the team of that town. . . . Next Wednesday afternoon the drug clerks of this city intend to show their brethren of Waterbury how to play ball on the White street grounds. The Knights of Columbus base ball club have challenged The News nine to play a game, and undoubtedly a match will be arranged. The News nine is made up entirely of men employed in the office. The Alerts [a team for which Ives played] and a team from the Boys' club will play Decoration Day on the White street grounds. The Alerts are going to make a strong bid for the championship of Danbury this season, and the result of their first game will be watched with interest by the many admirers of the National game in Danbury. They have scored neat uniforms.[11]

Illustration 3.1.   The Alerts, Ives's amateur baseball team in Danbury, Connecticut, July 1890. Charles Ives appears in the middle row, seated on the left.
MSS14, The Charles Ives Papers in the Irving S. Gilmore Music Library of Yale University.

Clearly, a wide variety of teams participated in the sport locally, there seemed to be keen interest in these games, and the press gave each team at least some attention. The White Street grounds was a frequent site of ball-games in which Ives played. Based on the *1875 Bird's-Eye Map of Danbury, Connecticut*, the location of this ball field probably was the single large vacant field that later became the campus of Danbury High School, now Western Connecticut State University, where baseball is still played today.[12] "The Alerts" was likely a team sponsored by the local fire department. Fire companies frequently were involved in baseball in the nineteenth century, and fire-fighting companies often were known by the name "Alerts."[13] Illustration 3.1 shows Ives in his Alerts uniform in a team photograph taken in 1890. Ives's membership on the Alerts provided him with a tremendous sense of pride: His diary is full of references to his participation on the team.

The Pleasures of Baseball

Ives's entries in his first diary, beginning in 1886 at the age of eleven, bear witness to the importance he placed on his own participation in organized

baseball games; yet, at the same time, the entries suggest that music remained an essential aspect of the boy's life. Stuart Feder noted the conflict
between these two activities, yet showed how baseball also exerted a positive influence on Ives's life and music:

> At this time, Charlie was discovering the pleasures of baseball—the com-
> pany of men, the assertion of leadership, the discharge of aggression, and the
> exercise of aptitude. And as Charlie's interest in the game was developing,
> he was also becoming increasingly involved in music and beginning to es-
> tablish his identity as a musician and composer. The two activities were ap-
> parently polar, competing for time and dedicated practice. On a deeper level,
> sports provided an avenue for both the discharge of aggression against men
> as rivals and the expression of love toward them as teammates. In accom-
> plishing these, the exercise of sports could exert a liberating and enabling ef-
> fect on the practice of music.[14]

Thus, as also suggested by Ives's diary, the apparent gulf between these
two pursuits may not have been as wide as it first appears.

Ives kept up *daily* entries in his first diary only during January of the
year for which the diary was printed; afterwards, his entries are placed
without regard to the preprinted dates on the diary pages. Sometimes Ives
crossed out the original dates and inserted entirely new ones, and other
times Ives just changed the year and crossed out the day of the week in
order to use the preprinted month and day for an entry. Although the diary as a whole is devoted mainly to baseball (and sometimes football),
brief notations pertaining to music appear periodically. For example, the
entry on one page lists both a music lesson and a team meeting called by
the captain, and the entry on the facing page similarly displays a mixture
of baseball and music:

May 30
    Rained. Beat Fountain Boys Park Ave. 26 to 12. No Lesson by Mr. Hall.
    Played at City Hall Memorial Service.
May 31
    Fri. 4th Lesson Mr. Hall
    Rainy. Special Meeting of Alerts by Clark.[15]

A newspaper clipping about the game that is mentioned on May 30 in the
diary accompanies the entry, placed immediately above it. Both of these
days featured rain, and rain was a fairly frequent theme in Ives's diary, so
much so that a rainy day preempting baseball seems to have been a suffi-
ciently important event as to prompt an entry. The plain entry "Rained no
ball game" appears on two different pages in the diary in reference to
dates in two different years.[16]

Most of Ives's other handwritten entries about baseball simply log the outcomes of various games—in the majority of cases, strangely enough, recording his team's *defeat*:

May 18, 1889
   Got beat by Flusky of Stevens nine score 7 to 10, Ballground
June 22, 1889
   Go beat by Flushing 9 to 3
   North Meadow
July 6, 1889
   Got beat by YMCA
   16 to 6
   White St. grounds[17]

In some cases Ives inserted newspaper clippings between the pages of the diary, and these clippings primarily record his team's victories. Most of these clippings are probably from the school newspaper started by his brother Moss. John Kirkpatrick revealed the origin and early history of this publication:

In 1891 Moss and two other boys started a school paper first called *The New Street Weekly*, each issue a single leaf mimeographed on both sides, [the first surviving issue] Vol. 1, No. 3 dated February 15, 1891. The next year it became *The New Street Monthly*, a printed double leaf, [the first issue] Vol. 1, No. 1 dated March 1, 1892. . . . It covered local athletics with frequent mention of Charlie.[18]

Perhaps Charles Ives felt the need to *acknowledge* the losses through handwritten entries, but he understandably chose not to commemorate these games by saving newspaper clippings. A victory, on the other hand, called for the full newspaper report:

On the White Street ball grounds this morning the Alerts and Flus[h]ings contested a game of ball, which this time resulted in victory for the former team [Ives's team], the score being 10 to 5. The battery for the Alerts were Millard and Howland, and for the Flushings Moore and Davis.[19]

The Alerts and a picked nine, two juvenile base ball teams, played a game of ball on Pearl Street yesterday afternoon. The Alerts won by a score of 21 to 20.[20]

In several, but not all, of the clippings, Ives is listed as the pitcher in the list of players, certainly another reason to save a newspaper clipping. One such clipping contains a detailed box score showing that Ives batted fifth in the order, scored three runs, made two errors, and handled two balls successfully. As pitcher in this game, Ives struck out nine and walked one—an outstanding pitching performance by any measure.[21] In the back of the diary, under the heading "Memoranda," Ives neatly and in ink produced a table of twelve teams, showing what appears to be his own performance as a hitter and fielder against each of these teams:[22]

Club	Hi[ts]	Runs	PO [Put outs]	Er[rors]
1st Picked nine	2	5	1	0
Aemes	4		1	0
2nd Picked nine	4		0	0
Flushings[1]	2		0	0
Fountain Boys	2		0	1
Flushings[2]	1	1	0	0
Flushings[3]	1	0	4	0
Flushings[4]	1		2	0
Norwalk 1/2 game	1	3	1	0
Y.M.C.A.	0	0	4	0
3rd Picked nine	1	2	0	0
4 P.N. Men	2	2	0	0

(The superscripts after "Flushings" probably refer to four different times that Ives played against that team.)

This record of Ives's achievement as a ballplayer over some period of time, probably a single season, suggests that he performed impressively on the baseball field. The chart shows only one error, whereas errors were a frequent occurrence in these games, based on the evidence in newspaper accounts. Although the number of at bats is lacking from this chart, making it impossible to calculate Ives's batting average, the seemingly large number of hits in some of these games (especially against Aemes and the 2nd Picked nine) suggests that Ives was an excellent hitter as well. Overall, throughout this diary, the handwritten entries and clippings from newspapers suggest the seriousness with which Ives approached his own participation in baseball.

Charles Ives's first mention of baseball appears in a letter to his aunt Amelia (his father's sister, Sarah Amelia Ives) on September 14, 1886. This letter is written on paper stamped at the top with the company letterhead, "Ives Bros, Groceries, Main St Danbury," a "play store" that he and his brother Moss pretended to run when they were children:

Dear Auntie

I have just returned from the chicken coop & I have closed up the chickens for the night. I have got the sour milk & watered the chickens every day. I do not play in the store every day but I keep it a going. Momma has pickled some pears yesterday up home & little Amelia came over to see her. Momma has canned & pickled some peaches down here. Tell Grandma there was a meeting of the Childrens Home here last evening before last. Papa has fixed most all the doors & the blinds in the house so they will work easier. Every body has the base ball fever up here & I have it a little, We were playing base-ball up to Ned Tweedys satery [Saturday]. Moss was 3rd base Ned fired the ball to Moss to have have [repetition sic] him put him out, but Moss dodged it, & the ball struck him & knocked him down. That was Moss's last playing of base-ball. I have a new bat. I am going to get the cracked corn to-morrow. . . . I have given the leaves of the corn to the chickens. Our Orchestra have got to play again we expect to have some new members Ned Tweedy 2nd vi-olin & Harry Biddiscond piano instead of Fannie Blasderd. How many baths do you take, Please tell Uncle Leyman to take a bath for me because I have to work, study, etc. From love & all to love to all

    Yours Truly

    Charlie[23]

The letter reveals Ives's budding interest in baseball ("Every body has the base ball fever . . . & I have it a little") and in music at an early age, and it also shows that his activities were much like those of any eleven-year-old boy—playing at the store, feeding livestock, watching his father work on the house, and avoiding baths!

Two letters written to his father when he was fifteen bear witness to his continued enthusiasm for baseball. These letters, dated August 14 and 15, 1889, tell of his trip with his extended family to the shore of Long Island Sound in southeastern Connecticut. Along with discussing the latest news and describing some of his other recreational activities, Ives recounted his baseball activities:

Saturday the Westbrook base-ball nine played the Essexs. I played with The Essex asked me to play with them and I did. but the Essex got beat. 18 to 10. The Stamards Beach ball club asked me to pitch for them against the Clintons next Sat.[24]

He crossed out the phrase "I played with," apparently preferring to em-phasize the honor of being asked to play. His second invitation to pitch with another ball club, after the game, suggests that his pitching skills were in demand, despite the inflated score, by today's standards, of the earlier game he had pitched. The second letter from the shore simply tells of a ballgame Ives planned to attend—"I am going to see ball-game be-tween Westbrook and Essex"—but he does not reveal any hopes he may have held to participate in that game as well.[25]

In addition to his avid participation in baseball throughout his youth, Ives also excelled in other sports. His interest in football—which he en-joyed particularly due to the extra roughness involved—seems to have peaked during his high school years when he was elected captain of the combined Danbury High and Danbury Academy team.[26]

To some degree he may have inherited his enthusiasm for baseball from his family's involvement with the hat-making industry and from his father's military service in the Civil War. Although these two activities seem totally unrelated to sports on the surface, both hatmakers and soldiers were active participants in baseball.

Hat making was the principal industry of Danbury throughout most of the nineteenth century. Danbury historian William Devlin described the importance of the hat-making industry to Danbury and to the Ives family:

> Hat manufacturers were well-represented on the founding boards of all the local banks, and their descendants, like Charles Ives . . . , were active in the town's social and cultural life. In the mid-19th century the town's civic leadership— George W. Ives [Charles's grandfather], Frederick S. Wildman, and Edgar S. Tweedy—were all sons of early figures in the town's hatting industry.[27]

Baseball contests between the employees of rival factories were a natural way to build good working relationships after hours. The hats themselves played an important role on at least one such team, the Middle River Cowboys baseball nine, from the Mallory factory:

> All of the men wore derbies except for the pitcher, Rob Hall, who donned a baseball cap after his hat kept falling off every time he threw the ball. Hall developed an effective curve ball that attracted the attention of professional scouts. The team was successful for many years, and was one of the many amateur and semi-pro teams in Danbury that engaged in a variety of sports. Baseball was an especially popular sport among hatters.[28]

With his family's strong historical connection to the hat-making industry, Charles Ives likely was in attendance at many of these games from an early age, and his family's almost certain acceptance of the sport as an important social activity for the workers in hat-making factories would have influenced Ives's devotion to baseball that he carried throughout his life.

Baseball and the Civil War

According to Stuart Feder, who recognized the importance of the Civil War in Ives's life and music:

> The spirit of the Civil War and Ives's idealization of it in musical reminiscence persisted throughout his life. It had a deeply private meaning for Ives in addition to the shared common memory of America. For through much of Ives's lifetime the Civil War remained alive in cultural history, [in] the living presence of veterans whose number was inexorably diminishing, and in the music of the War.[29]

Ives remained deeply concerned about war throughout his life, and he composed numerous pieces about American involvement in wars including two movements of *Three Places in New England*—"Putnam's Camp,

Redding, Connecticut," referring to a revolutionary war site near his hometown, and "The Saint-Gaudens in Boston Common," a piece based on a bas-relief sculpture of a Civil War regiment and its commander on horseback, mentioned previously in chapter 2.[30] In addition, Ives's *Decoration Day* from the *Holidays Symphony* commemorates the holiday originally set aside to remember the Civil War dead, which later was expanded and renamed as Memorial Day. Several of Ives's songs treat American involvement in the First World War including "Tom Sails Away," "In Flanders Field," and "He Is There!" Later, in 1942 Ives transformed the latter song into a tribute to American soldiers fighting in World War II, revising the song and renaming it "They Are There!" also as mentioned in chapter 2.

The participation of George E. Ives, Charles's father, as a bandmaster in the Civil War is well documented in the literature.[31] The association of baseball with the Civil War is a function of the sort of war that pit "brother against brother," and the association of that war with music, in general as well as in Ives's works, is undoubtedly also related to its familial nature. It was a war fought by boys, as suggested by the youthful terms for soldiers from the two sides, "Johnny Reb" and "Billy Yank," as well as by some of the song titles, such as "Bear This Gently to My Mother."[32] Charles's music is full of Civil War references, and because baseball was a prominent recreational pursuit for soldiers during their free time between battles, it is possible that stories of baseball games played by soldiers at encampments were among the tales Charles's father told when remembering the war to his son.

Although baseball served as an essential form of release for soldiers on both sides of the war, Civil War scholar Patricia Millen urged restraint from overstating the influence of the war on the development of the game into the national pastime: "Long before the first shot of the Civil War was fired at Fort Sumter, South Carolina, the game of baseball had already entrenched itself into American society and was well on its way to becoming 'America's National Game.'"[33] Yet the idea that the Civil War helped spread the popularity of baseball is difficult to dismiss, even if, as Millen noted, baseball "was slowed by the four year interruption of the war, rather than accelerated by the intermingling of Civil War troops."[34]

> The men from the Union and Confederate armies had marched off to war [already] knowing how to play baseball. By examining available sources on the leisure time activities of Civil War soldiers, it is clear that baseball was indeed played with great enthusiasm by northern and southern troops. Soldiers played in army camps, in winter quarters and while pausing between marches.[35]

But of course the soldiers were involved in any number of other leisure activities besides baseball, as Millen pointed out. Nevertheless, truths are sometimes distorted by memories, and Charles Ives's conception of the war was primarily dependent on his father's recollections. Therefore, the role of baseball in the Civil War may have been elevated in Charles's mind, just as it was in the minds of many of his contemporaries who claimed that the Civil War was instrumental in the spread of baseball across the nation.

For example, Albert Spalding, former standout pitcher for the Boston Red Stockings and Chicago White Stockings, as discussed in chapter 2, waxing poetically, claimed that the Civil War was primarily responsible for the development of baseball into the national pastime:

> During those years of unhappy conflict, on both sides of the line "Yanks" and "Johnnies" were playing ball and laying the foundation for a game which, when war's alarms should cease, would be national in its spirit and national in its perpetuity.
>
> No human mind may measure the blessings conferred by the game of Base Ball on the soldiers of our Civil War. . . . Base Ball had been born in the brain of an American soldier. It received its baptism in bloody days of our Nation's direst danger. It had its early evolution when soldiers, North and South, were striving to forget their foes by cultivating, through this grand game, fraternal friendships with comrades in arms. It had its best development at the time when Southern soldiers, disheartened by distressing defeat, were seeking the solace of something safe and sane; at a time when Northern soldiers, flushed with victory, were yet willing to turn from fighting with bombs and bullets to playing with bat and ball.[36]

Although his account cannot be accepted literally as historically accurate, in light of recent research by Millen and others, Spalding's view was widely accepted for years. His enthusiasm for baseball may not have been shared equally by all of those soldiers who participated in the war; however, such ideas surely had an enormous influence on younger people like Charles Ives, whose views of the war were shaped only by the memories of others, through stories such as these, rather than by first-hand experience.

George may have participated in or at least observed baseball games during the war, because any distraction from the main matter at hand must have come as a welcome relief. According to Stuart Feder:

> Life at Fort Richardson [where George initially was assigned] was for the most part humdrum, and he had ample opportunity to practice his instruments. Rehearsal requirements for a band such as his in such an installation were far from demanding. Musicians had much spare time and usually spent it in whatever recreation could be devised.[37]

Charles's father also may have brought back to Danbury the idea of baseball as a refuge:

> One can almost hear the crack of the bat and imagine the dusty, weather-worn soldiers striking up a game . . . and for a brief time, forgetting where they were and all the possible outcomes of what lay ahead.[38]

And perhaps he transferred this general notion of baseball as a solace to Charles, who looked to baseball not as a solace from war but as a solace from his fears of the feminine implications that music making carried at that time. At the same time, baseball's association with the war may have conjured up masculine images of battle that equally appealed to Charles as a fitting diversion from music. However, baseball soon became a source of conflict between Charles and his father, as the Civil War became only a distant memory and the proper education and musical development of Charles dominated his father's attention, despite Charles's intense emotional need for baseball.

BASEBALL AND MASCULINITY

As a boy growing up in Danbury, Charles Ives was torn between his musical interests and his desire to fit in with other boys.[39] Even as a youngster he must have sensed that his father as a musician was not as highly regarded among townsfolk as some of his other male relatives who pursued more traditional business paths. Stuart Feder explained that "a fear of the feminine lurked in largely working-class Danbury and in the rough-and-tumble atmosphere that pervaded America. In its endeavors to conquer the West and make as much money as possible, masculine entrepreneurship was hailed as the ideal."[40] Nevertheless, Ives could not deny his musical leanings, despite his feelings of embarrassment. Later in life he was able to look back at his earlier feelings about music and recognize his erroneous beliefs. Ives recalled:

> As a boy [I was] partially ashamed of it—an entirely wrong attitude, but it was strong—most boys in American country towns, I think, felt the same. When other boys, Monday A.M. on vacation, were out driving grocery carts, or doing chores, or playing ball, I felt all wrong to stay in and play piano.[41]

Clearly, feelings of inadequacy as a male, compared to other boys, were deep-seated, even if later in life he seems to have been able to recognize his mistake. His fervent choice of words, that the attitude "was strong" and that he felt "all wrong" to be pursuing music with such devotion, makes his ashamed feelings about music at the time poignant.

Swafford claimed that

> social dilemmas were not unusual for an American boy growing up an artist, then or later. Some of Ives's solutions were common ones—lambasting sissies,

playing sports, becoming profane and 'manly' in personality. This pattern
turns up time and again in male American artists. . . . At length Ives would arrive at a perverse view of dissonance as a token of manliness in music.[42]

While Ives perceived dissonance as emblematic of masculinity in music,
he also early saw baseball a way to prove his own masculinity. Baseball
gave Ives a chance to be more like other boys, and it must have been
tremendously gratifying to him to have been able to develop some high-
level skills on the baseball field. His participation in baseball and other
sports provided a fitting balance in his life between music and more aggressive activities. Although his extraordinary musical talent was immediately recognizable even as a boy, he gained more acceptance, at least
among his peers, through success on the ball field—competing with other
boys in terms of physical skills, which he equated with masculinity.[43]

He certainly was not the only boy seeking masculine identity though
baseball. Donald Mrozek concluded that

> the sexual isolation of the male in most sport made it an institution into
> which men might flee, spend their time, use their energies—avoiding con-
> frontation with women [and, in Ives's case, with "feminine" pursuits] and
> defining personal values in a largely homosocial environment.[44]

Contemporary publications about baseball, such as *The Dime Base-Ball
Player for 1881*, went so far as to emphasize baseball's "demands upon the
vigor, endurance and courage of manhood."[45] Moreover, this publication
noted both the masculine and American associations of the sport, both of
which would appeal to Ives greatly:

> The National Game of Base-Ball is now undoubtedly the most popular sum-
> mer pastime in America. In every way is it suited to the American character.
> It is full of excitement, quickly played, and it not only requires vigor of con-
> stitution, manly courage, and pluck, but also considerable power of judg-
> ment to excel in it.[46]

Such burly attributes surely would have appealed to a young Charles Ives.
    Furthermore, in nineteenth-century society in general, baseball was
viewed widely as a decidedly masculine pursuit—not just a sport played
by males, but a place where masculine traits might best be developed. According to Colin Howell:

> The early development of team sports such as baseball . . . fell to an emerg-
> ing middle class that regarded organized sporting activity as a social training
> ground for young men entering adulthood. Many bourgeois reformers be-
> lieved that team sports inculcated respectable social values. The lessons
> learned on the gentlemanly field of play, it was hoped, would help young

clerks, merchants, bankers, and professionals to provide future leadership and social refinement to their respective communities. In virtually every town of any size throughout the Maritimes and New England, middle-class reformers advocated a more disciplined and rational approach to leisure, seeking to replace irrational and often turbulent popular or working-class recreations with more genteel and improving leisure activities.[47]

Howell, furthermore, concluded that "most people believed that baseball inculcated manly virtue, an assumption that in turn relegated women to observer status. The presence of women in the stands, moreover, was thought to civilize the audience and curb usually aggressive play."[48]

Like Howell, other scholars also have linked participation in baseball with success in business, another important component of Ives's life, as discussed in chapter 1. Michael Kimmel saw baseball as an integral component of the transformation from youth to maturity, which would have been extremely important to Ives, given his self-image and his positive view of successful businessmen in his family:

> Baseball is about remaining a boy and becoming a man. Like other sports, baseball fuses work and play, transforming play into work and work into play, thus smoothing the transition from boyhood to manhood. Play as work generates adult responsibility and discipline; work as play allows one to enjoy the economic necessity of working.[49]

Perhaps Ives's phenomenal success in business, outlined in chapter 1, was also due in part to his personal development on the baseball diamond.

Steven Riess concluded that the time was ripe for the rise in sports as a measure of masculinity, as boys prepared to take their place as adults in the increasingly complicated world of business:

> Sport boomed as a middle-class recreation in the late nineteenth century and contributed significantly to the redefinition of middle-class manliness. The rise of bureaucratization, the threat posed by the new immigrants, an uncertainty of measuring up to brave ancestors, and the feminization of culture encouraged middle-class young men to test their manliness through vigorous physical activity, especially team sports. Participation in strenuous, if not dangerous, clean outdoor sports would develop strength, courage, and virility, while restoring self-confidence. Sport tested one's mettle and prepared one for adulthood. Followers of the strenuous life would grow up to become self-controlled, disciplined men of action who were team players in the workplace . . . [and would] surmount the feminization of American culture.[50]

Thus, through his participation in baseball and other sports, Ives was preparing himself physically to excel in the workplace, and at the same time he was participating in an inner battle against the feminization of

American culture that he saw most prominently in contemporary views of music and musicians.

Like this linking of masculinity attained through sports and the development of business skills, the linking of masculinity and baseball occurred in perhaps even stronger ways in the church, which saw baseball as a means to develop virtuous qualities in young men and at the same time to serve as an evangelical tool:

> The YMCA, a Protestant organization transplanted from England in 1851, aided baseball both directly and indirectly. By 1900 it had more than 1,400 branches throughout the country and 250,00 dues-paying members. It owed its growth largely to the backwardness of churches in attending to the troubling social problems of the changing times. The "old-time religion" that in a rural age may have been "good enough for pappy" left many city youth cold. The Y, which at first served the poor but soon began appealing to the lower middle class, took a practical route to carrying out its evangelistic mission. Perceiving the need for "wholesome" recreation to counteract "the allurement of objectionable places of resort," and wishing to temper the largely feminine aspect of American Protestantism by means of the idea of "muscular Christianity," Y leaders capitalized on the mounting interest of the young in athletics by adding sports, baseball included, to the Y's many-sided program as bait to lure youth into the fold.[51]

Other church organizations turned to baseball for similar reasons:

> The churches played a critical role in the fostering of physical notions of manhood. . . . Baseball seemed to be one possible solution to what social gospellers called the "young boy problem" and the declining involvement of young males in the work of the church. As sports such as baseball were increasingly seen as contributing to Christian manliness, moreover, ministers were finding it useful to employ baseball analogies in their sermons, warning their congregations not to become stranded on the third base of life.[52]

Ives seems to have adopted this convention of incorporating baseball analogies into nonbaseball situations, and he often used such analogies in his later writings, as will be described later in this chapter.

Baseball was more than simply a momentary amusement in Ives's life. As Rossiter concluded:

> Charles Ives maintained his manhood by becoming a baseball player. . . . Undoubtedly he enjoyed these sporting activities; but he seemed to place an unnatural and strained emphasis, both for his own benefit and for that of other people, upon his role as a player and enthusiast. And there is good reason to believe that this emphasis was a counterweight to the connotations of emasculation and effeminacy which his activities in music of the cultivated tradition had in his own mind and which, he knew, they had for other people as well.[53]

Illustration 3.2. Standout pitcher for the Hopkins Grammar School baseball team, Ives appears on the left, next to his catcher, Franklin Hobart Miles,1894.
MSS14, The Charles Ives Papers in the Irving S. Gilmore Music Library of Yale University.

Similarly, Feder summarized the issue succinctly: "Charlie's avid pursuit of sports in the midst of his involvement with music provided an answer to the gnawing question of whether he was truly a man."[54] Thus, as suggested at the beginning of this book, Ives saw the baseball field as a *proving ground*—where he could prove himself as a man.

BASEBALL AT HOPKINS AND YALE

When Charles Ives left Danbury for preparatory school, he devoted himself to academics in order to achieve high enough grades to qualify for entry into Yale. Yet, despite his father's concerns about his son's grades and participation in extracurricular activities, Charles continued to play baseball actively at Hopkins Grammar School in New Haven, Connecticut, in the spring of 1893 and 1894.[55] Illustration 3.2 shows Ives with his Hopkins team catcher. Baseball was Hopkins's strongest sport, and the school had a long history of very successful teams.[56] "On 3 April he pitched a game in which Hopkins beat the Yale freshmen (the Hopkins *Critic* reported: "Ives is a little apt to be wild, but he plays coolly and is very quick at catching men napping at bases")."[57] Jan Swafford recognized the importance of this particular event in Ives's life, classifying it as

> an experience that unequivocally excited Charlie, and which he would recall proudly for the rest of his life: he pitched for Hopkins in their 10-9 defeat of the Yale freshman baseball team. . . . It was only the second Hopkins victory over Yale.[58]

This was an important enough event in the life of the preparatory school that "in celebration Rector Fox gave the school a 'holiday hour.'"[59] "Athletics were the main excitement at the school; earlier in 1876 a Hopkins baseball nine, with Walter Camp on the mound, had first beaten the Yale freshmen. At Hopkins that was the pinnacle of success."[60] Ives's Hopkins team photograph appears as illustration 3.3.

His pitching skills at Hopkins certainly helped build his self-esteem, and the recognition given to him by an important male authority figure, the school headmaster Fox, surely contributed to his feelings of manly achievement. At the beginning of the spring baseball season, Ives wrote a letter home relating that Fox "asked how my arm was for baseball. . . . Unless someone else comes I feel as if I was needed to pitch."[61] But Charles's father apparently did not see the importance of baseball for developing his son's confidence and self-respect. George was concerned that baseball would overshadow his son's studies, and he questioned the motivations of the school headmaster in encouraging Charles's baseball pursuits. George expected his son to be focused

Illustration 3.3.   Ives's baseball team at Hopkins Grammar School, 1894. He is seated in the front row on the right.
MSS14, The Charles Ives Papers in the Irving S. Gilmore Music Library of Yale University.

solely on the goal of qualifying for entry into Yale during this time, other than the continuation of his musical development, and he discouraged wasting time playing ball.[62] Charles, in turn, complained to his father: "And [I] don't see why you insist on blaming everything on ball."[63] Notwithstanding, in a letter a few days later, Charles attempted to ease his father's worries about baseball competing for time with academics, reminding him that "the baseball season is nearly at an end."[64] Nevertheless, despite his father's concerns about how his son spent his time at school, Charles did get accepted into Yale and began his studies in the fall of 1894.

After trying out for the Freshman Baseball Nine unsuccessfully in the spring of 1895 at Yale, Ives no longer participated in baseball.[65] His father had forbidden his participation at Yale so that Charles would be able to devote himself fully to his studies.[66] Clearly, baseball (and other sports) threatened the close bond that the two shared through music. Thus—ironically, when compared to relationships between many fathers and sons in connection with sports—baseball, the proverbial "boy's game," served to separate the boy from his father rather than to deepen their relationship through a shared passion for the sport, as is the case in many families today.

However, this negative viewpoint about sons' ball playing was not an isolated opinion at the time. Baseball scholar Ronald Story claimed that late nineteenth-century baseball players approached the game with

> love and passion—strong but appropriate words. Because these boys and young men not only played baseball but played it in the face of adult disinterest and disapproval. This is one of the most important differences between the 19th and 20th century games. Nineteenth century adults did not really want their adolescent sons playing baseball. Stories abound of 19th century fathers tracking down sons and whipping them off the ball field, of mothers throwing iron pots and boiling water at team organizers, of tempestuous quarrels over ball playing instead of chores and serious work.[67]

Fortunately for Charles, his father and mother stopped short of these remedies. But his father's concerns about sports taking precedence over his son's education and musical development were a constant source of conflict between them. Despite this friction, however, Charles does not appear to have been restricted from these activities during his youth, as indicated by the record of his participation in baseball, football, and other sports. But when Charles matriculated at Yale, his father seems to have become more insistent about the issue.

It must have been especially difficult for Ives to be faced with the idea of giving up sports at Yale. According to Feder:

> The single most acceptable college passion was sport. . . . The position of sports in college life cannot be overestimated. Yale led American universities in its programs of physical education and intercollegiate sports. . . . It is no wonder that the ethos of sports endured among the Yale men as they became older.[68]

Furthermore, for Yale men sports took on a higher moral or spiritual significance:

> "For God and Yale" on the athletic field and the fields of war was a youthful sentiment scoffed at by some but keenly and earnestly felt by most. . . . Athletics was life not merely in miniature but distilled and concentrated, a field like the battlefield where young men proved their valor and devotion to cause and principle.[69]

However, except for his initial attempt to make the baseball team (perhaps in a moment of rebellion), Charles adhered to his father's wishes, despite his father's untimely death in November 1894.

But the loss of sports participation in Ives's life seems to have demanded a replacement, and Ives filled this void through his entrance into fraternity life at Yale.[70] Although Ives's playing days effectively were over, sports continued to be an important fixture in Ives's life;

however, from this point forward Ives's involvement in sports mainly as a spectator, both at Yale, where football again took the upper hand, and after completing his college studies when he began his professional life in New York City. This latter period in Ives's life will be discussed in detail in chapter 5, in conjunction with Ives's musical sketches involving baseball.

LOOKING BACK

Baseball Memorabilia

Although Ives's regular participation in organized baseball had ended, Ives continued to play baseball whenever the opportunity arose. Ives played ball on company teams, usually serving as his team's pitcher.[71] And he frequently played backyard ball with his nephews and other family members during visits.

Ives's youngest nephew, Chester Ives, remembered his uncle's continued devotion to baseball:

> Everything for us with Uncle Charlie was always built around baseball and other sports. As a child, my impression of him was this enthusiasm to be a sportsman, and he could always share your enthusiasm and give advice if you were a ballplayer. I remember I said I played second base. "Oh, no. You want to get over to shortstop. Anybody goes to sleep on second."[72]

When Charles was not pitching for the Alerts and Hopkins Grammar School in his youth, he usually played shortstop. Jacques Barzun saved his highest praise for

> that transplanted acrobat, the shortstop. What a brilliant invention is his role despite its exposure to ludicrous lapses! One man to each base, and then the free lance, the trouble shooter, the movable feast for the eyes, whose motion animates the whole foreground.[73]

Charles Ives seems to have shared Barzun's admiration for the position by insisting that his nephew switch positions.

Chester also remembered his uncle's affinity for and sustained abilities in pitching:

> Of course he pitched. I can remember going up on top of the hill alongside of the barn at Redding and he'd show us how to pitch. He'd wind up—he really had a classic way of the windup, just as any professional player. My poor father was always catching for him. Father used to lose his interest in catching the ball for him, and Uncle Charlie would get mad and say, "Come on, Moss. Pay attention when I'm throwing."[74]

Barzun's view of the position of pitcher was almost as compelling as his praise for the shortstop: "The pitcher . . . is the wayward man of genius, whom others will direct. They will expect nothing from him but virtuosity."[75] It seems from Ives's behavior with his family that he continually aimed for virtuosity on the mound.

Bigelow Ives, another of Charles's nephews, remembered playing baseball with his uncle as well. His memories, too, focused on his uncle's baseball skills:

> We saw a great deal of them [Charles and Harmony Ives] when they were in Redding in the summertime, and that was always a lot of fun. We would pitch a tent down by the pond and stay there for several weeks at a time. Uncle Charlie would always take time out from his composing in the music room to come out and play ball with us. He'd insist on a game of catch at least once a day. I thought he was a little unfair, because I was still a little fellow and he'd throw the ball really hard at me. I was rather frightened to be faced with playing catch with the real ballplayer I thought he was. He'd put on his old baseball cap when he did this.[76]

These memories reveal Charles Ives's continued interest in baseball, and his competitive behavior in playing catch with his brother and his nephews suggests the seriousness with which Ives approached the game. The fact that he saved his old baseball cap and wore it even for informal games of catch in the yard is indicative of Ives's nostalgic approach to the game and the importance he placed on his baseball memories.

In addition to sharing his passion for baseball with his nephews, he also tried to introduce baseball to his adopted daughter, Edith. The only record of her participation in the sport appears on the first page of a diary for 1919, during the Ives's trip to Asheville "for rest and recovery," though "Charlie did little of either."[77] Apparently the story was not intended as an entry for New Year's Day, because the entry continues from January 1 to January 2, and a parenthetical date, though difficult to read, suggests that the event occurred later in the month. Nevertheless, this diary entry shows that his daughter unfortunately was not as compellingly drawn to the sport as he was, though she was only five years old at the time:

> Edie, who had tried to play base ball with Hugh & Bobby (Minturn), in the back yard (1-20) said she didn't like baseball very well, as she couldn't "base it" much [Ives must be using Edith's childlike term for hitting], and that she couldn't seem to catch the ball when it staid [stayed] up in the air all the time.[78]

The fact that Charles Ives included this story in this diary, along with other "cute" stories of his beloved daughter, again suggests that baseball continued to occupy a prominent place in his life as he matured.

Illustration 3.4.   The doors of Ives's studio in West Redding, Connecticut, where Ives had tacked baseball team photographs and other memorabilia.
Photo by Lee Friedlander, Courtesy Fraenkel Gallery, San Francisco. MSS14, The Charles Ives Papers in the Irving S. Gilmore Music Library of Yale University.

A few years later—May 7, 1922—Ives wrote a "Letter to Editor of The New York Times" in which he extolled the virtues of college athletics. Although the letter is not signed by Ives, instead signed "Another Yale Graduate," anyone familiar with his rhetoric and idioms could not fail to attribute it to him, and he kept a clipping of the letter among his papers:

> I'll admit that I went to college for athletics. I played on all the teams at prep school and wanted to do the same at college. The one thing that interested me in those days was athletics. But the fact that I had to put myself through college—in other words, a lean purse—did not keep me off the teams; my inferior playing did that well and efficiently. . . . It would be hard to prove that prominence in athletics in college does or does not tend to soften instead of toughen the life-work muscles, or that it creates less lasting qualities, less fighting spirit, or stimulates less constructive, creative, or original thinking.[79]

Though he never played at the college level himself, which was clearly still troublesome to him, even as he wrote this letter—and which he blamed on his inability to make the Freshman Nine, rather than his father—he certainly continued to appreciate the importance of sports for young collegians to develop life skills, not just athletic ability, through participation in sports.

Ives's love for baseball continued into his old age, long after he had retired from the insurance industry. He often would take his barber into the garage to show "a football, the knee pants, baseballs, spiked shoes, and a lot of stuff like that."[80] But he kept many of his cherished baseball possessions much closer to his workspace. The inside doors of his studio at his home in West Redding, Connecticut, as shown in illustration 3.4, were covered with various programs, photographs, and newspaper clippings, and prominent among these items were baseball memorabilia.[81] Ives preserved three photographs of baseball teams scattered on the doors among his other items. One of these shows his Hopkins Grammar School baseball team, and the other two are difficult to identify precisely but may be other teams for which Ives played.

More importantly, his studio contained a baseball bat, prominently placed near the piano, and the top shelves of his bookcase held a large, battered old sign saying "Ball Field" with an arrow pointing to the right, as shown in illustration 3.5 (the bat is not visible in the photograph). Perhaps Ives had this baseball bat in mind (and in hand) when he composed a sketch [f4822] that ends with a huge cluster chord, containing all black and white notes from C2 to B♭5, with a dynamic marking of *fffff* and the indication, "a Knock Out Chord play with BASE Ball BAT, Elk Lake."[82] Material from this sketch, but unfortunately not the fabulous baseball bat chord, was reworked into Ives's Study no. 23, a piece to be discussed further in chapter 6. Finally, according to Feder, "he kept two hats on the top

Illustration 3.5. Ives's studio. An old "Ball Field" sign appears in the upper left on the bookshelves.
Photo by Lee Friedlander, Courtesy Fraenkel Gallery, San Francisco. MSS14, The Charles Ives Papers in the Irving S. Gilmore Music Library of Yale University.

of the bookcase in his studio—one crushed old Danbury felt hat and a baseball cap with the insignia 'Yale '98.'"[83] This is probably the cap to which his nephew Bigelow referred. Even after so many years, Ives chose to surround himself in his primary workspace with treasured items reminding him of his baseball-playing days.

In addition to these baseball objects, Ives kept a photograph of his father in his military uniform with his cornet, and Ives kept the cornet itself, a beloved token of his father's spiritual presence, prominently displayed on a shelf in his study.[84] Clearly, this instrument served to remind Charles of his father throughout his life, especially while at the piano in his studio. In this way he likely could draw strength from his memories of his father as he composed. In the same way, it appears that Ives's baseball memorabilia, with which he also surrounded himself in his studio, conjured up the continued strength to battle his longstanding and lasting fears of effeminacy. Seeing these associative objects surely reminded him of his past athletic successes and may have served as a constant counterbalance to his own complicated views of himself as a musician. Put differently and more bluntly, in the same way that the old cornet reminded him intimately of his father, the baseball photographs and objects reminded him that he was a *man*.

Talking Baseball

Surrounded by all of this baseball memorabilia, Ives included many baseball analogies in his writings. Most of his writings came during his mature years, and relating his ideas to baseball seems to have aided him in expressing himself. The use of baseball idioms in American expression can be traced to the nineteenth century, as far back as when the first ball-games were played, according to baseball scholar, Maggi Sokolik: "Baseball lingo . . . has become an integral part of everyday American speech; metaphor that seems to have become a necessary part of our expressive powers, filling a gap in our language."[85] By tapping into the language of baseball to make his points, Ives, again, was establishing himself as an American through association with the American pastime. His use of baseball metaphors offered him new picturesque ways to address topics and also revealed his own personality and interests in the course of his discussion. His use of baseball metaphors, too, can be attributed to his difficulties with gender identity. By associating himself directly with the sport through his choice of language, again, he attempted to distance himself from his artistic side, which he feared might be perceived as too soft or feminine.[86]

In challenging his readers to accept some of the unusual musical traits contained in his self-published collection of songs, for example, Ives called upon baseball to make his point vivid:

> Does not the sinking back into the soft state of mind (or possibly a non-state of mind) that may accept "art for art's sake," tend to shrink rather than toughen up the hitting muscles,—and incidentally those of the umpire or the grand stand, if there be one?[87]

In baseball Ives saw a toughness that he equated with the ability to appreciate new kinds of music, and he saw perhaps the performer (the hitter), the critic (the umpire), and the audience (the grandstand) all as needing to be toughened up to properly appreciate the kind of music that interested him most.

By invoking the umpire, presumably in reference to the music critic, perhaps Ives had in mind the kind of ultimate objectivity expected from an umpire in baseball. Albert Spalding captured this impartiality by claiming that an umpire

> must be absolutely without prejudice. Did you ever think what that means? Consult your own feelings at the next contest you witness. Note how perfectly free you are from bias against the visitors. Put yourself in the umpire's place for a little while. Let a team bluster, and kick, and play horse, and dispute your decisions from the opening of the game. Let them play rowdy ball, seeking thereby to gain unfair advantage not only of the adversary, but of you. Let

them encourage rooters in the grandstand to hoot, and howl, and insult and browbeat you in your earnest efforts to be just. Let them encroach upon the rules far enough to strain without breaking them. . . . All this let players do—you being the umpire—and remain without prejudice, *if you can*.[88]

Spalding's umpire (or Ives's critic) would not carry a bias against individual players (or composers) or against teams (styles of music), would be free from the influence of the grandstand (or general audience), and would make decisions (or write reviews) fairly. This is the kind of music critic that Ives certainly would have desired. However, as Ives surely perceived in his harshest critics and as Spalding concluded concerning umpires, "To secure the presence of intelligent, honest, unprejudiced, quick-witted, courageous umpires at all contests in scheduled games has been one of the most vexatious problems confronting those in control of our national sport."[89]

Elsewhere, Ives also equated the incompetent or corrupt umpire to the music critic. Violence against umpires was a common part of the early decades of the sport, as will be discussed in more detail in the following chapter, and Ives seems to have condoned this behavior against umpires (and, by extension, critics) when warranted: "It is right to throw a bottle at the umpire who closes his eyes and yells 'foul!'"[90] In addition, Ives portrayed an incompetent music critic (he apparently thought *all* music critics were incompetent) as an umpire:

You see, onct [sic] I got in wrong somethin' awful a-umpiring a baseball game. I seemed to get the base hits and foul balls all mixed up. I got tired of receiving bottles, so I decided not to yell fair or foul, but just chase the small boys away from third base every time a hit was made.[91]

In Ives's story, unable to distinguish between good music and bad music (base hits and foul balls), the critic instead tried to prevent innovative composers (depicted as small boys to represent their innocent and imaginative approach to music) from *significant* achievement (by chasing them away from third base, which obviously suggests a greater degree of achievement than first or second base because it is one base away from home).

A few of Ives's baseball analogies involved the importance of taking risks in music. Perhaps Ives's memories of the personal and strategic risks inherent in playing baseball aided him in trying to make himself clear. In response to an unnamed music professor's criticism of using hymns in original compositions, Ives's wrote that "he never took a chance at himself, or took one coming or going."[92] In a footnote to this comment in Ives's *Memos*, Kirkpatrick speculated that

these may be baseball terms from the days when Ives played pitcher, fielder, shortstop, etc. A former Cornell varsity player, Jim Oliphant '68, suggests that "never took a chance at himself" could mean [a pitcher] not risking a fastball that might rebound as a home run, and that "took one coming" could refer to a fielder catching a fly on the run that was dropping in front of him, and "took one going"—that was dropping behind him.[93]

In other words, the professor was unwilling to take the risks necessary to make great plays (or, apparently, to compose great music). These baseball terms may have been used informally by spectators at games in Danbury to discuss impressive fielding plays with each other; however, these terms do not appear in any of the surviving contemporary written accounts of games in newspapers and weekly sporting newspapers that I have examined. Since the descriptions of games are rather brief, as discussed earlier in this chapter, usually only describing the scoring highlights and unusual plays, fielding plays in general are given scant attention in these columns. Nevertheless, Oliphant's interpretation of these phrases as baseball oriented is compelling.

In a similar vein, Ives wrote, "It is better to go to the plate and strike out than to hold the bench down—for by facing the pitcher he may then know the umpire better, and possibly see a new parabola."[94] Here again, Ives used baseball to say that only by taking risks (going to the plate), even if failure results (a strikeout), can a person grow as a composer or perhaps even as a human being. In a similar manner, Ives espoused the view that an author or composer must not be overly influenced by the audience: "A home run will cause more unity in the grandstand than in the season's batting average. If a composer once starts to compromise, his work will begin to drag on *him*."[95]

Regarding innovation in musical composition, Ives again turned to baseball:

This boy's way—of feeling, if you can have two 3rds, major or minor, in a chord, why can't you have another one or two on top of it, etc.—[is] as natural to a boy as thinking, if three bases in baseball, why not four or five, Mr. Gumbo? A boy doesn't deserve much credit in anything like [this]—it's an obvious and natural way of having a little fun![96]

Burkholder fittingly interpreted this remark as indicating that Ives felt that musical rules were "just as artificial, conventional, and man-made as the rules of baseball" or were "a set of arbitrary conventions invented by humans for the purpose of having fun."[97] However, the analogy may be extended further. As discussed in chapter 2, the rules of baseball changed in significant ways almost annually during Ives's formative years. Fundamental concepts, such as the number of balls required for a walk, the number of strikes required for an out, and the distance between pitcher and batter, changed often. To Ives the rules of baseball were not only arbitrary and manufactured, but they were also subject to change, based on the whims or desires of the league owners. A boy growing up with baseball—where the rules were *always* subject to modification, prompting the boys to change the way they played the game on a regular basis—might easily see the rules of music in the same light. If baseball officials could alter the rules of the game to shift the balance between hitters and pitchers in any way that they wished, surely a composer could transform the conventions of music and assumptions about musical structure in significant and profound ways.

A more technical baseball analogy appears in reference to Ives's quarter-tone music. In this case Ives attempted to explain how his quarter-tone music could be perceived, at times, as humorous: "The quarter-tone family, like most other families, has a sense of humor. But that's a rather dangerous thing to refer to; it depends as much on where the catcher's mitt is as on the pitcher's curves."[98] Thus, the recognition of humor in the music depends on the listener's receptiveness (or the location of the catcher's mitt as the ball is received) as much as on the composer's intentions (the break on a pitcher's curve ball).

Moreover, as Feder noted, even

> in humorous remarks or figures of speech, Ives juxtaposed music with sports. He once said that he enjoyed playing the last variation of the *America Variations* nearly as much as he liked playing baseball. (The analogy has some literal, motor basis, the feet fairly running over the pedals as fast as they can, especially in the sixteenth-note figure.)[99]

Such baseball references abound in his writings.[100] Finally, one baseball reference has a special significance for Ives's own life. Regarding Thoreau, Ives wrote: "Somehow one feels that if he had kept this balance [between public and private life] he would have lost his 'hitting power.'"[101] Ives used this baseball analogy to refer to Thoreau's supreme abilities as a writer, using hitting *power*, not just hitting, to suggest the *depth* of Thoreau's work, not merely its quantity. The parallel between this observation and Ives's own life and approach to composition is unmistakable; by keeping his own public life of business separate from his private life as a composer, Ives, likewise, retained his "hitting power" in music—swinging for the fences rather than just meeting the ball, to sustain the analogy further, or aiming for profound musical expression and not just simple, likeable ditties.

All of these baseball analogies have one thing in common: They really are unnecessary to Ives's point, and in some cases they may even distract from his point. So why did Ives turn to baseball so frequently to express his ideas? Probably for the same reason that he was attracted to the game in the first place. By calling forth baseball images, Ives was able to give some of his ideas a "manly" connection—again serving to prove himself as a man during his lengthy sermonizing about music. Perhaps the only non-musical connections that Ives employed in his writings more than sports are those involving females and femininity as a form of derision. "Ladies," especially in reference to his critics, both real and imaginary, are peppered throughout his writings. Ives even referred to certain composers' music as feminine, such as Frédéric Chopin whom Ives characterized as "pretty soft, but you don't mind it in him so much, because one just naturally thinks of him with a skirt on, but one which he made himself."[102] Baseball gave Ives a more "manly" metaphor for his own approach to music.

As Rossiter concluded,

> Baseball, football, and other sports, then, helped Ives to maintain his masculinity as a boy; but the danger, from the point of view of the future composer, was that Ives's boyhood musical experiences would sour him on music of the cultivated tradition and cause him to be perpetually embarrassed by his connection with it.[103]

However, Ives managed to overcome his fears about music, and baseball in some ways helped him deal with negative associations of cultivated music by providing opportunities to create new connections between the music he composed and the sport that continually served to offset these feelings. Chapters 4 and 5 detail how Ives formed even more specific connections between baseball and music by writing compositions that depict baseball situations, scenes, and players.

Chapter 4

Playing the Game— Baseball in Completed Compositions

BOYHOOD MEMORIES

Whereas Ives's fascination with baseball extended throughout his life, as described in the previous chapter, ranging from his involvement as a young ballplayer to his memories as a older man, his *completed* musical compositions pertaining to baseball all seem to relate mainly to baseball in his youth. According to Charles Ward, "the roots of his music were inextricably found in the heritage of rural Danbury—the music, the literary heroes, and the social activities of pastoral America."[1] Baseball was an important leisure activity of pastoral America in the nineteenth century, and Ives's completed pieces about baseball, for the most part, represent the rural version of the game.

This chapter discusses Ives's five completed pieces that contain baseball references. Two of these pieces, *All the Way Around and Back* and *Some South-Paw Pitching!*, are instrumental works with baseball references in their titles; one piece, "Old Home Day," is the only song Ives composed that includes a baseball reference in the text; and the other two pieces, *The Fourth of July* and the First Piano Sonata, have programmatic baseball associations.

In some of these baseball-related and other similarly programmatic pieces, Ives constructed various musical experiments through which he was able to explore new ways of making and combining sounds to recreate a scene or picture. In this way, Ives was able to provide a familiar context for his only audience at that time, his housemates in his New York apartment, because he had given up on pursuing music as a profession, as described in chapter 1. By writing pieces about baseball, he offered some common ground, from which his housemates might be able to approach some of his radical musical ideas. As Ives noted:

> Around this time, running say from 1906 (from the time of Poverty Flat days)
> up to about 1912–14 or so, things like *All the Way Around and Back, The Gong
> on the Hook and Ladder, Over the Pavements, Tone Roads, The Unanswered Ques-
> tion,* etc., were made. Some of them were played—or better tried out—usu-
> ally ending in a fight or hiss (as in Tams later on). I must say that many of
> those things were started as kinds [of] studies, or rather trying out sounds,
> beats, etc., usually by what is called politely, "improvisation on the key-
> board"—what classmates in the flat called "resident disturbances."[2]

Apparently, despite Ives's best efforts to shape the results into something
palatable, his ideas were not always well received by his housemates.
Nevertheless, at least some of his attempts to depict baseball were met
with approval by his friends, and all were indispensable to Ives's development as a composer.

Ives's music depends heavily on extramusical associations: Among
these are the associations he developed to connect his music with baseball. Carol Baron aptly characterized the essential role that such associations played in Ives's music:

> The extramusical elements serve various functions in the music. They deter-
> mine the individualized and unique forms of Ives's musical motives, formal
> designs, notation and musical language. The pitch organizations and rhyth-
> mic conceptions result from the interaction of Ives's innovative musical ideas
> and the extramusical subject matter he portrays.[3]

In at least the first piece about baseball to be discussed in this chapter, as well
as the first two sketches to be discussed in chapter 5, baseball totally shaped
the form or content of the music. On the other hand, the other pieces carry
only partial baseball implications in the musical or conceptual design.

In much of his music, Ives attempted to imitate sounds, a habit he inherited from his father. As Burkholder noted:

> Such imitation was possible only by listening closely to environmental
> sounds, recognizing their intrinsic interest, and trying to construct a similar
> sound from musical tones. While originating in an attitude of listening, this
> kind of imitation of extramusical sounds in music also depended to some ex-
> tent on experimentation, as nontraditional musical techniques often had to
> be invented in order to reproduce the sound.[4]

In addition to the representation of sounds, Ives also composed music
that reflected his yearning for idyllic baseball settings in his completed
baseball pieces. Thus, he portrays the momentary excitement of a long
foul ball, the idiosyncratic approach of a left-handed pitcher, an informal
game played by schoolboys in a corner lot, a holiday contest between rival towns, and a father's enthusiastic reaction to his son's big hit.

Reflecting on rural scenes from childhood in Ives's music helped him mitigate the effects of the hectic pace and stress of urban business life. Whereas New York City offered an environment that was comparatively rich in cultural opportunity and diversity, Ives often was drawn to the simpler life of Danbury, where folks were more united by sharing similar cultural viewpoints, religious devotion, and amusements.[5] Thus, these baseball pieces refer back nostalgically to his experiences as a boy growing up and playing baseball in his hometown, instead of focusing on major league ballplayers, as he did in several sketches to be discussed in chapter 5. The pieces to be discussed in the present chapter revert to earlier days of baseball, where boys learned the rules and language of baseball in corner lots and local ballfields by playing the game.

ALL THE WAY AROUND AND BACK

The chamber work *All the Way Around and Back* depicts a specific baseball scenario through music. Philip Lambert succinctly summarized this piece as "a brief scherzo . . . where a pitch palindrome depicts the journey of a base-runner in a baseball game from first to third base and back during a foul ball."[6] From Ives's perspective,

> *All the Way Around and Back* is but a trying to take off, in sounds and rhythms, a very common thing in a back lot—a foul ball—and the base runner on 3rd has to go all the way back to 1st.[7]

The baseball-related inspiration of this piece seems to have been in Ives's mind from its inception; a page of Ives's first sketch [f3056] contains the indication "(Practice scrimage!) All the way around to 3rd &—back again! = Foul!"

At first glance, this piece seems to present a humorous musical impression of what Ives viewed as a relatively commonplace baseball scene from his childhood. As noted by Rossiter:

> For Ives, however, the term *takeoff* could mean not only a caricature, but also a reflection (or even an idealization) of something. His takeoff of the music with which a serious idea or attitude was associated was usually not intended to satirize that idea or attitude, but was rather the most effective way he knew of showing how much that idea or attitude really meant to him.[8]

The scene he musically depicted, or at least the scene of backyard baseball in general, was a meaningful part of his boyhood memory, as established in the previous chapter. Furthermore, the musical techniques he utilized in these baseball takeoffs are technically sophisticated and challenging. Ives later recalled:

> I'll have to admit that some of these shorter pieces . . . were in part made to strengthen the ear muscles, the mind muscles, and perhaps the Soul muscles too . . . —not so much in *Tone Roads*, but for instance *All the Way Around and Back*.[9]

The basic scheme of *All the Way Around and Back* is to build up polyrhythms gradually to a point of maximum tension among the various voices of the chamber ensemble and then to do the entire process in retrograde.[10] This basic musical scheme, in addition to the baseball idea, also was present from the inception of the piece. A page of Ives's earliest sketch [f3054] contains only the first half of the piece written out in notation, then at the end of the score Ives indicated "the backway to [a symbol presumably denoting the beginning of the piece]." Finally, acting as a miniature coda, the piece concludes with a reprise of the two most complex measures, which first appeared at the center, the climax, of the palindromic musical process. Clearly, the gradual building up of tension produced by the gradual imposition of polyrhythms represents the gradual increase in tension and excitement among the players as the ball sails down the line and deep into the outfield and as the baserunner rounds second base on his way to third. And of course the retrograde section of the piece depicts the gradual release in tension as the ball is determined to be foul, and the runner who has progressed from first base "all the way around" to third is obligated to return by the same path "back" to his original location.

The whole process seems to take place in slow motion, however, as Ives lays out the musical scene very deliberately at first. The polyrhythmic aspects of the piece are hinted at from the very beginning, where Piano II presents the notated meter in whole notes in the bass while Piano I syncopates a pair of six-beat chords against the four-beat bass notes (mm. 1–7). The violin (in consort with, or more accurately in "discord" with, the top voice of Piano I) seems to represent the runner's progress. After waiting for the ball to be hit during the slow opening of the piece, the violin (supported by the upper notes of the piano) begins an additive process and eventually a subtractive process that is remarkably similar to the processes devised by Philip Glass over a half century later. Glass's "additive technique" gradually builds a long and complex pattern of individual notes by presenting one note at a time until the pattern is complete. In Glass's case these patterns are ametric, with each added note extending the length of the original pattern, whereas Ives's additive and subtractive processes work within the confines of the meter by increasing the number of notes contained in each beat. In this way, Ives builds a long and increasingly

Example 4.1. *All the Way Around and Back,* mm. 9–14, violin.
© Peer International Corporation.

complex pattern by gradually adding notes over the course of the first half of the piece, as the runner on first makes his way to third, and then Ives (and the runner) reverses direction and dismantles this pattern by gradually subtracting notes from the complete pattern over the second half of the piece. As illustrated in example 4.1, the violin begins with a D♭ whole note (m. 9), then in successive measures adds C to produce a pair of half notes, D to form a half-note triplet, E yielding quarter notes, and finally the double-stopped F♯ and A to create a measure-long quintuplet (m. 13). Next, Ives, showing a preference for one-measure asymmetrical patterns, moves immediately to a septuplet by adding B and C to the original pattern (m. 14), rather than by employing the next successive beat division of a sextuplet, a more common and even division. He then repeats the septuplet two more times before moving directly to a one-beat undecatuplet (11-tuplet) by adding four more notes to the original pattern (m. 17), continuing a preference for asymmetrical patterns and prime numbers.

The additive process aptly represents the gradual process of the runner. If the initial D♭ that begins each measure symbolizes first base, then each added note tracks the runner's progress toward third. The skipped additions (moving directly from five to seven and from seven to eleven notes) seem to depict the runner's increased speed as he builds up momentum heading for third. Finally, the complete pattern is repeated once more, running as fast as he can, before the whole process is reversed beginning with an extra two measures of the final undecatuplet, as the runner returns to first base in the same way that he traveled in the first place—rapidly at first, then easing up as the base is reached.

At first glance the symbolism of the baserunner, speeding up as he rounds the bases and then slowing down as he returns, seems to be lost in this palindromic reversal, since a runner presumably might easily trot back to first base after a foul ball. However, the rule that determined how quickly one must return to the base after a foul ball changed over the years. The rules of 1883 state that "a baserunner who fails to return to his base at a run following a foul ball is liable to be put out by being touched by the ball while off his base."[11] In other words a runner must hustle back to his original base after a foul ball. Later, the rules of 1887 removed the danger of being tagged out, and consequently eliminated the need to return to the base as quickly as possible: "Baserunners need not return to their bags on the run following a foul ball etc., provided

Example 4.2.   *All the Way Around and Back,* **mm. 13–17.**
© Peer International Corporation.

they do not unnecessarily delay the game."[12] Since Ives's piece depicts the runner returning to first base after the foul ball in exactly the same manner and speed as he advanced, as embodied in his perfect palindrome, Ives's memories of this event that he tried to capture in this piece likely were from before 1887, when Ives was twelve years old.[13]

In addition, through this palindrome, Ives is able to depict one additional, important aspect of this reversal: The runner would have to return to first base by retracing his identical path, crossing second base rather than taking the shortest possible route across the diamond and over the pitcher's mound. The rules in place when Ives played baseball clearly stipulate that a player must, in effect, go "all the way around and back" on a foul ball. But this assumption, still in effect in the game today, was not *always* a rule. According to the rule *changes* for 1861: "Players running the bases must make them in the following order: first, second, third, and home, and in returning must reverse this order."[14]

Meanwhile, throughout this whole process, each asymmetrical pattern is constantly maintained by a subsequent instrument to create intricate polyrhythms that build tension as the baseball sails down the foul line through the air. Upon their entrance, the bells continue with the violin's quintuplets, as the violin moves on to septuplets (m. 14), as shown in example 4.2. Likewise, the clarinet maintains the violin's newly formed septuplets, entering as the violin shifts to undecatuplets (m. 17). Underlying this entire polyrhythmic structure, Piano II constantly maintains half-note triplets to further complicate the composite rhythmic articulation.

Against these conflicting rhythmic patterns that are gradually built by the other instruments of the ensemble, a typical bugle call builds in tension, not by any rhythmic device, but by gradually moving higher in register, as seen in example 4.2. This bugle call, though it differs markedly from the present-day one, immediately brings to mind the (now hideously digitalized) bugle calls that still echo through most baseball stadiums today in an effort to rile up the crowd into yelling, "Charge!" Amusingly and appropriately, after the hit is ruled a foul ball in Ives's piece, even the bugle retraces its melody, moving progressively lower in pitch, as the runner dejectedly retreats back to first base.

After the palindrome has been completed, the middle two measures of the piece, symbolizing the height of tension, suddenly reappear unexpectedly and unprepared. Musically, these measures serve as a miniature coda to close the piece, but in baseball terms, with this musical reminder of the climax of the baseball play, *could Ives be anticipating "instant replay"*? The bugle does not reprise its measures in this codetta. Instead, the bugle repeats a different segment of its earlier material to intone an altered and abbreviated version of the end of *Taps*—signifying the death of the rally.

SOME SOUTH-PAW PITCHING!

Another baseball-related composition completed by Ives—*Study no. 21: Some South-Paw Pitching!* for piano—offers a different perspective on the

STUDY NO. 21:
Some South-Paw Pitching!

and to toughen up the

CHARLES E. IVES (1909?)
Edited by John Kirkpatrick (1973)

Example 4.3. *Some South-Paw Pitching!* title page, mm. 1–5.
© Mercury Music Corporation, used by permission of the publisher.

association of Ives's music with baseball. In this piece Ives attempted to create a study for piano that would strengthen and improve a piano player's left-hand abilities. But rather than simply stating the purpose of the study, Ives makes use of a baseball term to colorfully and playfully make his intentions known. His initial pencil sketch [f4814] contains the title "Some South Paw Pitching!! and to toughen up the . . . "—here a line points back to the word "Paw" in the title to suggest that the study will toughen up the left hand, as shown in example 4.3, as retained in the critical edition.

Although "southpaw" is now a well-known nickname for a left-handed pitcher, the use of the term in Ives's time was relatively new. As sports historian Christine Ammer explained:

> This term allegedly was coined in Chicago in the 1880's because the Chicago Cubs' home plate faced east. When a left-handed pitcher faces west (home), his throwing arm is then to the south. The reason for this orientation supposedly was that during an afternoon game it kept the sun out of the batter's eyes as well as shielding the eyes of customers in the expensive seats behind home plate.[15]

Although other theories have been advanced about the origin of the word, most professional ballparks are indeed laid out in this manner, making right field a "sun field" for late afternoon games, even today in the age of night baseball.[16]

The earliest documented reference to a left-handed pitcher as a southpaw was in 1885:

Morris and Carroll had never seen the St. Louis team play ball, and as they had always been accustomed to having their opponents hug their bases pretty close, out of respect for Morris' quick throw over to first with that south-paw of his, they were supremely disgusted by the reckless manner in which the Mound City gang ran the lines [to steal bases] on them.[17]

Since this term likely took some time to spread across the country among the general populace, Ives's relatively early adoption of this term for the left hand *in general* again suggests how important baseball was in Ives's life and thoughts—going beyond the norms of everyday discourse, since widespread nonbaseball uses of the term, such as left-handed boxers or left-wing politicians, did not appear until the 1930s.[18]

Two significantly different versions of this piece have been published. The first, edited by Henry Cowell and appearing in print in 1949, was based on a "probable (but now missing) set of photostats of [Ives's pencil sketch of ca. 1909, the original of which is still extant] with a few revisions by Ives."[19] The second, a critical edition published in 1975, was edited by John Kirkpatrick in cooperation with and with the approval of the Charles Ives Society, and was based on a combination of the original pencil sketch [f4814–15] and an ink score [f4816–17] that apparently was unavailable to Cowell.

When Cowell produced the earlier edition of this piece, "Ives may not have been able to find [the ink score]—his manuscripts were habitually in that much confusion," as Kirkpatrick noted.[20] Noel Magee, who was perhaps the first to transcribe the ink score, provided an explanation for the primary musical discrepancy between the two versions:

> The *piu mosso* section at the bottom of page one should be a pattern of six-teenth-notes in fours, not in sevens. On the pencil sketch Ives wrote two bass parts for this section; the top bass staff in groups of four was to be played first, and he indicates with "II" that the lower bass line in patterns of sevens was to be played on the repeat. In the pencil copy it was his way of abbreviating material to be repeated in the coda. In the ink copy he writes the coda out in complete form and shows what he explained on the pencil sketch.[21]

Cowell, working only from the original pencil sketch, apparently missed this important detail. Keith Ward, on the other hand, found an unfortunate omission from both editions, in terms of baseball significance. An upper-register accented dyad, which appears in the first measure of both the pencil sketch and the ink manuscript, would force the pianist to cross the left hand over the right to play it—giving the visual impression that the performer, by throwing the left hand over the right, is "throwing" a left-handed pitch.[22]

In addition to the musical discrepancies between the two versions, one additional error in the earlier edition is the footnote on the first page that must have been added by Cowell or the publisher: "This piece was written in fun and excitement after seeing a good baseball game (Ives played on the Yale ball team himself)."[23] Of course, as discussed in the previous chapter, Ives never played baseball for Yale, which undoubtedly was a sore point with him, and on his own copy of the published work [f4826] Ives crossed out the word Yale, leaving "Ives played on the ball team himself."

Since the later edition combines aspects of both of the original manuscripts, my analytical comments on this piece will adhere to this critical edition by Kirkpatrick. Ives's methods for toughening up the "southpaw" may be divided according to the sectional layout of the piece.[24] While the right hand plays constantly throughout the piece, the left hand is nearly always moving at a faster rate. However, in addition to presenting the problem of speed and fluency for the left hand, Ives also offered a number of specific challenges for the pianist to meet with the left hand. The piece may be divided into subsections based on the texture of the music in the left hand: mainly block chords but with intricately shifting voices (mm. 1–3), disjunct and rapid bass activity (mm. 4–14, 30–31, 44–48), block chords (mm. 15–17, 32–36), a fast-moving tenor line above a slower-moving bass line (mm. 18–29, 37–43), and sweeping septuplet runs (mm. 49–52).

The piece begins with octaves in the left hand, quickly evolving into trichords. Many of these chords feature single voices shifting in intricate rhythmic patterns to form new resulting sonorities, as shown in example 4.3 (mm. 1–3). The right hand joins the left for most of these chords, creating larger, more complicated chords.

After this slow introduction, a faster section commences with a new kind of left-hand activity, consisting mainly of a disjunct bass line in sixteenth notes. In some parts of this line, Ives orients the bass line around interval cycles that sometimes conflict metrically with the right hand.[25] For example, in the first measure of this section (m. 4), the bass line initially presents pairs of ascending perfect fifths (forming quintal chords)— beginning on C2, C♯2, and E2, respectively, as shown in example 4.3 (mm. 4–5). These three-note groupings conflict with the metric accents that are clearly presented in quarter-note beats in the right hand. The fifth-based patterns are quickly replaced by ascending perfect fourths (m. 5), but these quartal patterns—beginning on F♯2, D♯2, and D3—immediately start shifting octaves rather than preserving the *pitch* idea of ascending fourths—unlike the true fifths of the previous measure. Still, the conflict with the meter of the right hand is preserved, if the left hand continues to be perceived in terms of these intervallic groupings. The remainder of this section moves away from these predictable intervallic patterns, but the stretch of a ninth formed by the overall shape of each initial ascending fifth pattern continues to play a prominent role in the passage, adding to the toughening of the left hand.

This rapid disjunct bass activity leads directly and without pause into a passage containing block chords in the left hand (mm. 15–17). Some of these block chords project triads and tertian seventh chords—for example in m. 15: Bb major (chord 1), A major seventh (chord 3), C# diminished seventh (chord 5), and C major (chord 6). Meanwhile, others of these block chords present less traditional sonorities—a favorite seems to be the interval of a perfect fourth below a diminished fifth (m. 15, chord 2; m. 16, chord 2 excluding the tie), or an (016) in set class terms. In addition to the challenge of forming these disparate block chords in the first place, moving between these chords sometimes involves leaps as large as a sixth (for example, m. 15 chords 2–3; m. 17, chords 1–2).

After this section of block chords and using a metric modulation in a similar manner to Elliott Carter's famous technique of a half century later, Ives returns to rapid melodic activity in the left hand—here in triplet eighth notes that are now equivalent to the sixteenths of the previous section (mm. 18–29). But instead of a single-line bass, Ives again increases the difficulty a notch for the "south-paw" by shifting the active line to the tenor and by including sustained notes in the bass against the moving tenor line.

The conclusion of the piece offers one final technique that Ives employs to "toughen up the south-paw" (mm. 49–52). Here, septuplet runs form a large-scale ascending chromatic line across the lowest notes of each septuplet, as shown in example 4.4. Each of the septuplets individually forms a major triad with a passing tone between the third and fifth of the chord. Then the "passing tone" that ends each septuplet forms a common tone

Example 4.4.   *Some South-Paw Pitching!* mm. 49–52.
© Mercury Music Corporation, used by permission of the publisher.

with the third of the ensuing major triad. This planing effect takes the line through all twelve major triads of the octave, the most systematic compositional device in the piece. The wedge-shaped design of these gradually ascending chromatic lines in the bass against the primarily descending borrowing of Stephen Foster's *Massa's in de Cold Ground* in block chords in the right hand provides a dramatic and effective conclusion to the piece and provides a Civil War reference in this baseball-related piece.[26]

Ives also tries to ensure this dramatic conclusion by the tempo indication, "Allegro molto, spirito, agiganto, hitopo, conswato!"[27] His Italian seems to get worse the further along he goes; the first three words are proper Italian terms that are common in music, but the last three are self-invented Italian-sounding words that have no meaning in Italian. "Agiganto" seems to be a combination of the Italian words *gigante*, meaning "giant," and *agitato*, a common musical term meaning "agitated." For Ives, clearly, the arpeggiated triads contained in the septuplet sweeps are huge and the effect is excited. "Hitopo" and "conswato" apparently are words completely manufactured by Ives. Similar to the apparent intent of "agiganto," these faux-Italian words seem to indicate that the pianist should "hit" this passage hard, or "hitopo," and to play the keys with swat or "conswato" to properly execute the passage. Through the use of these irregular but inventive terms, however, Ives manages to provide two additional, if obscure, references to baseball—as the batter "hits" or "swats" the ball. (Babe Ruth later was known as the "Sultan of Swat.")

Baseball is suggested by these expressive indications, the borrowed Stephen Foster tune and its Civil War implications, and of course the title, even if none of the musical techniques used in the piece to "toughen up the south-paw" seems otherwise related to the sport. However, Ives returns to the baseball orientation of this piece at the very end of the composition. Here, Ives presents a drawn-out plagal cadence with fermatas everywhere except on the last chord, a single quarter-note containing an unexpected major triad. Ives places above the staff the words "after a 2nd thought look for a boy in front row!" as shown in example 4.4. Placing a boy in the front row by this comment seems to call forth a picture of a baseball grandstand, rather than a concert hall. Practically, Ives seems to be trying to assure that the proper amount of silence will take place on the held quarter note rest before the final chord, but Ives also may have envisioned the self-imposed silence of an eager young baseball fan in the front row at the ballgame watching in awe as a crafty lefthander throws a curveball.

"OLD HOME DAY"

Despite the importance of baseball in Ives's life and music, only one of his nearly 200 songs, about a third of which have texts written by Ives, contains any text related to baseball. Ives's own text in "Old Home Day" (ca. 1913), #52 in *114 Songs*, presents an obvious reminiscence of his childhood. The scene is typical of small-town Americana in the late nineteenth century—an opera house, a parade down Main Street, a church-bell, and boys playing baseball in "a corner lot, [with] a white picket fence, daisies almost everywhere, there, We boys used to play 'One old cat,' and base hits filled the air." Throughout the text the narrator, presumably Ives, represents himself as a young boy. He twice uses the phrase, "we boys"; he depicts the narrator as a child too young to play in the band by means of the words "as we march along . . . behind the band"; and he remembers "another sound we all know well . . . that little red schoolhouse bell." According to Stuart Feder:

> Charles's account of his own early life is a celebration of boyhood—of his own, of his father's (still implicit in the sounds and sights of a town rapidly changing but still imbued with a post-Civil War atmosphere), and of boyhood in general. There was a reverence in Ives's use of the term, *we boys*, which only intensified as he later idealized these earlier years.[28]

Ives's fond memories of playing baseball with other boys in "a corner lot"—memories that he carried into his old age, as discussed in chapter 3—are an important component of this song as reflected in his reminiscence of playing "one old cat" in the text.

The term "one old cat" (also known as "one-hole cat" and "one o'cat") refers to an early variant of baseball. Baseball scholar Paul Dickson identified it as

> an informal game that is usually played by three children. Rules vary depending on circumstances but a typical game has one base with one player at the plate, one pitching and one in the field. Outs occur when a ball is caught on the fly or there are three strikes. The batter can score on a hit, which enables him to run to the base and return before being put out. The players rotate and each keeps his own score.[29]

With only two children in the field to catch the ball, it is easy to see why "base hits filled the air" in a game of "one old cat."

"Old cat," in general, was a pickup game named "according to the number of batters available, 'one old cat,' 'two old cat,' etc."[30] Tristram Coffin, another baseball scholar, explained that the name for this informal version of baseball likely developed from "rounders," a British game played with a ball and stick that is clearly related to baseball, despite Al Spalding's attempts to counter this claim, as discussed in chapter 2:

> Colonial versions of rounders were apt to be casual. One variant that became popular was called "one hole catapult" or in slang "one old cat." . . . When a batter was put out, each fielder moved up a position toward his turn at the plate. If a fielder caught a ball on the fly, he exchanged positions with

the batter at once. When there were enough people, two stakes were provided and the game was called "two old cat." In towns, where a lot of people got together of an evening, three stakes were used, four or more men
were put to bat, the rest sent out to field, and the name of the game was
"town ball."[31]

From another perspective, Harold Seymour claimed that

the most elementary version of "old-cat" was borrowed from the English
game of "tip cat," in which a wooden "cat," shaped like a spindle, was placed
on the ground, tipped in the air, and struck with a stick. "Old-cat" merely
substituted a ball for the spindle.[32]

The melodic line that sets this baseball-oriented text borrows an entire
phrase from *John Brown's Body*, or *The Battle Hymn of the Republic*, as shown
in example 4.5.[33] The tune is chromatically altered from the original diatonic model, but it harmonically outlines an A major triad and at the same
time expands upon the melodic line of the previous phrase. Thus, instead
of beginning on E and ending on A, as would be expected in the original
tune in A major, Ives's chromatically altered version begins and ends on
the same note. But Ives's well-conceived chromatic alterations to the tune
preserve the contour, tonal center, and triadic outline of the original tune
(an A major triad between the beginning, ending, highest, and lowest
pitches of the passage) while substantially altering its melodic and rhythmic details.[34]

Ives uses this music for the parallel spot in the first stanza of his text,
"We boys used to shout the songs that rouse the hearts and the brave
and fair," which also seems to fit well with the Civil War associations of
the borrowed tune. This first-verse text is the only one that appears in
the only surviving manuscript of this passage [f6802], though this manuscript does not appear to be a first draft, based on the clear organiza-
tion of the page, the ruled bar lines, and the uncharacteristically neat

Example 4.5.   "Old Home Day," mm. 14b–17.

notation. Borrowing a Civil War tune for this baseball-related text again provides a connection of baseball and the Civil War.

THE FOURTH OF JULY

In the orchestral work *The Fourth of July* (1911–1913), Ives made a prominent reference to baseball in his program note that precedes the score. This piece is the third movement of his *Holidays Symphony*, a collection of four separate movements that Ives later grouped into a symphonic work. The other holidays included in the symphony are *Washington's Birthday*, *Decoration Day*, and *Thanksgiving and Forefathers' Day*. Although in some ways Ives considered this collection of movements as a complete work, he composed each movement separately and thought of them equally as individual works. In his *Memos* Ives noted that "these movements have been copied and bound separately, and may be played separately."[35]

In *The Fourth of July*, Ives depicted a boyhood memory of the midsummer holiday celebration. Ives again turned to Danbury and his own childhood for inspiration for this piece:

> I remember distinctly, when I was scoring this, that there was a feeling of freedom as a boy has, on the Fourth of July, who wants to do anything he wants to do, and that's his one day to do it. And I wrote this, feeling free to remember local things.[36]

Apparently, among the things a boy "wants to do," who can "do anything he wants to do," is play baseball, and among the "local things" that Ives remembered from the many activities on the Fourth of July was a baseball game. (Fireworks are a big part of this piece as well, but I will confine my remarks to baseball for now, though fireworks *at* baseball games of course now have become a commonplace and, especially for young fans, very welcome phenomenon.)

In the program note Ives listed a number of specific events associated with this celebration of "a boy's Fourth," including a "baseball game (Danbury All-Stars vs. Beaver Brook Boys), pistols, mobbed umpire."[37] (Obviously, the Danbury area took its baseball very seriously!) Ives, however, minimized the importance of the program of this piece by maintaining that "all this is not in the music—not now!"[38] But some aspects of the piece suggest that the references to baseball in the program indeed may be depicted in the music, and Ives, contradictorily, claimed that "this is pure program music—it is also pure abstract music—'You pays your money, and you takes your choice.'"[39] Although the music stands well on its own as abstract music, I will take Ives's advice and take my choice: "pure program music."

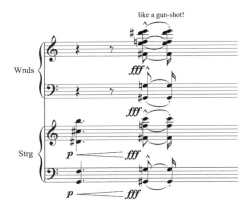

Example 4.6.   *The Fourth of July*, "gun-shot," m. 39, short score.
Associated Music Publishers.

First, Ives borrows from several Civil War–related tunes, including *Battle Cry of Freedom, John Brown's Body* (or *The Battle Hymn of the Republic*), and *Marching through Georgia*. These Civil War references again may be associated with baseball, as discussed earlier in this chapter and in chapter 3; however, these borrowings also might simply represent the festivities in general. Although the Civil War had long since passed before Charles Ives's birth, a celebration of the nation's independence may well have included reference to its most recent war, especially by honoring veterans.

In addition to this indirect reference to baseball by means of the Civil War, more compelling programmatic baseball references appear directly in the music of *The Fourth of July*. The "pistols" mentioned in the program, as the crowd mobs the umpire, fire in the piece through an immediate crescendo from piano to fortississimo arriving on a syncopated and accented six-note open cluster chord (using all chromatic pitch classes between D♯ and G♯) marked "like a gun-shot!" in the score (m. 39), as shown in short score in example 4.6. Regrettably, violence against umpires was far too common in the nineteenth century, as suggested earlier in this book, and fans often used projectiles to back up their heckling. Fortunately, as Bill James concluded: "As nearly as I can figure out, the fans never actually killed an umpire. They tried."[40]

Another, more subtle reference to baseball occurs when Ives borrows part of his own song, "Old Home Day," in *The Fourth of July*. As identified by Wayne Shirley, who edited the critical edition of the piece:

The "minor tune from Todd's opera house" (cited verbally and vocally in the song *Old Home Day* is the basis of mm. 44-53 of *The Fourth of July*. . . . Measures 45-53 also use parts of the accompaniment of *Old Home Day*, and come

Example 4.7. *The Fourth of July*, mm. 50–53, first violins.
Associated Music Publishers.

as close to common-practice harmony as anything in *The Fourth of July*; curiously, their effect is not one of relaxation but of heightened tension.[41]

Included in this passage is a direct quotation of the line of music that evokes baseball in his earlier song through its text—"We boys used to play 'One old cat,' and base hits filled the air" (compare example 4.7 with example 4.5). In *The Fourth of July* the line is played in parallel perfect fifths by the first violin using double stops, and this line, of course, also quotes *John Brown's Body*, a Civil War reference, as noted previously.

Other than these three references—the association of baseball with the Civil War tunes, the depiction of a gunshot mentioned in the program in connection with baseball, and the use of his earlier baseball-related piece—*The Fourth of July* seems to contain no other allusions to baseball. Perhaps Ives at one time planned to depict more details of the ballgame he mentions in the program note, but later changed his mind, as suggested at the end of his program note: "All this is not in the music—not now!"[42] However, like most any kid, he seems to have become more interested in the fireworks: "In the parts taking off explosions, I worked out combinations of tones and rhythms very carefully by kind of prescriptions, in the way a chemical compound which makes explosions would be made."[43]

FIRST PIANO SONATA

The First Piano Sonata contains a brief reference to baseball in the program note that Ives wrote on the back of a manuscript page [f3723], but these rough ideas toward a program for the work were never completed and carried forth into published versions of the piece.[44] As is the case with many of his other pieces, Ives never put this piano sonata into final form. In his *Memos*, Ives explained that

> not all of this sonata has been copied out in ink, although it is all there in lead pencil. It was finished in 1909 or 1910. Not getting it into more legible shape is one of the peculiar psychological things hard to explain. When I finished it, I had expected to get [going] right off and copy it out plainly. Then, as in many other cases, I got started on something else, and I kept putting it off and putting it off, and for so long a time, that, when I did look back at it, I lost interest.[45]

Later, in 1948–1949 the work was copied into performable and publishable form by Lou Harrison and premiered by William Masselos.[46]

The sonata is in five movements—or seven, if the two subdivisions of the second and fourth are considered separately—an arch shape with unifying cyclic thematic references.[47] Jan Swafford called this sonata "one of Ives's most ambitious and important works."[48] The program for the piece appears on a page of an early ink score of the first movement:

> What is it all about?—Dan S. asks. Mostly about the outdoor life in Conn. villages in the '80s & '90s—impressions, remembrances, & reflections of country farmers in Conn. farmland.
>
> On page 14 back, Fred's Daddy got so excited that he shouted when Fred hit a Home Run & the school won the baseball game. But Aunt Sarah was always humming *Where Is My Wandering Boy*, after Fred an' John left for a job in Bridgeport. There was usually a sadness—but not at the Barn Dances, with their jigs, foot jumping, & reels, mostly on winter nights.
>
> In the summer times, the hymns were sung outdoors. Folks sang (as *Ole Black 'Joe'*)—& the Bethel Band (quickstep street marches)—& the people like things as they wanted to say, and to do things as they wanted to, in their own way—and many old times worse there were feelings, and of spiritual fervency![49]

The baseball reference in the piece's program—"Fred's Daddy got so excited that he shouted when Fred hit a Home Run & the school won the baseball game"—at first seems out of place among the surrounding text, but the entire program is clearly another example of Ives's frequent nostalgic reminiscences, many of which include baseball.

One important component of this programmatic reference—subconsciously, or even consciously—is that Ives's mention of Fred's father's reaction in this program note seems to carry connotations beyond the scene itself. The reference may evoke Charlie's disappointment that his own father's reaction to his son's exploits on the ballfield were decidedly unenthusiastic, as discussed in chapter 3. The emphasis is on Fred's *father* in this story, rather than on the boy who hit the home run. Again, it must have been tremendously disappointing to Ives that his father did not share his enthusiasm for baseball, as some of his teammates' fathers almost certainly did. On the other hand, the reference may not hold such negative connotations, instead reflecting the thrill of the situation, a joy that Ives certainly would have shared, even if he had to gain his father's approval in other ways—through music.

Unlike *The Fourth of July*, where a clear depiction of a gunshot links the music directly to the program, and the other pieces cited earlier, where baseball situations and memories are portrayed in specific musical ways—the First Piano Sonata does not seem to contain any obvious musical depiction of Fred's home run or his father's excited reaction. Ives's mention of Robert Lowry's *Where Is My Wandering Boy?* is of little help; although Ives alludes to fragments of this source tune throughout the movement, presumably to depict Aunt Sarah humming, no clear-cut borrowing of a significant portion of the tune helps suggest a location for the musical depiction of the home run.[50] However, one notable possibility is a passage early in the first movement, where the music gradually builds in terms of register, then just as gradually the tension created is released (mm. 18–19). The circular nature of this brief passage may be an attempt to portray Fred circling the bases after his home run. The passage certainly portrays the excitement that would result from a home run, but Ives, unfortunately, made no mention of this specific passage in the program.

On the other hand, Ives provided a specific reference to "page 14 back" for the passage containing "Fred's Home Run," but this reference is difficult to trace. He may have been referring to page 15 [f3728], which appears on the back of page 14 of the second ink copy.[51] However, page 15 contains only a brief sketch of the sweeping left-hand arpeggios (mm. 21–24), which occur immediately after the passage previously mentioned as a potential depiction of the home run. These arpeggios—which, in contrast to the finished version, are measured in the sketch—seem wrong for the excitement of a home run in a local ballgame. The arpeggios underlie and support soft and pensive melodic material in the right hand of the finished version. Though circular in construction, these arpeggios do not give an impression of an excited youngster circling the bases. The "page 14 back" to which Ives refers may be from some other lost manuscript version of the piece; the slightly earlier passage seems like a better explanation for this portion of the program. From a broader perspective, however, rather than an actual baseball scene to be depicted through music, it seems more likely that Ives's picturesque baseball reference in this program note—which continues to remain buried in the sketch and in biographical references to the piece—was a broad reflection of the romantic character of the piece in general, a nostalgia for baseball enthusiastically played by amateurs and schoolboys, to represent his memories of a simpler time.

MEMORIES OF BALLGAMES

In summary, Ives's completed baseball-related pieces are each about his own memories—of playing the game, of general baseball concepts, or of local ballgames he apparently watched—and bear no specific relation to major league baseball. Instead, for each of these pieces Ives invoked his sense of musical nostalgia, whereby he represented some of his fondest recollections by attempting to recreate the sounds associated with his memories or the emotions he attached to them. In each of these pieces,

Ives looked back on his baseball-playing youth: running the bases according to the rules, observing the distinctiveness of left-handed pitchers, playing pickup games in corner lots, watching ballgames on holidays, and seeing schoolboys hit home runs to their fathers' delight. Although Ives's memories of the sport seem to revolve around amateur baseball in these pieces, major league baseball did enter Ives's life when he arrived in New York as a young man starting out in the insurance industry where, for the first time, he had a chance to follow the national pastime at its highest level. And in several incomplete musical sketches dating from around 1906, to be discussed in the next chapter, Ives left a record of his attendance and his enthusiasm for major league baseball by means of his musical portrayals of several prominent ballplayers.

Chapter 5

Musical Sketches of Ballplayers—A Baseball Fan's Record

BURSTS OF CREATIVITY

The first decade of the twentieth century brought about a significant change in Ives's compositional approach. As suggested in chapter 1, Ives's overreaction to the public presentation of his cantata, and his subsequent abandonment of his long-held role as a church musician, afforded him the liberty of creating music that was free of the perceived pressure of public reaction. According to Stuart Feder:

> Ives's "giving up" of music in 1902 had paradoxically brought about a greater commitment to it. But by 1905, the vigorous and innovative thrust of the music seemed spent, a symptom of the depression Ives rationalized as composer's "slump" [another example of Ives's use of a baseball term in general discourse]. When the creative spirit broke through once again the following year, it required an exhausting effort for Ives to organize. Ideas for experimental works bubbled over and were realized in brief, highly unique works which had to be sketched in a hurry.[1]

Included among these hurried, distinctive, and experimental sketches were musical depictions of contemporary baseball players.

The musical language in the sketches he worked on at this time expanded Ives's compositional technique considerably by becoming increasingly dissonant and rhythmically complicated.[2] As mentioned previously, these pieces evoked strong reactions from his housemates, who called them "resident disturbances."[3] Yet, according to Burkholder,

> even these pieces were carefully tailored to their intended audience. The primary audience was of course Ives himself, as he tested new ideas in his com-

positional workshop. But he also shared several of them with friends and tried them out with fellow musicians, usually in private. Ives was well aware of the resistance his experiments were likely to provoke, and so he couched many of them as "jokes" or "stunts." This made them more palatable, while at the same time allowing listeners—himself among them—to come gradually to accept the new sounds as interesting in their own right and as potentially valuable additions to the musical palette.[4]

Furthermore, connecting these new musical experiments directly to major league baseball—a rapidly growing pastime, especially among young urban men—would have made these pieces even more attractive, to his housemates as well as to himself.

ARRIVAL IN NEW YORK

Although Ives seems to have been unaffected by professional baseball in his youth, as discussed in chapter 3, his attention to the professional game increased dramatically shortly after his arrival in New York in 1898. This shift of interest parallels the development of the sport during these years. The idea of baseball as primarily a spectator sport did not develop until the end of the nineteenth century; before this time baseball was mainly, according to baseball historian David Nasaw,

> a sport played by boys in vacant lots. . . . Baseball, as a spectator sport, took off in the early 1900s as major league clubs built new stadia just outside the central business districts at locations served by as many trolley, subway, and railroad lines as possible. . . . Big-league admissions doubled between 1903 and 1908.[5]

With this unprecedented access, Ives for the first time was able to become a genuine fan of major league baseball. As Ives was working his way into the insurance industry and living with similarly minded recent graduates of Yale and their associates, he must have seen professional baseball as both an interesting and appropriate amusement:

> The limited number of inexpensive seats, all of them far from the action, uncovered, and uncomfortable, and the placement of the games on weekday afternoons guaranteed that the bulk of the spectators would be professionals, white-collar workers, and self-employed businessmen.[6]

Ives, as a budding professional and future business owner, was among the spectators of at least some of the games.

The record of Ives's interest in major league baseball appears in the sketches he composed during these early years in New York, and the record this baseball fan left is unique in historical baseball literature, because few if any reflections of individual fans were written down and none were documented through music. Ives's sketches contain specific references to baseball players, and these baseball references were based on firsthand experience of games from the grandstand. Although these sketches are incomplete and in some cases occupy less than half of a page, Ives gave full titles to these sketches and provided descriptive commentary between staves and in the margins. As Jan Swafford indicated, this programmatic treatment was not exceptional among Ives's sketches:

> Most of Ives's ideas, even ones coming from sheerly technical experiments, had programmatic titles, and usually in some degree expressed those titles. . . . He tended, in fact, to name nearly every sketch, even if it lasted just a few lines, and sometimes referred to such sketches as if they were pieces.[7]

Parts of three pieces based on major-league baseball players have survived among Ives's autograph manuscripts. Apparently, Ives completed none of these pieces, or at least none of these pieces survived in their entirely. But the music that does survive suggests much about Ives's personal view of the professional sport and his approach to composition.

Ives's apartments as a bachelor in New York from 1898 until his marriage in 1908 all would have provided convenient access via public transportation to both of the New York baseball teams in Manhattan. Ives lived at West Fifty-Eighth Street until moving "a few blocks to Central Park West in 1901, then to elegant digs at 34 Gramercy Park in 1907."[8] Although Brooklyn's Washington Park would not have been completely inaccessible, the Polo Grounds at Eighth Avenue and 155th Street or Hilltop Park at Broadway and 165th Street offered convenient public transportation access and probably would have been much more suitable locations for Ives to watch an occasional ballgame than Brooklyn.[9] Swafford mentioned "the Giants-Dodgers rivalry at the Polo Grounds" as one of the primary "diversions" of Ives and his friends.[10] Of the four players portrayed by Ives in these sketches, one played for the New York Giants (at the Polo Grounds), one played for the New York Highlanders (later renamed the Yankees) at Hilltop Park, and the other two played for opponents of these two teams. The Giants were a powerhouse in 1904 and 1905, winning the National League pennant in each year with over 100 wins, while the Highlanders were much less successful, finishing only as high as second place in the American League in 1904 and 1906. However, Ives seemed to show no preference for one team over the other in his choice of material for these compositions, and in fact he paid as much attention to players on visiting teams as to players on the home teams in the two ballparks.

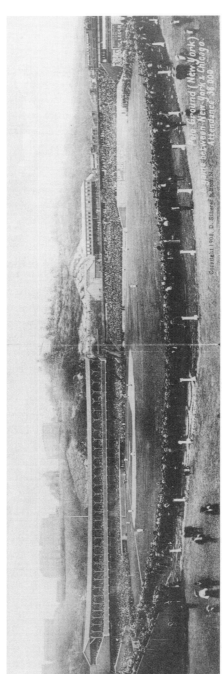

Illustration 5.1.   The Polo Grounds, home of the New York Giants, ca.1908. Coogan's Bluff can be seen behind the grandstand and an elevated train car, which could pull directly up to the stadium, can be seen to the right in the photograph.

Courtesy National Baseball Hall of Fame Library, Cooperstown, New York.

Several different structures have used the name "Polo Grounds" over the years.[11] The initial stadium, the New York Giants' first home, was a double-decked wooden structure located on 110th Street. This ballpark was demolished by the city following the 1888 season, and the Giants relocated for the next two years to Manhattan Field, which was located in the same tract of land as where the new Polo Grounds would be constructed. The Polo Grounds that Ives would have known was built in 1890, was initially known as Brotherhood Park, and was used by the Players League for its initial year. In 1891 after the Players League dissolved, the New York Giants moved next door from Manhattan Field to the newer, larger stadium, and brought with them the name of their old ballpark, the Polo Grounds. This ballpark, shown in illustration 5.1, was rectangular in shape and narrow in order to fit between Coogan's Bluff, a high rock formation forming a cliff behind the stadium (shown in the background of the photograph), and Manhattan Field located adjacent to the stadium. Public transportation was especially convenient, as elevated train cars could pull up directly adjacent to the stands for unparalleled easy access for fans, as seen in the far right of illustration 5.1. Sadly, the entire stadium was destroyed by fire in 1911, but a mammoth new concrete and steel facility was built that summer in the same location and with the same basic layout—a structure that was originally called Brush Stadium, after the owner at that time, but was soon renamed and is now remembered simply as the Polo Grounds. This is the ballpark that most people familiar with the name associate with it, not the older version that Ives would have attended during the first decade of the twentieth century.

Hilltop Park, built in 1903, served the New York Highlanders for only ten years.[12] It was relatively small (seating capacity of approximately 15,000) and "consisted of a flimsy edifice, free of ornamentation, made entirely of wood except for a masonry foundation. . . . The field was dirt thrown on top of rock, and no money was ever put into upkeep."[13] The ballpark was not especially attractive, and the seating capacity was sometimes vastly exceeded, as shown in illustration 5.2, causing the eager fans to spill out onto the field in some cases.

Attending games at these two ballparks, Ives obviously was a very good judge of baseball talent. Of the four players to whom Ives chose to pay tribute in these sketches, three of them have been inducted into the National Baseball Hall of Fame in Cooperstown, New York. The one player who was not inducted, Mike Donlin, voluntarily cut his career short in order to pursue other interests, as detailed later. But he certainly was playing Hall of Fame–caliber baseball when he left the sport.

The *Mike Donlin—Johnny Evers* sketch contains some narrative description of what appears to be an event that happened in an actual baseball game witnessed by Ives, and *Willy Keeler at the Bat* contains a

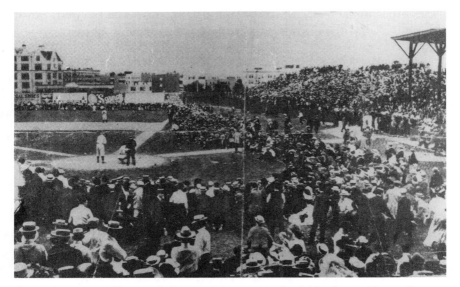

Illustration 5.2.   Hilltop Park, home of the New York Highlanders, with overflow at-tendance.
Courtesy National Baseball Hall of Fame Library, Cooperstown, New York.

narrative account of Keeler's legendary batting ability.[14] Ives's sketch of
Rube Trying to Walk 2 to 3!!, on the other hand, contains no narrative elements in the score to help identify the situation described through music. The baseball references in this piece are much more difficult to pin-
point, but some clues may be found in the biographies of the various
"Rubes" that played professional baseball in the first decade of the
twentieth century.

MIKE DONLIN—JOHNNY EVERS

The Manuscript

Only a half page of the first page of an orchestral sketch in short score
for *Take-off #7: Mike Donlin—Johnny Evers* survives [f2660], shown in facsimile as example 5.1. The sketch is written on the top half of a 13¾ by 10½
inch manuscript page, marked page 4 in the upper left corner. On the bottom of the page, upside down, are six measures of a sketch marked "Echo
Piece," which Ives later used in *The Pond* for chamber orchestra. However,
the entire sketch at the bottom of the page is scribbled out. The sketch of
Mike Donlin—Johnny Evers occupies the first eight staves of the total sixteen available on the page. The sketch is in pencil; clefs appear only on the

Example 5.1.   Facsimile of *Take-off #7*: Mike Donlin—Johnny Evers

first system. On the back of the sheet is the third and last page of a pencil sketch for a piece marked "Largo—*Hymn*" (mm. 20–32), which later became part of the first movement of *A Set of Three Short Pieces* for string quartet, double bass, and piano. "Trade mark Melodie No. 6" identifies the source of the paper on the bottom left-hand corner of the side containing the baseball sketch.

Example 5.2 provides my diplomatic transcription of the sketch. Ives identified this piece on the manuscript as "Take-off" #7. This piece is probably the seventh movement of Ives's planned but never completed "Athletic" set of cartoons or take-offs, referred to in his work lists. Ives's earliest surviving work list includes "*Take-offs* (academic, athletic, anthro-politic, economic, tragic) for large and small orchestras, about 1896–1916."[15] A later work list prepared by Ives similarly includes "Pieces for orchestra, *Cartoons or Take-offs*—Undergraduate and other events (academic, anthropic, urban, athletic, and tragic) 1898–1907."[16] According to James Sinclair,

> among Ives's extant works, the only such pieces referred to by a number that might be part of the [athletic] set are *Take-Off No. 3: Rube Trying to Walk 2 to 3!!*, *Take-Off No. 7: Mike Donlin—Johnny Evers*, and *Take-Off No. 8: Willy Keeler at Bat*.[17]

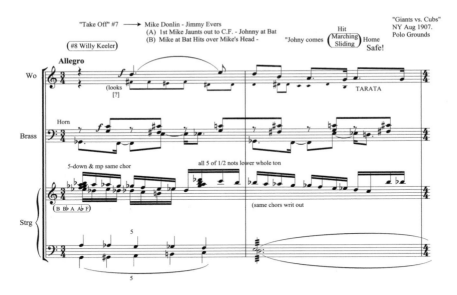

Example 5.2. Diplomatic transcription of *Take-off #7*: *Mike Donlin—Johnny Evers.* Clefs at the beginning of each system are provided editorially, but otherwise my transcriptions try to stay as close to the original sketches as possible. Other editorial comments and insertions are enclosed in brackets.

Reprinted by permission. All rights reserved. By Peer International Corporation.

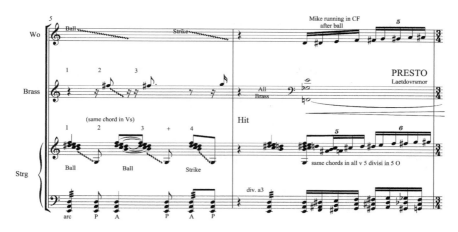

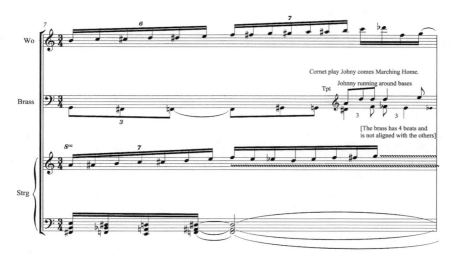

Example 5.2.   (*continued*)

These are the three baseball sketches to be discussed in this chapter. The title on the manuscript indicates Johnny Evers as "Jimmy," but references to Evers throughout the rest of the sketch identify him correctly as Johnny. The sketch includes only the first nine measures of the piece; at the end of the sketch Ives indicated "to Sheet back p. 8," but this page is lost.

Example 5.2. (*continued*)

Johnny's Home Run

The piece begins with some introductory material that explores different metric configurations simultaneously.[18] While the piece is notated in
three-four time, only the violins seem to adhere to this meter. Ives indicates that the violins should play *5-divisi and mp* the same chord, a five-
note cluster, through the first two or three measures in a chromatically descending series of sixteenth notes. Ives seems to have had some trouble
deciding on the structure of the cluster. The notes marked on the first beat
of the sketch appear to be E♭, F, G♭, A, and B♭—an (01457) set class, or a
cluster with two half steps (F–G♭, A–B♭), a whole step (E♭–F), and an augmented second (G♭–A). However, Ives writes in the following letter
names below this first beat and enclosed within a circle: B, B♭, A, A♭, F—
an (01236) set class, or a cluster with three half steps and a minor third. A
lower line, which does not move chromatically in parallel motion with the
upper line, complicates the identity of the desired notes further. Finally,
the ultimate goal of the chromatically descending passage is a tremolo
cluster (m. 3) with the following letter names written in a circle by Ives: A,
A♭, G♭, G, E—an (01235) set class, or a cluster of three half steps and a
whole step. If Ives wanted the same chords throughout the three-measure
passage, including the tremolo, as suggested by his two indications of
"same chor[d]s writ out" on the manuscript, then either the first chord or
the last chord, or both, must be wrong, whether marked with letter names
or using the notes on the staff. Another written indication by Ives, "all 5
of ½ nots lower whole ton," may shed some light on this problematic passage. The phrase is somewhat ambiguous as it stands, but it may mean

that the top four violin parts should be a half step apart, and the lower violin should be a whole step below the others—or interpreting Ives's words, all five of the "not[e]s" are a half step lower except the lowest note, which is a "whole ton[e]" lower. This reading corresponds with Ives's indication for the tremolo chord and may be more accurate.

Against this descending cluster that articulates the three-four meter, the lower strings divide the three-beat measure into five equal parts and move through a chromatic wedge, with two voices moving chromatically in contrary motion, to arrive on a D-E whole-step tremolo, one measure before the violins arrive on their tremolo (mm. 1–2). Meanwhile the lower brass divide the measure into four equal parts, written as dotted eighth notes and their equivalents, and present a chromatically based pattern, generally grouped into pairs of notes. At the same time the horns insert a syncopated pattern—adhering to the structure of the notated triple meter but grouped in two-beat units, both by notes and the beamed notation, to result in a duple metric feeling against the written triple meter, or a hemiola. The implied meter of the horns ultimately triumphs as the meter switches to four-four upon the arrival of the cluster tremolo in the violins (m. 3). Above all of these conflicting metric patterns, an upper woodwind instrument (unspecified or unclearly indicated by Ives) floats a melodic line that immediately turns into a fragment of the tune *When Johnny Comes Marching Home*, the main thematic material of the piece, and a clever reference both to one of the title characters, Johnny Evers, and to baseball's home plate. A third baseball-related reference is to the Civil War, like those in some of his other baseball-related pieces but enhanced by referencing the specific text of this tune in this sketch.[19] The triple reference to baseball in this borrowing is particularly remarkable, since this piece was "Ives's first piece to use borrowed tunes solely in a symbolic manner."[20] Another apparent woodwind part appears below this melody (marked in the sketch with smaller noteheads), but this fragment is both incomplete and incompatible with the meter.[21]

After these introductory measures, as "Mike jaunts out to C.F. [center field]," the main action begins with "Johnny at Bat" (m. 4). Ives's notation omits many rests, but he generally makes the metric placement of notes clear by writing in beats and half-beats numerically. The strings, labeled "Pitcher on mound," depict the pitches, marked "ball" or "strike" in the score, with descending glissando clusters in the violins along with open-string fourths alternating between tremolo and pizzicato in the double basses. A single trumpet personifies the umpire with ball and strike calls depicted with, what Ives fittingly calls, "slide down yell" glissandos.

A sudden one-beat silence, marked "Hit," suggests the hush of the crowd at the crack of the bat (m. 6), followed immediately by the return of the violin cluster and double-bass tremolo. Ives depicts "Mike running in cf [center field] after ball" with a written-out accelerando in the woodwinds and violins. These increasingly rapid chromatic scales are out of synchronization with each other, at first by pitting sixteenth notes in the woodwinds against a quintuplet in the violins then by contrasting a quintuplet in the woodwinds against a sextuplet in the violins. Each of these nonsynchronized scales continues to increase by one note per beat and ascend chromatically. The low brass and double basses add to the excitement generated by these polyrhythms, as well as by the baseball play depicted: The brass present a single held chord that increases dramatically in volume through a crescendo followed by a low chromatic pattern in triplets, while the basses offer rapid ascents and descents through the chromatic scale in perfect fourths *divisi a 3*.

Just before these chromatic runs have been completed, Ives depicts "Johnny running around bases" with the trumpets and cornets playing another fragment of *When Johnny Comes Marching Home* in a newly marked *Presto* tempo—taking up the triplets begun in the low brass. Ives adds the inscription "Johnny comes marching home, Johnny makes Home Run" above the trumpet line, making his intended pun on the borrowed tune clear. He adds the words "great excitement" in parentheses over the strings to characterize the descending and ascending glissando cluster chords in the violins (or, in Ives's words, "all fiddles rove up & down Scratchy") over a held chord in the lower strings. The woodwinds accompany "Johnny's march" around the bases with a descending sequence of first two-note, then three-note, ascending chromatic figures.

Ives outlined the program of this piece in his subtitles and other identifying marks at the top of the page of the sketch. The first subtitle, marked "(A) 1st Mike Jaunts out to C.F.—Johnny at Bat," sets the scene to accompany the opening three measures of the sketch, the polymetric structures mentioned previously. The second subtitle, marked "(B) Mike [Ives meant Johnny] at Bat hits over Mike's head!! Johnny comes marching (sliding) Home Safe!" describes the action in the rest of the piece, though the slide home safe is presumably on the missing page(s). (If only we could see that musical cloud of dust!) In the upper right corner of the manuscript, Ives wrote, "'Giants vs. Cubs' NY, Aug [written over and apparently replacing July] 1907, Polo Grounds." At first glance it appears that Ives must have composed this piece based on an actual game he watched at the Polo Grounds in the summer of 1907. However, the record of Mike Donlin's career emphatically calls this date into question. A brief outline of the two players involved will help sort out the problem with the date, will provide some additional baseball context for the piece, and will shed some light on why Ives chose to depict their heroics in a composition.

The Actor and the Crab

Michael Joseph Donlin (1878–1933), shown in illustration 5.3, "became the most popular of the 1905 Giants by hitting .356 in 150 games and performing well in the famous five-shutout World Series. He played only one complete season (1908) thereafter."[22] Donlin's popularity continued even after his participation level and skills had waned: Returning to the club after a long absence, he was presented with a gold bat by his teammates, marked "'Welcome Home' Mike Donlin 1914" on the trademark and with all of his teammates' names inscribed. His popularity also was strong at opponent ballparks: He was awarded a silver cup "presented by the Chicago American [newspaper] to Michael Donlin 'The Most Popular Visiting Ball Player in Chicago' Winner in the Voting Contest Open to All 'Fans' 1908 April-June."[23] His playing abilities alone at the height of his career certainly would have attracted Ives's attention:

> He soared in 1905. He and [Christy] Mathewson, ranked to this day the greatest pitcher the game has developed, were the heroes of a baseball-mad New York. The picturesque Donlin, an athlete by day, a playboy at night, knew everybody and was known to everybody. . . . When the world series with Connie Mack's "Athletics" started in October he and Mathewson were the men to whom New York looked for victory.[24]

Even after his death, "the Giant fans never forgot him, and they placed him high in the list of immortals."[25]

In addition to his playing abilities, Donlin's flamboyant character also may have caught the interest of Ives: "On the field Mike had color. He clowned and strutted, argued with the umpires, chatted with the fans and between times caught fly balls and hit .330."[26] His nickname, "Turkey Mike," came not from his hitting or fielding prowess but from his showy style, his appearance, or simply how he walked out to his position in centerfield. According to one report of his antics,

> "Turkey Mike," they called him, because when he'd make a terrific catch or something he'd do a kind of turkey step and take his cap off and throw it up like a ham, a real ham; but he was a great one, he could live up to that stuff in the field or at bat.[27]

Other reports, on the other hand, indicate that his nickname came from his long sunburned neck or his distinctive turkey-like strut.[28] In any event, his distinctive manner of walking, in addition to his abilities on the ballfield, must have attracted considerable attention:

> He was idolized by the "fans," and the "kids" adored him. They imitated his every action, and the proudest boy in the universe was he who could mimic Mike Donlin's walk to the extent of being nicknamed "Turkey."[29]

Illustration 5.3.   Mike Donlin, center fielder for the New York Giants.
Courtesy National Baseball Hall of Fame Library, Cooperstown, New York.

Illustration 5.4.   Mike Donlin strikes a pose in a publicity photo for the theater, but strikes out in the hearts of Giants fans.
Courtesy National Baseball Hall of Fame Library, Cooperstown, New York.

Based on these attributes, it appears that the awkward interaction of four different implied metric beat patterns in the opening of Ives's piece (mm. 1–3, shown in example 5.2), as "Mike Jaunts out to C.F.," is Ives's attempt to mimic Donlin's distinctive walk through music.

Even at the time of his death, Donlin was remembered as much for his style as for his performance. An obituary recounted that

> he had color and swagger. He was rough, tough and profane—likeable. He wore his cap at a belligerent angle, over one ear, and there was always a prodigious plug of tobacco stuck away in a corner of his jaw. He was the most picturesque player of his time, and in the year of his greatest popularity and his greatest diamond deeds—1905—he shared with Christy Mathewson, the pitching king, the honor of being the baseball idol of Manhattan.[30]

After missing most of the 1906 season with a broken ankle, Donlin missed the 1907 season completely because of a contract dispute or his desire to begin a career in vaudeville, or both. Following his marriage to a leading vaudeville actress, Mabel Hite, in January 1907, Donlin—seemingly more interested in the stage than in the diamond, as suggested by his "uniform" of choice shown in illustration 5.4—became involved in a bitter contract dispute with the New York Giants and his manager John McGraw.[31] Early reports of his demand for a $600 raise in salary suggest that no one took his demands very seriously: "It is believed that unless Mike Donlin gets off his high horse his bluff will be called."[32] As the start of the regular season approached, however, the seriousness of his salary demands in light of his considerable baseball skills began to look more ominous to Giant fans. The dispute apparently was settled by the end of March as the Giants agreed to the increase.[33] Any lingering doubts in Giant fans' minds were erased when they heard

> that Donlin "made a sensational debut" [and that he was to receive] the $600 increase on the conditions originally proposed by Donlin, that is to be dependent upon the big outfielder keeping in condition all season. Manager McGraw personally assumed the responsibility in this instance. Nobody really cares how the matter really was adjusted, but the fans are glad the hard-hitting outfielder is in line.[34]

The fans seemed as forgiving as baseball fans today who flock back to the ballparks immediately after long-lasting strikes, now over millions of dollars rather than six hundred. This charitable attitude among Giant fans quickly changed, however, when reports came that Donlin had left the team due to a number of conflicting reasons, ranging from his doctor finding that his leg would not stand up to rigors of the season to a rumor that he had retired for good or that he would play occasionally only with independent clubs.[35] Both the fans and the press finally seemed to have tired of Donlin's unreliability. A popular sports magazine concluded that "Mike Donlin's frequent change of mind has made Gotham fans sore, and they do not care whether he reports or not."[36] The same issue summed up the apathetic attitude of the press: "Mike Donlin, the base ball star, has vanished. Hereafter he will be known only as the husband of Mabel Hite, an actress."[37]

Donlin's abandonment of baseball at the height of his career spawned many conflicting ideas and reports of the circumstances that led to his decision. The contemporary baseball literature contains many different accounts of his actions and the timing of his actions, including some distortions of the dates involved—similar to the problems associated with Ives's dates on his sketches. Donlin's own description of the situation, in a full and final report detailing his actions, gave a medical excuse for his behavior, which may or may not have been true or even accepted as accurate by his fans:

> Mike Donlin, formerly star slugger of the Giants, has definitely abandoned professional baseball and is now installed as house manager of the Whitney Opera House in this city [Chicago], where his wife, Mabel Hite, is playing in a musical comedy stock company. Said Donlin today: "After McGraw and I had come to a satisfactory agreement on the salary question, I joined the Giants in New Orleans, with every intention of playing throughout the season, and I remained with the club for ten days until we arrived at Louisville. At that time my foot, which I injured early in the last season, began to give me some trouble and my physician told me, after an examination, that I would not be able to stand the strain of playing every day. After this there was, of course, nothing for me to do but give up the idea of remaining with the Giants. . . . I shall not abandon baseball, as I have arranged to play first base with the semi-professional club managed by Jimmy Callahan. I will play Saturdays and Sundays through the season."[38]

Despite his insistence otherwise in this account, Donlin returned to major league baseball the next season, in 1908, immediately reprising his earlier success by playing 155 games and hitting .334. However, he missed the next two and a half seasons to continue his vaudeville career before finishing his baseball career in abbreviated stints with the Boston Braves, Pittsburgh Pirates, and again the New York Giants.[39]

Since Donlin did not play in the summer of 1906, due to his broken leg, and did not play at all in 1907, due to his continued injury, his contract dispute, and especially his budding stage career, Ives's date of 1907 cannot be accepted as the date of an actual baseball game involving the two players. Either the piece was composed in some other year than Ives indicated on his manuscript, or Ives did not compose the piece immediately following an actual game.

Additional evidence that might help date this sketch are the two pieces appearing on the same page of manuscript paper. The sketch of "Largo—*Hymn*," which occupies the first three pages of the set of manuscripts that contains the baseball sketch, was probably composed in August 1904, according to Kirkpatrick.[40] The sketch of *The Pond* at the bottom of the fourth page must have been composed before May 1906, also according to Kirkpatrick's date. Thus, based on Kirkpatrick's dates, the sketch of *Mike Donlin—Johnny Evers* that appears on the back of the earlier sketch and above the later sketch that is written upside down below it may have been composed between these two dates, strongly suggesting 1905—Donlin's best season—as a possible date and therefore making it possible that Ives indeed composed the piece in response to a specific baseball game. On the other hand, Gayle Sherwood, who has examined Ives's handwriting in detail, "dates the hand between 1907 and 1914, closer to 1907."[41]

Based on Maynard Solomon's often-debated essay that questions the veracity of Ives's dates, perhaps Ives intentionally fabricated some or all of the dates or dateable references listed on this sketch.[42] Certainly, the evidence in this case strongly supports this assertion. Donlin never played a single game in 1907, yet the handwriting on the sketch suggests 1907 as the composition date. Ives might have composed the sketch in 1907, based on his *memories* of the flamboyant and distinctive player, then much later in his life added the "Giants vs. Cubs" and "Polo Grounds" descriptions in an attempt to make his work seem more authentic. This addition would certainly raise the level of novelty in the sketch by indicating that it was composed based on an actual baseball game that Ives observed. Alternatively, if Ives composed the piece earlier than 1907, such as during the 1905 season at the height of Donlin's career, the date obviously must have been added later. The placement of the date, which appears to have been inserted between the surrounding lines of text, and the handwriting, which appears to be different than some of the other markings on the score, supports the idea that Ives added the date later.

Stuart Feder, in an essay that contradicts Solomon's findings about Ives's motivations for assigning dates on manuscripts, acknowledged the likelihood of such postdating. Feder also conceded that Ives harbored wishes for the priority of his compositional ideas and that Ives possessed the capacity for carrying out these wishes due to his physical and emotional instability in his later years. However, although Ives certainly was motivated to backdate his manuscripts to make himself seem more groundbreaking as a composer, Feder claimed that Ives was psychologically incapable of doing so deliberately. Nevertheless, Feder admitted that many of the dates on Ives's manuscripts were added later, but he attributed these later insertions to Ives's compositional style, where Ives worked on multiple compositions at the same time rather than finishing and dating each one in turn.[43]

Although on the surface this case seems to provide more evidence disputing the veracity of Ives's dates and questioning his motivation in assigning dates and datable references to pieces, it seems more likely that Ives mistook the date by two years, and the piece was actually composed in 1905 at the height of Donlin's career and as suggested by the presumed dates of the other sketches on the same paper. As Swafford noted, "Ives quoted dates for all kinds of things off the top of his head and was often wrong . . . [but] he is as likely to be late as early."[44] If Ives composed the piece in 1907, as suggested by Sherwood's reading of the manuscript clues, it seems unlikely that he would have included the absent ballplayer in his piece without including some sly remark about Donlin's disappearance from the team, and no such reference seems to appear. My earlier conjecture—that Ives mistook the date by two years, composing the sketch in 1905 and adding the wrong date later—seems like the most compelling interpretation.

As colorful as Donlin was as a character, Johnny Evers (pronounced *eee-vers*), the other subject of Ives's composition, equaled or bettered Donlin's accomplishments in this regard. A typically smirking Evers appears in illustration 5.5. One story, developed from the reminiscences of the two players years later, places the two opponents together, though in a different situation than Ives's scenario. Recalling their confrontation, Donlin said to the second baseman Evers:

> "Remember when I got to second base once I got hold of your ear and kept pulling it to get you sore so you would smack me and get put out?"
> "And what did I do?" asked Evers, blandly.
> "What did you do?" bellowed Donlin. "You grabbed my hand so I couldn't let go of your ear and hollered to the umpire: 'Look what he's doing to me? Are you going to let him get away with that? Put him out!'"
> "Those were great old days," sighed [Evers's teammate Joe] Tinker.[45]

Stunts like this, in full view of the spectators, certainly would have appealed to the aggressive and combative nature of Ives, especially in regard to his own views of sports and manliness, as outlined earlier in this book.

John Joseph Evers (1881–1947) played second base for the Chicago Cubs during the team's best years to date. Johnny Evers is perhaps best known for being part of the immortal double-play combination, "Tinker to Evers to Chance," featured in Franklin P. Adams's poem, "Baseball's Sad Lexicon," first published in July 1910:

Illustration 5.5.   Johnny Evers, second baseman for the Chicago Cubs.
Courtesy National Baseball Hall of Fame Library, Cooperstown, New York.

These are the saddest of possible words:
  "Tinker to Evers to Chance."
Trio of bear cubs, and fleeter than birds,
  Tinker and Evers and Chance.
Ruthlessly pricking our gonfalon bubble,
Making a Giant hit into a double—
Words that are heavy with nothing but trouble:
  "Tinker to Evers to Chance."[46]

This well-known poem neatly summarizes the rivalry between the Chicago Cubs and the New York Giants during the first decade of the twentieth century, in addition to the legendary skills of the Cub ballplayers mentioned. The Cubs ousted the Giants for the National League pennant in 1906, 1907, 1908, and 1910. Of course, "division champions" and "wildcards" were not even a dream at that time; only the top team in each league reached the postseason. The poem mentions the players' speed, "fleeter than birds" (Evers stole as many as forty-nine bases in 1906); it immortalizes their celebrated fielding ability, "making a Giant hit into a double" (referring to a double play, not a two-base hit); and the Cubs' continual success, "pricking our gonfalon bubble" (defeating the Giants for the pennant).

Bill James attempted to put this famous double-play combination into perspective through statistical analysis, comparing the double-play totals of the Cubs each year with the average number of double plays for the teams in the rest of the league, and found that the combination was only slightly better than that of the average team: "Tinker to Evers to Chance surely was not the greatest double play combination of all time, and probably was not the best in baseball at that time."[47] However, their reputation for turning the double play, based on this poem, has become legendary.

The poem's reference to "trouble" takes on new significance in light of the kind of player that especially Evers was. According to James Skipper, he was called

> "The Crab" because of the crab-like way he gripped the ball when throwing it, but the nickname took on a new dimension when National League President John Tener announced that Evers was the number one problem player in the league.[48]

However, he was distinctive in his achievements on the field as well as in his demeanor, as Donald Honig observed:

> Evers was the team's spark plug. Small, feisty, combative, Johnny was a nonstop chatterbox on the field, to the extent that both Chance and Tinker sometimes wished he was in the outfield. One of the game's all-time sharp thinkers, he was called "the Crab." Some say the name was bestowed for the way he moved on the diamond; others say it was for his often briny disposition.

Johnny was in constant battle, with umpires, opponents, even teammates. Tinker finally tired of his partner's querulous nature and stopped talking to him, except when necessary in the heat of combat.[49]

Since the Cubs were the chief rivals of Ives's New York Giants, Ives fittingly chose Evers to combat Mike Donlin in his piece.

Illustration 5.6.   Johnny Evers comes marching (sliding) home.
Courtesy National Baseball Hall of Fame Library, Cooperstown, New York.

Of them all [Tinker, Evers, and Chance], John Evers was the most picturesque. A wonderful all-around player, a firebrand on the attack, a heckler of
umpires, one of the gamest men this world ever saw, the "Crab" faced every
vicissitude that human frailty is heir to. On the diamond and off he faced
enough troubles to whiten the hair of almost any man, but he faced them so
courageously that he won even the admiration of his enemies.[50]

The fact that Ives depicted Evers hitting the ball over Donlin's head,
rather than the other way around—besides the obvious enticement of being able to use the *When Johnny Comes Marching Home* reference—seems to
be an indication of Ives's admiration for this opposing player, shown sliding home in illustration 5.6, spikes up! The fact that Evers hits a home run
in Ives's piece is remarkable given that Evers hit only *five home runs* between 1902 and 1910.

Evers's career offers no help in determining the appropriate date for
Ives's piece. While Donlin sat out in 1907, the date written on the manuscript, Evers played a complete season but batted only .250—though he
stole forty-six bases, second in the league.[51] In 1905, Donlin's best season,
Evers only played ninety-nine games, batting .276, a much more re-
spectable average. Perhaps Evers's and Donlin's performance in a single
game in 1905 peaked Ives's compositional interest. Evers did hit at least
one home run in each of these years, and perhaps Ives was there to see it.
In any event, their idiosyncratic playing style and colorful behavior, more
than anything else, likely influenced Ives's decision to depict their
ballplaying skills in a musical composition.

WILLY KEELER AT THE BAT

The Manuscript

Only a little over half a page of a sketch for *Take-off #8: Willy Keeler at
the Bat* survives [f0891], shown in facsimile as example 5.3. The pencil
sketch appears upside down on the fourth page of an ink and pencil
score-sketch of *Thanksgiving and Forefathers' Day*, which became the
fourth movement of the *Holidays* Symphony. The *Willy Keeler* sketch is
written on two five-stave systems with a blank staff between the two
systems on "trade mark Melodie No. 6" paper, the same paper as for the
Mike Donlin—Johnny Evers sketch. The bottom five staves of the page—
or really the top five staves, because the *Keeler* sketch is upside down,
based on the trademark—is part of the *Thanksgiving* sketch, while the
remainder of the page contains the *Willy Keeler* sketch. Clefs appear on
only the lower three parts in the first system but on all parts in the second system. A large round ink spot appears in m. 5 covering half of the

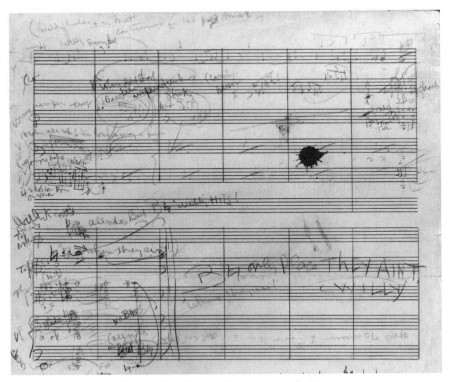

Example 5.3.   Facsimile of *Take-off #8: Willy Keeler at the Bat*.

fourth system as well as the space between the fourth and fifth systems, but apparently not obscuring any music. The sketch page has been folded in half.

Ives listed this piece as #8 of his planned, but incomplete, "Athletic" set of Take-offs. The surviving sketch includes only the last eight measures of the piece. Perhaps it was complete at one time, but if so the remaining pages are lost. Kirkpatrick dates this piece as July or August 1907, though 1907 was one of Keeler's worst seasons. The use of the definite article in the title of the piece, *Willy Keeler at the Bat*, may have been a reference to Ernest Thayer's famous poem, "Casey at the Bat" (1888), especially since Ives uses the simpler and more natural phrase "Johnny at Bat" in part of the subtitle of *Mike Donlin—Johnny Evers*, rather than the fuller variant "Johnny at the Bat," which would be parallel to the version used here in the title.[52]

Wee Willie

William Henry Keeler (1872–1923), a right fielder who played major league baseball from 1892 to 1910, played primarily in the early part of his career in the National League for the Baltimore Orioles (1894–1898), no relation to the present team of that name, and the Brooklyn Superbas (1899–1902), later to be called the Dodgers.[53] But his longest stint was with the New York Highlanders (1903–1910), an American League team that also, coincidentally, relocated from Baltimore, and Ives surely would have seen him with the Highlanders. Keeler also began and ended his baseball career in abbreviated seasons with the New York Giants (1892–1893 and 1910), but these dates are too early and too late, respectively, to have been relevant to Ives's musical sketch of the ballplayer.

Keeler obtained his well-known nickname, "Wee Willie," from his stature at 5' 4½" and 140 pounds; however, despite his diminutive size he remains one of the best hitters of all time.[54] According to an early newspaper report,

> Keeler was the smallest big man of baseball. His equals and his peers in batting were men physically equipped and Keeler was not. Keeler was contrary to all the accepted requirements, for besides being small, he in no other way resembled the masters of the wallop on the diamond.[55]

Yet, he holds the third-highest batting average of all time for a single season, .432 in 1897, and the fifth-highest lifetime batting average, .345.[56] His forty-four-game hitting streak (forty-four consecutive games with at least one hit in each game) is still the National League record, tied by Pete Rose in 1978, and was the major league record for over forty years (until Joe DiMaggio's fifty-six-game streak in 1941, mentioned in chapter 2).[57]

Keeler was perhaps best known for the phrase "Hit 'em where they ain't," which first was applied to him by Abe Yager, a sportswriter for the Brooklyn *Eagle* newspaper.[58] A contemporary reporter explained the slogan:

> While Willie Keeler was never a slugger, it is questionable if the game ever developed a greater hitter than he. [Honus] Wagner, [Nap] Lajoie, [Ty] Cobb and [Shoeless Joe] Jackson are of the slugging variety. They drive the ball a great distance, but when it comes to making effective hits just out of reach of the fielders, none of them compared with Willie Keeler when the latter was in his prime. There was real science in Keeler's hitting. He could place the ball just about where he wanted to, and it was only on very rare occasions that a pitcher succeeded in striking him out. Keeler led the old National League in hitting for several years, and yet only a few of his hits were hard-hit balls. But when it came to placing the ball where it could not be handled Keeler was an expert in a class by himself.[59]

Ives misspelled Keeler's nickname as "Willy" rather than "Willie," but perhaps he did so deliberately to conjure up associations with Keeler's *wily* style of hitting. The fact that Ives puts quotation marks around the nickname only when describing his hit supports this assertion.

Keeler also invented new ways to keep the ball out of reach of the defense and new strategies for maximizing his unique abilities:

> With the Orioles, he and John McGraw [a Baltimore player at the time, who later managed Donlin and the New York Giants] perfected the hit-and-run play [where a baserunner begins to run just as the ball is pitched, anticipating that the batter will make contact and keep the runner from being thrown out stealing]. Keeler originated the "'Baltimore Chop,'" whereby he swung down, pounded the ball into the ground, and reached first base by the time the ball finally came down.[60]

Clearly, his intelligent approach to the game and his speed were major factors in his success. According to his teammate McGraw:

> It was uncanny how Willie managed to keep the ball just out of the reach of the fielders. His mind always was active, and frequently he would not decide where to hit until a moment before he tapped the ball. For hitting ability Keeler was baseball's foremost artist. But he was a grand, all-around player and a hustler for his team. I consider Keeler the fastest man that ever streaked down to first base, and he always had to be watched on the bases. He was a splendid fielder, smart and a student of hitters. He knew just where to play for opposing hitters, where other fielders never could play just right for him.[61]

Thus, his defensive skills were as highly praised, though not nearly as often, as his hitting abilities.

It is not surprising that Ives noticed Keeler and honored his baseball skills by writing a piece about him. Keeler's distinctive size and manner of batting, shown in illustration 5.7, must have made him easily recognizable even at great distances:

> Keeler used a short thick bat and gripped so far up on the handle only half of the bat extended beyond his hands. He poked the ball just over the heads of infielders. When outfielders moved in to stop his short drives, he swung at the ball and sent it over the outfielders' heads.[62]

His instinctual approach to the game also must have fascinated Ives, who seems to have had a similar instinctual approach to his music. According to Thomas Rice, Keeler:

> could hit a ball outside as well as one inside; and whether a ball was high or low made little difference to him. His co-ordination of brain and muscle was as near instantaneous as could be conceived in an athlete. He did in a flash

what other players had to work out by more or less involved processes, and that was largely the secret of his success.[63]

Finally, as with other players that caught Ives's imagination, Keeler seems to have had a somewhat deviant nature in making the most of his chances on the ballfield. For example, early in his career when a bunted foul ball was not counted as a third strike according to the rules at that time, he would purposefully bunt pitches foul repeatedly until he was thrown a pitch he wanted to hit, as shown in illustration 5.8.[64] His ability to avoid striking out became legendary; according to one report, he went through the entire 1896 season without striking out.[65]

> Keeler could judge a pitched ball to a fraction of an inch. He is said to be the only player who ever umpired his own games. When he let a ball pass, umpires were satisfied it was not over the plate and called it a "ball."[66]

Although he was known as a practical joker, Keeler does not seem to have brought his somewhat deviant style of play off the field, as did the other players that caught Ives's attention. One columnist eulogized:

> Out of all the columns of tribute paid to Willie Keeler, one gathers the paramount impression that he not only was one of the game's greatest ball players of all time for performance, but one of its most admirable characters as well. Keeler made records that stood the test of time, he originated ideas in playing the game that made him a pattern to be followed in years to come—but above all he was an ideal character, a lovable personality.[67]

Willy's Hit

In Ives's musical tribute to Keeler, rather than using a single instrument to represent the ballplayer, Ives characterized him by means of several different instruments, possibly suggesting his multifaceted personality and varied skills. At the beginning of the sketch, as shown in a diplomatic transcription in example 5.4, Ives depicted Keeler's warm-up swings, "Willy swings bat," with a flute or oboe—or perhaps some other high woodwind instrument, as the sketch is unclear; the upper woodwinds are marked simply as "I." These musical swings of the bat consist of a flowing three-note pattern of a descending octave leap compensated by half-step motion in the opposite direction (mm. 1–6). The rhythmic pattern for these swings, a quarter note followed by two dotted quarter notes and an eighth rest, lasts one half-beat longer than a measure, moving the hitter's swings more and more out of synchronization with the meter, suggesting the lazy swings of a batter awaiting a pitch, and creating a constantly

Illustration 5.7.   Wee Willie Keeler, right fielder for the New York Highlanders, chokes up on the bat to "hit 'em where they ain't."
Courtesy National Baseball Hall of Fame Library, Cooperstown, New York.

Illustration 5.8. Willie Keeler was a masterful bunter and could bunt balls foul on purpose (when it was legal) until he got a good pitch to hit.
Courtesy National Baseball Hall of Fame Library, Cooperstown, New York.

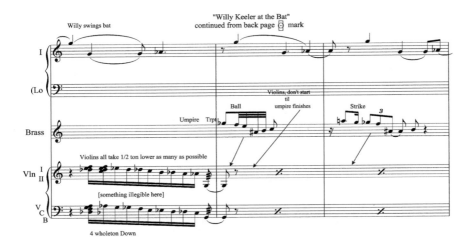

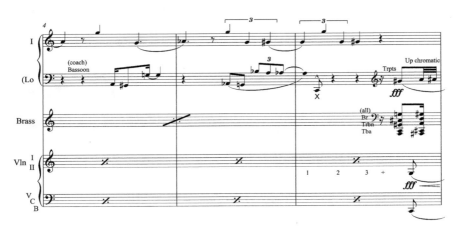

Example 5.4.   Diplomatic transcription of *Take-off #8: Willy Keeler at the Bat*.

changing pattern of metric dissonance. A sudden switch to quarter-note triplet rhythms (mm. 5–6) increases both the velocity and frequency of the warm-up swings immediately before Keeler hits the ball.

Between these warm-up swings, each time beginning when the "bat" is at rest, an umpire calls out first a ball and then a strike (mm. 2–3) in the form of a trumpet. The two calls by the umpire are remarkably similar to each other in pitch content, despite their vastly different intent; however, the strike call begins higher, ends lower, and is more drawn out in time— similar to the more dramatic strike calls still favored by many major league umpires even today.

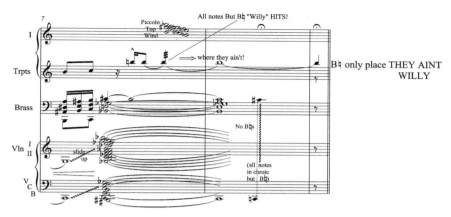

Example 5.4. (*continued*)

As Keeler continues to swing the bat in anticipation of the next pitch, the "coach," played by the bassoon, barks out instructions (mm. 4–6) in a retrograde and much quicker version of the gesture representing the practice swings of the bat. These instructions overlap and complement, or perhaps argue with, the umpire's ball and strike calls that continue in the trumpet, indicated by a two-measure repeat sign. The first set of coaching spans a diminished octave (from G#2 to G3), and the second set first spans a minor tenth (from G2 to B♭3) and then expands the motive through a concluding chromatic descent followed by a sudden leap down to an accented C2. This second attempt by the coach to inspire Keeler results in the batter's quickened warm-up swings and ultimately the hit itself.

For these final triplet swings Ives switches the chromatic note from A♭, as at the beginning of the piece, to the enharmonically equivalent G#. Although no pitch change would result from this shift (in an equal tempered system), perhaps Ives wanted to increase the tension further by using the upward pointing G# rather than the downward implication of the A♭. This enharmonic spelling change is especially significant, because Ives was very deliberate with his choice of accidentals. Nicolas Slonimsky related an instance in editing Ives's music when he suggested a change of a note from A# to B♭, to better approach the ensuing note for the ease of the player:

> But Ives said no. He said that A sharp was important because it was proceeding from A as a sort of an unfinished chromatic, that it would have gone to B but it just didn't, you know, and so therefore B flat would be wrong.[68]

Kirkpatrick related a similar story about Ives's idiosyncratic notation in which Ives declared, in regard to another similar enharmonic question,

"I'd rather DIE than change a note of that!"[69] Here the A♭ at the end of each warm-up swing connects musically down by half step to the G that begins each swing, but the initial G is raised via octave transfer in each case. The G♯ at the end of the last swing, on the other hand, moves up chromatically in the trumpet as the ball is about to be hit—representing very apt choices of chromatics.

During this time the strings present rapid chromatic descending patterns arriving in unison on a low G tremolo. Ives directed the violins to play half-step clusters below the indicated pitches: "Violins all take ½ ton[e] lower as many as possible." Following this direction each violin begins a half-step lower than the other—producing simultaneous, descending chromatic scales in a mass of sound. Meanwhile the lower strings, divided into four groups, play whole-tone clusters through similar descending chromatic scales, indicated in the score by means of the direction "4 wholeton[e] Down." These dramatic descending clusters in the strings, producing a "white noise" effect, represent the flight of the pitched ball; Ives wrote what appears to be a description between the staves of the string parts, but it is indecipherable. Ives coordinated each pitch with the umpire, by means of the indication "Violins, don't start til umpire finishes." Although the rhythmic notation is not coordinated in this way between the trumpet and strings, this inserted written indication shows the intended relationship between these instruments. If the strings represent pitches, each ensuing pitch must begin after the umpire has finished his call of the last pitch. These string statements repeat each measure throughout Willy's swings, the umpire's calls, and the coach's encouragements, continuing until the ball is hit. Musically, these string glissandos provide metric stability to contrast with the alternative polymetric grouping implied by Keeler's lazy warm-up swings.

The piece concludes with Keeler hitting the ball, represented by the trumpets at full volume (*fff*) continuing up the chromatic scale to C4 then dramatically leaping to B5, an inversion of the descending major seventh interval that spanned the warm-up swings. The switch from flute or oboe to trumpet for the depiction of the hit seems like a perfect way to indicate the "crack of the bat," or the different sound made by the bat hitting the ball. The heavier timbre of the brass instrument clearly indicates that a change in the swing has taken place as the bat meets the ball, rather than just floating through air in practice swings as before in the lighter woodwind timbre. Using trumpet for this depiction, however, at first seems like a curious choice since the trumpet is indicated for the umpire's ball and strike calls, but here in Ives's piece, as in the quotation cited earlier, Keeler really is "the only player who ever umpired his own games."[70]

At this point the strings, fittingly marked "slide," and the low brass join with the trumpets in an ascending glissando, with all of these instruments joined also by the woodwinds, and land on a massive cluster. This cluster, marked "no B♮s," includes all of the chromatic notes except B♮, extending from C♮2 (or B♯1) to C♯4 in the strings and low brass and from B♭4 to B♭5 in the woodwinds. With B♮ missing from this chromatic cluster—and marked "where they ain't!"—the trumpets "hit" the missing note at full volume, with an added flutter tongue tremolo for emphasis. Thus Willy "hits 'em where they ain't"—or, as Ives joyfully declared in large letters at the end of the sketch, "B♮ only place THEY AINT WILLY." This final B♮ in the trumpet continues to hold, after the massive cluster cuts off, by means of an additional held quarter note marked in the trumpet while all of the other instruments rest. The insertion of this final note looks like an afterthought, especially because an eighth rest is placed under the trumpet quarter note and an unruled double bar line is inserted tightly and hastily at the end of the piece. Ives probably recognized the need to emphasize this note further—by holding it longer, without the interference of the chromatic cluster—in order to make his baseball point more explicit.

RUBE TRYING TO WALK 2 TO 3!!

The Manuscript

Two complete pages of an unfinished draft of *Take-off #3: Rube Trying to Walk 2 to 3!!* survive [f3051–3052].[71] These pages appear to contain the entire thirty-two measures of the piece but are labeled as pages 5 and 6 in the upper right and upper left corners respectively. These pages seem to include the beginning of the sketch, rather than a continuation of any possible lost opening pages, so perhaps the pages were planned for some other piece, but unused. The sketch is written in pencil on the front and back of a single sheet of the same kind of "trade mark Melodie No. 6" manuscript paper as the other sketches, suggesting all three pieces indeed date from around the same period. On each side, the sixteen staves are divided into three five-stave systems with a single blank staff between the second and third systems. Ives provides no clefs at all. The bar lines are carefully drawn with a ruler, though the notes and other indications are much more untidy and are sometimes difficult to read. A three-inch piece of ¾-inch clear tape repairs a tear on the right middle of page 5, between staves 7 and 8 on the fold line.

Ives labeled this piece as "Take-off #3," along with the descriptive title, on the first surviving page of the manuscript. My diplomatic transcription of the sketch appears as example 5.5. Ives scored this piece, in transposed score, for B♭ clarinet, bassoon (or saxophone), B♭ trumpet, and piano. Later Ives reworked some of the material from this piece into at least five other

Example 5.5.   Diplomatic transcription of *Take-off #3: Rube Trying to Walk 2 to 3*.

pieces, as discussed in chapter 6. Before attempting to uncover the baseball references in this piece, I will describe some essential features of the music.

2 to 3 Rhythmically

Rube Trying to Walk 2 to 3!! deals mostly with rhythmic issues of two against three, as suggested by the title. While the sketch is notated in

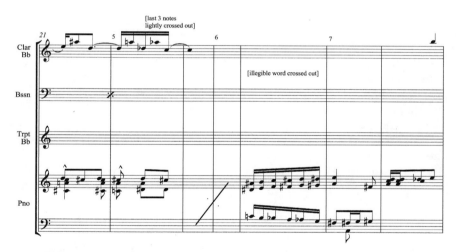

Example 5.5. (*continued*)

three-eight time, except for the last two measures, accent marks produce duple groupings in some instruments in various ways throughout most of the piece. The sketch begins with the clarinet presenting the main thematic material, a sequential five-note scalar pattern beginning with an upper neighbor figure, in triple groupings with the last beat of each measure accented. Meanwhile, the bassoon offers a bass accompaniment to the clarinet in a pattern that suggests two-four meter, with repetitive octave

Example 5.5. (*continued*)

leaps providing the eighth note divisions of the beats, pairs of eighths articulating the beats, and accents placed on the down beats of the implied two-four meter. Thus, the bassoon and clarinet present two different views of two against three, two eighth notes in the bassoon against the three eighth-note meter of the clarinet, and two quarter-note beats in the bassoon, presented as pairs of eighth notes grouped by an initial accent mark, against the clarinet's triple meter. At the same time, the pitch-class content of the bassoon, six eighth notes of A followed by six eighth notes of F, suggests a grouping of three quarter notes against the two quarter-note grouping implied by the accents. Expanding this idea further, the three quarter-note beats on A in the bassoon, articulated by pitch class repetition, act in opposition to the two groups of scalar material presented by the clarinet in the first two measures of the sketch. Therefore, in the first three measures and in only two voices, Ives presents four different ways of combining two against three—or, as in the title, "2 to 3!!"

The entrance of the piano (m. 4) initiates additional groupings of two and three. The piano repeats the first two measures of the clarinet and bassoon material; however, Ives alters the metric subgroupings slightly. Instead of a three-measure melodic statement as in the clarinet, the right hand of the piano presents only the first two measures and repeats this two-measure statement. The left hand takes up the pairs of eighth-note octave leaps from the bassoon, but the accents suggesting duple meter are gone. Instead, the left hand joins with the right hand in accenting the third beat of the written three-eight meter, first with a written accent in the bass and then with a pitch accent created by a descending octave skip (m. 5, last beat). Nevertheless, Ives still achieves two two-against-three patterns between the hands of the piano. The two-note patterns consisting of octave leaps in eighth-notes in the left hand contrast with the three-beat meter of the right hand articulated by the sequential melodic line. Meanwhile, from a more expanded viewpoint, the left hand presents three pairs of eighth notes against the two measures of sequential scalar material in the right hand. Finally, in the first five measures the main melodic material as a whole, in the written meter, forms a three-measure group (in the clarinet) followed by a two-measure group (in the piano)—again suggesting the title.

At the entrance of the piano, the trumpet (also entering for the first time) and clarinet begin to articulate new two-note groupings produced by constant syncopated eighth notes, accented in pairs. This new two-note pattern acts in direct opposition to both the triple groupings of the right hand of the piano (articulating the written meter) and the duple groupings of the left hand by occurring in syncopation. In addition, producing a scheme similar to that of the piano alone, the clarinet and trumpet present three groups of their duple pattern, indicated by the accents but displaced by a sixteenth note, against the two groups of the right hand's triple pattern, producing another two-against-three opposition. These patterns of two and three in the clarinet and trumpet become more pronounced as the clarinet begins to move up chromatically in pitch, with octave transfers, through (written) B♭ and B♮ (mm. 8–11).

Just before the end of the sketch, which repeats in its entirety by means of a da capo sign, the material from the first extant page of the sketch, described previously, returns with its duple and triple opposition. The conclusion of the piece (marked as a second ending in the sketch) abruptly leads to a written meter of two-four time, through a metric modulation (keeping eighth notes constant), where the duple patterns in the left hand of the piano ultimately triumph (mm. 31–32). The clarinet and trumpet, notated on the bassoon's second staff of the system, articulate beats one and three of the three-eight meter, then beats one and two of the two-four meter—emphasizing the written change in meter at this point. The piano also abandons its three-beat patterns and joins with the other instruments in articulating the new duple meter.

My reading of the second line of the sketch as the trumpet part, rather than the bassoon in this passage, is first suggested by Ives's notation of C♯ in the clarinet against E♮ in the bassoon (m. 16). Ives carefully lined up the two notes with a dotted line, indicating their relationship, and the natural sign on the lower part suggests that this note is actually a C♮ in the trumpet, since there seems to be no other explanation for the natural sign on this note. Later pieces that derive from this sketch confirm this interpretation.

In the intervening music (mm. 12–28), the piece largely articulates the written three-eight meter in the piano while the clarinet and trumpet (incorrectly placed on the bassoon staff) play intricate and largely irregular syncopated patterns against this metric stability. The only remotely consistent opposition of two against three occurs in the clarinet part, where pairs of notes lasting for three sixteenth notes appear in opposition to and syncopated with the written meter (mm. 14–21). On the other hand, Ives continued to conceive of this passage in terms of two measure groupings, as in the opening of the sketch. Here, measure numbers—written above the staves every two measures, rather than cross-measure beamings—project the two-measure groupings. With three beats per measure and two measures per group in this passage, Ives again portrays the numerical associations of the title.

Clearly, the idea of "2 to 3" in the title is an important compositional aspect of the piece. However, the exact meaning of the title in baseball terms is more difficult to trace. It is certainly possible that the piece is not baseball related at all. David Wooldridge suggested that "Rube" in the title "could be a contraction of [housemate] Bill Maloney's middle name—Raymond—spoken by a New Yorker through a heavy cold."[72] From another point of view, it could be just a reference to the nickname for a country bumpkin in general. Stuart Feder and others, on the other hand, have identified the title of this piece as a baseball reference.[73] In many respects the baseball implications seem too strong to ignore. Nevertheless, the exact relationship between this piece and baseball is difficult to establish. First, there have been at least thirty major league baseball players who were nicknamed Rube, and Ives does not identify the reference further in the score or in any of his writings.[74] Second, although the word "walk" in the title seems to be a reference to a pitcher walking a batter, the phrase "walk 2 to 3" is not a common baseball phrase. Finally, although the numbers two and three occur naturally together in baseball terms of balls and strikes, the numbers appear in the opposite order as a part of the phrase "3 and 2," as in a count of three balls and two strikes, not "2 to 3." In an attempt to come to a better understanding of the title, I will begin by trying to identify Ives's "Rube."

The Rube

Rube was a common nickname assigned to players who were from, or appeared to be from, the country. The name was "general slang for a farmer or country man, which appears to derive from Reuben, a name long-associated with country bumpkins."[75] Of the many ballplayers named Rube, three pitchers—Rube Marquard, Rube Foster, and Rube Waddell—might be singled out as the most likely choices among possible subjects for Ives's piece. All three of these Rubes were highly successful pitchers during Ives's era, and two of them were distinctive personalities of the game.

John Bowman and Joel Zoss claim that Rube Marquard is the subject of Ives's piece.[76] However, Marquard's first major league game was in 1908, when he pitched in only one game, and Ives's date on a photostat of the manuscript is earlier, 1906. Ives's date does not appear on the original pencil sketch; it appears only in the bottom left-hand corner of a photostat reproduction of the original manuscript, which is identical to the original except that it has numbered measures and the date added. While Ives's date again may be called into question, especially since it does not appear on the original copy of the score, Marquard's best seasons were in 1911–1913, far too late for this sketch, which must have been composed before Ives's marriage due to other clues on the manuscript.[77] Ives's annotation at the end of the score—which appears on both copies, "Wally McCormack only one to see it! + Harry Farrar! at 2.45 Am"—clearly suggests that the piece was composed at Poverty Flat, where Ives lived with friends and associates from Yale between 1898 and 1908.

John Kirkpatrick interpreted the name "Wally" as "Watty," which was repeated by James Sinclair and various Ives biographers.[78] The sketch has a horizontal mark through the double-L, but this mark appears to me to be a stray mark rather than a cross through a double-T. The double-L is looped, and the horizontal mark is slightly lighter than the letters. Kirkpatrick identified the individual as "Walter McCormick [Ives misspelled his last name], a cousin of Vance" (a Yale football captain). Wally, therefore, seems like a more likely interpretation for his nickname. Harry Farrar was a member the freshman class of '02 only, withdrawing from Yale after the first year. These two men arrived at Poverty Flat in 1903.[79]

Although Ives's dates and datable references are always open to question, as discussed earlier in this chapter, I see no evidence that suggests that Ives would have added both date and datable reference later, and I see no motivation for such fabrications. Ives's scrawled comment at the end of the manuscript seems to have been made spontaneously at the time of composition, rather than added in retrospect. Furthermore, it seems far more likely that Ives composed this baseball tribute in the company of his Poverty Flat friends, rather than with his wife, Harmony, whom he married on June 9, 1908. Although Marquard certainly would have been well-known to Ives once the New York Giants purchased Marquard's minor-league contract in 1908 for a record sum, prompting the nickname "the $11,000 beauty," this sketch likely was composed earlier, as suggested by Ives's annotation.[80] Finally, based on the handwriting, Gayle Sherwood dates this piece as circa 1907—still too early for Rube Marquard to have been the pitcher concerned.[81]

Another possibility for the subject of Ives's piece is Rube Foster, who was well-known at the time and is regarded as "the Father of Black Baseball."[82]

Foster's best seasons as a player were in 1903–1904, certainly soon enough to be recognized by Ives. Also, Ives's family background in abolitionism implies that he would not have excluded the player from consideration due to the color of his skin. However, Foster was only allowed to play in racially segregated leagues, and he played for teams outside of New York. Although Foster's brilliance as a player and Ives's comparatively open racial attitude suggest Foster as a possibility, I believe another player was the subject of Ives's composition, the Rube after whom both Foster and Marquard were named. According to James Skipper:

> As a 22-year-old pitcher, Foster defeated George "Rube" Waddell in an exhibition game in 1902. His teammates paid him deference by nicknaming him "Rube." Thus the nickname had a positive meaning when applied to Foster, rather than its more common use in baseball to refer to a country bumpkin; Honus Wagner thought Foster was the smartest pitcher he had seen in all his years of baseball.[83]

Marquard, similarly, was named simply for showing similar pitching successes as the elder player, Rube Waddell, rather than for any lack of sophistication:

> After [Marquard] won the Indianapolis home opener, 2 to 1, against Kansas City in 1908 [in the minor leagues], a newspaper account said, "He is so tall and skinny (6'3" 180-lbs) he looks like a big number one when he stands on the mound, but he pitches like Rube Waddell."
> They called him Rube ever after.[84]

However, in the case of Rube Waddell, the original intent of the nickname was a fitting choice. George Edward Waddell (1876–1914)—pitcher for the Philadelphia Athletics during the prime of his career; Louisville, Pittsburgh, and Chicago upon breaking into major league baseball; and St. Louis during his last three years—was the complete opposite from Marquard and Foster in all regards except pitching ability. Waddell, shown in illustration 5.9, was never known for his intelligence, but his antics both on and off the field were sometimes so outrageous that it is difficult to know whether to attribute them to eccentricity or idiocy. As one reporter remembered:

> Most colorful of all players, of course was the eccentric Rube Waddell. No player that ever lived, not even Babe Ruth, has so captured the affections of the fans of his day as did Waddell. Wholly irresponsible and childlike in his mental functions, yet possessed of such great natural physical ability and mechanical pitching skill that he compiled pitching records that never before or since have been equaled in spite of the abuse that he accorded himself, Waddell presents the most unique personal picture baseball history has known.

Illustration 5.9.   Rube Waddell, pitcher for the Philadelphia Athletics.
Courtesy National Baseball Hall of Fame Library, Cooperstown, New York.

When he wasn't stealing away from his team to go fishing, or to tend bar in
some saloon, or to lead a circus parade, or to ride on fire engines, or to pitch
for some hick ball club up-state, the major portion of Waddell's big league career was spent under the calm and crafty consideration of Connie Mack.[85]

Waddell's longtime manager, Mack, claimed that Waddell

had four passions, and four passions only: He loved to fish. He loved the
stuff that the vintners sell. He loved fires. And he loved to pitch ball games.
In about that order. Only, sometimes he reversed the first two.[86]

His unpredictable nature affected both his opponents and his managers,
and his capricious personality made him difficult to manage:

Opponents learned that they could distract him with displays of children's
toys or pets. Managers learned that it was best to dole five or ten dollars out
to him at a time; a salary was an invitation to disaster, and twenty-five dollars might mean he disappeared for a week.[87]

Waddell was often tricked by opponents, but usually to no avail. For example, before a game that Waddell was scheduled to pitch, an opposing player
challenged him to a pitching contest to see who could throw a better strike
across the plate from center field. In hoping to wear down Waddell's arm,
the opponent duped him into throwing pitch after pitch from center field:

The St. Louis player remained "unconvinced," however, for the better part of
an hour, although Rube kept chunking one ball after another that long distance with almost incredible perfection. . . . Unable to control a grin, the St.
Louis player gave Rube his $5 and walked away . . . . "Boys, this game is in
the bag," he was telling his colleagues in the locker room a little while later.
"If Rube Waddell shows up on the mound, which is doubtful, he won't be
able to throw a pebble three feet." . . . Rube Waddell not only went out on the
mound but, if anything, he was in even more superb form than usual. His
control was well-nigh perfection itself, his speed blinding. He struck out a
dozen men. Philadelphia won hands down. When the final St. Louis out was
made, the Rube walked over to the player with whom he had made the $5 bet
and game him the money back. "Here, I don't want the money," he said. "I
owe you a lot of thanks for warming me up with that practice this morning."[88]

His manager, Connie Mack, also was known to try to trick Waddell on
various occasions:

He read Rube Waddell as no man had read him before. He understood what
a careless, big-hearted boy Waddell was. He knew when to plead, when to
cajole, when to threaten, and under his careful tutelage Rube rose to the
greatest height of his magnificent career.

Back in 1905 the [Philadelphia] Athletics were engaged in a double header with another Eastern club. Waddell, on the mound, apparently had little interest in that particular contest, for the enemy landed solidly on his delivery. He came back to the bench after a lucky double play had cut off two runs at the plate to find Connie Mack smiling grimly.

"'Do you know, Rube," said the chief, "I just heard [one of our opponents] say you were the easiest proposition his team ever faced, that you were just getting through on your reputation."

There was an instant change of expression on the southpaw's face. The muscles of his heavy jaw tightened; his mild eyes narrowed to a pair of blazing slits.

"I'm getting through on my rep, eh?" he snarled. "I'll show 'em."

Back he marched to the mound, and his speed was so blinding that for the rest of the game his opponents did not make a hit. Encouraged by his great work the Athletics rallied, and won by some wonderful work in the tenth inning. But that did not satisfy Waddell. The insult to his pride still rankled, and he pitched the second game without letting one of the enemy get past third base.[89]

Although Waddell pitched for Philadelphia in 1902–1907, not New York, Ives certainly would have heard and have been fascinated by at least some of these stories, and he likely saw Waddell pitch for the opposing team against the New York Highlanders. Ives would have had an opportunity to see Waddell in the 1905 World Series between the New York Giants and the Philadelphia Athletics, but Waddell did not play, complaining of an injured shoulder, though it was rumored that gamblers' money had convinced him not to appear.[90]

Despite the idiosyncratic aspects of Waddell's personality, Rube was one of the best pitchers ever to play major league baseball. Connie Mack, who managed the Philadelphia Athletics from 1901 to 1950, thought Rube could have been the best all-around pitcher of all time.[91] According to Mack:

He had terrific speed. He was a big, loose, lanky fellow who was almost as fast as [Walter] Johnson. And his curve was even better than his speed. . . . I've seen great hitters miss Rube's curve ball by more than a foot. I honestly believe the Rube's curve often broke at least two feet. But what is more important, it was a fast curve, one that came up in a hurry and then shot down like lightning.[92]

Unlike Foster and Marquard, Rube Waddell was at the height of his career between 1902 and 1907. Remarkably, he led the league in strikeouts in *each* of those six years, and his earned run average hovered around the 2.00 mark (two runs per nine-inning game).[93] If Ives composed the piece sometime during the middle of the decade, which seems likely—even if Ives's date of 1906 cannot be accepted with precision—Waddell seems like the correct attribution for Ives's Rube. Furthermore, Waddell's antics provide a possible explanation for the rest of Ives's title, *Rube Trying to Walk 2 to 3!!* What other major league pitcher would possibly *try* to walk batters?

> His team was leading 3–1 in the seventh when an enthusiastic fan suggested he fill the bases and strike out the side. Willing, always, to oblige, Rube called in the infield and outfield and walked the next two batters. With the count 3–2, Rube tossed a high, slow one and the opposing batter, stretching to the limit, sent the ball into center field, and scored two runs. The hitter, amazed by his own achievement [or perhaps laughing too hard], neglected to run, and was declared out; Waddell fanned the next two—and eventually won the game.[94]

Although this story seems impossible to believe, according to the contemporary literature Rube tried this stunt more than once. Perhaps Ives's title refers to stories such as this one, which depicts "Rube (*actually*) trying to walk 2 to 3"—batters!!

Clearly, the *potential* for this sketch to be interpreted as being inspired by baseball, and specifically Rube Waddell, is strong. Several secondary sources point to this reading, and the baseball implications of the title are vivid. Even the double exclamation points in the title and Ives's obvious delight with the reactions of his friends to this music, which he recorded at the end of the sketch, imply that there may be more to the story than a mere depiction of the unsophisticated walking pattern of a country bumpkin, as suggested by a literal and non-baseball-oriented interpretation of the name Rube in the title. The second half of chapter 6, which examines several pieces that derive from or are related to this sketch, will present more evidence that suggests baseball as the inspiration of *Take-off #3: Rube Trying to Walk 2 to 3!!*

MAKING CONNECTIONS

All four of the major league baseball players that Ives chose to depict through his music were undoubtedly notable for their abilities—Evers, Keeler, and Waddell were even elected to the Hall of Fame—but Ives seems to have been looking for something more than pure baseball talent in these pieces. The greatest pitcher of the era, and some say of all time, pitched for the New York Giants during this period, and yet Ives overlooked Christy Mathewson in favor of a visiting pitcher from Philadelphia. As shown in some of the quotations included earlier in this chapter, Mathewson was cited along with Donlin in nearly every source as the two best players of the New York Giants in the middle of the first decade of the twentieth century. But Ives chose to honor only Donlin, not Mathewson, in his music—instead choosing Rube Waddell as the only pitcher, Ives's own standout position when playing ball for the Danbury Alerts and the Hopkins Grammar School team, as described in chapter 3.

Ironically, the problem for Ives was not with Mathewson's pitching ability but rather with his character: "On the field he [Mathewson] was brilliant. Four times he won 30 or more games in a season. In some years he had more wins than walks."[95] However, although Waddell might have remained in Mathewson's shadow in terms of pitching, Waddell far out-shone the New York hurler in terms of eccentricity. In the words of present-day political writer and baseball enthusiast, George Will, Mathewson was "that elusive ideal, a gentleman a democracy could be comfortable with."[96] Contrarily, in all of his sketches about baseball players, Ives favored colorful, flamboyant, cantankerous, and eccentric individuals—ballplayers fashioned after himself. The people he mentioned were by all means excellent baseball players of the period, but Ives singled them out for their notoriety rather than their skills alone.

All of these ballplayers had colorful nicknames to further distinguish them from other major league baseball players of the time, but nicknames were much more common in the first decade of the twentieth century than in any decade since.[97] During the first decade of the twentieth century, 363 major league ballplayers had nicknames not derived from their names, whereas only 164 ballplayers had such nicknames in 1950–1959 and only fifty ballplayers, more recently, in 1970–1979.[98] However, although nicknames were much more common during Ives's time than today, the fact that all four of Ives's chosen ballplayers had nicknames, "which implies a degree of intimacy identification which is lacking with given names," is another indication that his selections were based in part on their "colorful, rough and ready . . . antics" and their status as "folk heroes, implying closeness, and personal identification."[99] There were plenty of other ballplayers whom Ives could have chosen without such distinctive monikers.

Also missing from his baseball sketches are the baseball heroes of Ives's youth. Clearly, Ives needed to choose ballplayers known to his friends at Poverty Flat in order to connect them with his music through baseball, and musical references to favorite Danbury amateur or semipro ballplayers certainly would be incapable of producing the desired response from his friends. The joy with which Ives writes, "Wally McCormack only one to see it! + Harry Farrar! at 2.45 Am," at the end of the *Rube* sketch suggests that, at least with these sketches of flashy major league ballplayers, Ives was able to delight his intended audience with these creative and fitting musical depictions.[100] According to Burkholder,

Ives's personal relationship with his audience made possible a friendly reception for his novel ideas; his friends liked him, so they were willing to give his music a try, and his light approach allowed them to accept the sounds they might otherwise never have approved.[101]

Certainly, in the pieces about major league baseball players, Ives was able to achieve a strong connection with his audience, even if his audience was only two of his friends in the middle of the night.

After watching major league baseball games with friends during his first decade in New York, and after composing music to reflect his impressions of some of the ballplayers he undoubtedly admired, Ives's interest in major league baseball seems to have waned. Ives composed no pieces on major league ballplayers after his marriage in 1908, and there is no record of his attending major league baseball games other than these sketches. His interest in the sport certainly continued, as suggested by his writings and memorabilia discussed in chapter 3, but musically and socially, he turned inward. According to Rossiter,

> At some point in the first decade of the century, Ives plainly began to be dissatisfied with the ways of his fellow Yale men and his business associates—not just with their attitude toward music, but with their whole approach to the conduct of life. Around the time of his marriage in 1908, . . . by immersing himself in his family life and his music, he cut himself off from his friends.[102]

Instead, he devoted himself to a private life and a more leisurely pace of reading and composing. His attendance at concerts virtually ceased. He and Harmony

> went out little and shunned participation in the social and civic life which was so important to other couples of their background and class who lived in New York. Nor was Ives interested in the male club and sporting life that his business associates favored.[103]

But although his attendance at baseball games and musical events seems to have ceased, he carried with him both the memories of the game and the compositional techniques he developed in these baseball-related sketches, and as discussed in the next chapter, Ives incorporated some of these techniques into later pieces.

Chapter 6

Baseball Techniques— From Sketch to Compositional Language

DEVELOPMENT OF A COMPOSER

The musical sounds that Ives devised to depict baseball scenes and individual ballplayers helped him to develop new compositional techniques that he was able to incorporate directly into his basic musical language. Ives used his "take-offs"—in general, not just the baseball pieces—to justify working with idiosyncratic and innovative musical ideas. As Burkholder noted:

> It is apparent in all of these pieces that the humorous context provided an excuse for Ives to play with dissonance, complexity, quodlibet, and other technical matters with a freedom he did not have in more serious works or in works that might potentially be played in public. Once techniques had been tried out in pieces that could be justified as mere jokes, experiments, or small descriptive pieces, they could be incorporated along with vernacular styles into the framework of large concert works.[1]

Consequently, a significant aspect of such experimental pieces, including the baseball pieces, in terms of his development as a composer, lies primarily in the reuse of techniques in later, more mature compositions.[2] Therefore, Ives used baseball not only to prove himself as a man, as discussed earlier in this book, but also as a proving ground for new musical ideas.

In fact, Ives himself recognized these pieces, as well as his other take-offs, as essential to his compositional development:

> Right or wrong, things like these—some hardly more than memos in notes— show how one's mind works. The only value probably of some of these things

133

was that, in working these sound-pictures out (or trying to), it gave the ears plenty of new sound experiences—it strengthened the ear muscles, and opened up things naturally that later were used naturally and spontaneously—that is, without thinking of it as "this chord" or "this way"—good bad, or nice![3]

In reference to his depiction of the *Yale-Princeton Football Game*, though his comments apply equally to his baseball music, Ives further stated that "doing things like this (half horsing) would suggest and get one used to technical processes that could be developed into something more serious later, and quite naturally."[4]

Swafford, also observing the importance of Ives's "cartoons or take-offs" in Ives's development as a composer, concluded, "These imitations of events or people or ideas are mostly scraggly, unfinished pieces. From them Ives gleaned technical lessons toward the works he really cared about."[5] The first section of this final chapter of this book will show how, in some of his later works, Ives employed compositional techniques that he earlier used to depict baseball scenes and personalities in his unfinished musical sketches about baseball. This section will focus on Ives's sketches of major league baseball players, discussed in chapter 5, rather than his completed baseball pieces, discussed in chapter 4, but aspects of the completed baseball pieces will be mentioned when they relate to techniques that also appear in the sketches.

The second section of this chapter will investigate how Ives used *Take-off #3: Rube Trying to Walk 2 to 3!!* as a model for later pieces. At least five significant pieces are related to this earlier sketch, including a song, both piano sonatas, a study for piano, and a work for chamber ensemble. Each of these pieces will be compared with the sketch of *Rube* in order to show how Ives derived or developed material from this sketch to be used in these later pieces.

Ives's reuse of musical techniques from his finished experimental works in general already has been addressed by scholars in some depth. For example, James Sinclair provided references to the earlier works, if any, from which every piece Ives composed is derived.[6] Other scholars have offered detailed commentary on how Ives composed new pieces based on earlier pieces and sketches.[7] Some of these scholars have addressed some of the pieces discussed in this book; however, their comments often appear in other contexts and therefore are less detailed than the account provided in this chapter. For example, Jan Swafford discussed the reuse of material from *Take-off #3: Rube Trying to Walk 2 to 3!!* in Ives's later chamber work, *Scherzo: Over the Pavements*.[8] John Rinehart also discussed this piece within a broader treatment of fifteen representative experimental works in which he isolated idiomatic compositional techniques appearing in each of these pieces; however, he did not trace the relationship between this piece and the earlier sketch, and the techniques he isolated in Ives's experimental music are very different from the ones that will be drawn from the baseball sketches in the section to follow.[9] Philip Lambert identified and traced the development of a number of experimental techniques, focusing especially on Ives's systematic compositional techniques.[10] Lambert discussed Ives's use of palindrome in several pieces, including the baseball-related piece, *All the Way Around and Back*, and he worked with a number of other important compositional techniques that appear in these experimental works. Thomas Winters, with similar aims, showed Ives's later employment of selected compositional techniques that first occur in his completed experimental pieces, also including *All the Way Around and Back*.[11] Winters, like Lambert, focused on specific compositional techniques, but not the techniques that will be explored in this chapter. By concentrating on techniques from Ives's unfinished baseball pieces, rather than the finished compositions discussed in chapter 4, this chapter will avoid retracing the material that appears in this scholarly literature.

ISOLATED TECHNIQUES

The first section of this chapter focuses on Ives's reuse of techniques from his baseball sketches that also appear in four representative masterworks. Examples are drawn from *The Unanswered Question*, "General William Booth Enters into Heaven," the Second String Quartet, and the Fourth Symphony. *The Unanswered Question* is a relatively early work (composed in 1908 but revised in 1930–1935) but is one of the pieces most associated with the composer. "General William Booth Enters into Heaven" is widely hailed to be Ives's best among his nearly 200 songs. The Second String Quartet (Ives's last string quartet) and the Fourth Symphony (his last completed symphony) also show Ives at the height of his compositional maturity.

According to Stuart Feder, "If any single work can be said to be Ives's 'signature' piece, it is *The Unanswered Question*."[12] Many people consider this piece to be among Ives's "experimental" music, but despite the experimental nature of its spatial orientation and the textural dissonance created by three contrasting and highly independent layers of music, this short piece for chamber ensemble is considered by most to be among Ives's finest and most probing compositions.[13] The strings play a supporting role throughout the entire piece with simple, diatonic, and triadic harmonies that shift slowly and quietly to create a smooth G-major based tonal landscape. Over this layer, "the trumpet intones 'The Perennial Question of Existence,' and states it in the same tone of voice each time" in a layer that creates considerable dissonance with the underlying strings.[14] This brief, angular, and chromatic melody undergoes only minor alterations on each repetition in the piece.[15] Meanwhile, a group of four solo flutes attempts to answer the trumpet's question each time it is stated. This third layer contrasts markedly with the other two layers in rhythm, harmony, texture, and phrase structure. The flutes play highly dissonant simultaneities, often forming wedges that propel the voices into tightly constructed dissonant chords at the end of each of their brief utterances. The flutes fail to answer the question each time, and they eventually incorporate some of the trumpet motives into their own part in a faster, "mocking" manner. Finally, the trumpet prevails, and the question is left unanswered while the strings slowly fade away into silence.

Ives's song, "General William Booth Enters into Heaven," provides a musical depiction of the founder of the Salvation Army, using a "folk-poetic memorial" penned by Vachel Lindsay.[16] This spectacular song draws heavily from the hymn tune *Cleansing Fountain*, but transforms the original both melodically and especially harmonically throughout the song. The song features the use of "piano drumming," Ives's simulation of Booth's "big bass drum," by means of cluster chords struck on the piano, as well as a number of other specialized compositional techniques—including bichords and bitonality; extended dissonant pedal points; ostinatos; whole-tone, octatonic, and synthetic scales; and polymeter and intricate polyrhythms. But Ives never loses sight of the spiritual and philosophical impact of the original poem. The song ends with the same bass drum with which it began, now fading away, along with a reiteration of the song's constant, probing question, "Are you washed in the blood of the Lamb?" Swafford summarized the final gestures of the song: "It is a microcosm of so much of what Ives was about—the mundane transformed into the spiritual, the comic into the sublime, paradoxes transcended before our eyes, and a final question awaiting answer."[17] Indeed it was yet another unanswered question.

Ives's Second String Quartet—in three movements, subtitled "Discussions," "Arguments," and "The Call of the Mountains"—was conceived "for 4 men—who converse, discuss, argue . . . fight, shake hands[,] shut up—then walk up the mountain side to view the firmament!"[18] The piece contains cyclic references "creating myriad interconnections—of motive, theme, harmony, texture, rhythm, gesture—among the movements."[19] H. Wiley Hitchcock neatly summarized the impact of this piece:

> The Second String Quartet is one of Ives's richest and most original works, on several counts. One is its programmatic conception, and the realization of it in sound. Another is its projection of a kind of musical discourse the implications of which are still being worked through by composers. A third is

the musical work as a whole, one of Ives's most subtly integrated, panoramically envisioned, and organically achieved.[20]

Ives later developed the closing portion of the quartet into part of the last movement of the Fourth Symphony.

The four-movement Fourth Symphony is one of Ives's most ambitious works, both in terms of scope and orchestration.[21] The second movement, to be focused on here, derives from an earlier work for piano entitled *The Celestial Railroad*, and both pieces derive from the second movement of the *Concord Sonata*.[22] These three pieces share the same program, a musical depiction of Nathaniel Hawthorne's short story of the same name in which a "locomotive speeds it passengers to the Celestial City in nineteenth-century comfort"—a New England gloss on John Bunyan's *The Pilgrim's Progress*.[23] The importance of the Fourth Symphony among Ives's works cannot be overstated. For example, Stuart Feder called this piece "a culminating work in several respects, not only with regard to the composer's entire output but within itself. . . . The *Fourth Symphony* is one of Ives's defining works."[24]

All four of these pieces have strong programmatic elements of their own, and these programmatic aspects certainly affected Ives's compositional choices. Therefore, it may seem somewhat tenuous to assign relationships between compositional techniques found in the baseball sketches and the same techniques found in these later pieces; ideas that Ives developed to depict baseball players and events might also have occurred to Ives in depicting the programmatic elements of these later pieces. Nevertheless, despite this potential for misinterpretation, these pieces are worthy choices to examine Ives's compositional development because of their status as being among Ives's principal masterworks. With Ives's penchant for programmatic music, it would be nearly impossible to select a repertory of representative works that have no programmatic influences. Furthermore, whether these later pieces have programs or not, Ives still used baseball images to help him explore certain compositional techniques in his earlier baseball sketches, and his use of these same techniques in his later pieces suggests that these earlier attempts to portray ballplayers and their heroics had at least some influence on his compositional development, as Ives himself claimed. Ives's later pieces certainly benefited from his experience with these compositional techniques, even if the same techniques might have occurred to him in these later programmatic contexts anyway.

In addition, no claims about the chronological priority of techniques found in the baseball sketches are being suggested in this book. Some of the same techniques may have appeared for the first time in other sketches or pieces; however, Ives still explored and developed these techniques in relation to the ballplayers and baseball scenes he was trying to recreate. Ives's use of these techniques in the baseball sketches would have furthered his compositional development, even if the techniques were not occurring there for the first time. In this section each technique is identified in one or more of the baseball sketches, and then its reuse is identified in later pieces. The techniques are grouped loosely by type, beginning with techniques related to pitch, followed by texture, then rhythm, and finally meter.

Cluster Glissando

In his sketch of *Mike Donlin—Johnny Evers*, Ives represents the pitches thrown to "Johnny at Bat," labeled "Ball" and "Strike," using cluster chords in the upper strings with descending glissandos, as shown in example 5.2 (on pp. 94–95), mm. 4–5. In each case the six-note chromatic clusters, spanning a tritone from B4 to F5, move directly to G3, the lowest open string on the violin. These cluster glissandos appear in alternation with single-note glissandos in the trumpet, representing the umpire's calls, as discussed in chapter 5.

The second movement of Ives's Fourth Symphony uses the same technique in several passages, unrelated to the flight of a pitched baseball. In the first such passage near the beginning of the movement (mm. 5–6), the *divisi* basses descend from their initial interval of a major third, between sounding B♭2 to D3, through a glissando, eventually arriving on a single note, E1, the lowest note on the unextended bass. Unlike the baseball sketch, however, the basses hold the note of arrival, rather than presenting a short eighth note, and the lower group of *divisi* basses arrives at the lower note earlier than the top note, whereas in the baseball sketch the violin glissandos all arrive on their low G at the same time.

In a later passage of the same movement, the basses, joined by the cellos, present similar descending glissandos, shown in example 6.1, but here the low strings begin with clusters rather than a consonant third—a remarkably similar configuration to the clusters in the baseball sketch. The only musical differences between this passage and the similar one from *Mike Donlin—Johnny Evers* are the lower register and the fact that the glissandos in the symphony movement descend to chords, rather than to a single note. The pictorial difference, however, is between the sound of the flight of a pitched baseball in the earlier sketch and the sound of a locomotive beginning to pick up steam in the symphony movement, as suggested by the movement's programmatic relationship to *The Celestial Railroad*. Later in the movement (Reh. 9, m. 2), Ives develops this basic technique further by reversing the direction of the glissandos, but still he retains clusters on each end of the glissandos. In this brief passage we

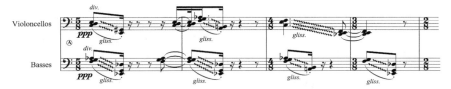

Example 6.1.   Fourth Symphony, mvmt. 2, Reh. 4, mm. 1–4, cellos and basses.
© Associated Music Publishers.

hear the locomotive beginning to accelerate, continuing to gain speed as the section continues.

In addition to the short glissandos in the *Mike Donlin—Johnny Evers* sketch, Ives also presents more extensive glissando chords in the violins in this sketch, as shown in example 5.2 (on p. 96), mm. 8–9. In this passage Ives attempts to depict the excitement of the crowd by having "all fiddles rove up and down" by means of these glissandos. Harmonically, Ives employs a triadic structure with added notes. The inverted-arch-shaped glissando begins with an F major triad with an added second above the fifth of the chord (D) and an added second below the root (E). This structure also could be interpreted as an inverted F major seventh chord with an added sixth or an inverted D minor ninth chord, but Ives drops the extended-tertian structure in the following two chords while retaining the triadic orientation. The nadir of the glissando is a D minor triad with an added fourth above the root, and the glissando concludes with a B diminished triad with an added fourth. The effect of each of these latter two chords is a three-note diatonic cluster above the interval of a minor third.

In the second movement of the Fourth Symphony, Ives makes use of the same technique with the same instrumentation, as shown in example 6.2. Whereas the earlier baseball sketch features triadic chords with added notes, the similar passage in the symphony movement features four-note clusters in the divisi first violins. Thus, the cluster plus interval approach suggested in reference to the latter two chords in *Mike Donlin—Johnny*

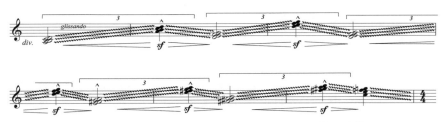

Example 6.2.   Fourth Symphony, mvmt. 2, Reh. 38, mm. 2–7, first violins.
© Associated Music Publishers.

Evers has much in common with the use of the corresponding technique in the symphony movement. In this later use of the technique, the violins rove up and down in the same way as directed in the original baseball sketch, but now for an even longer period of time. The glissandos in the baseball sketch occupy only two measures, whereas the similar glissandos in the symphony movement last for six measures. The chords or clusters in the baseball sketch are completely diatonic; each of the clusters in the symphony movement is also diatonic, but the clusters make use of three different diatonic collections (using notes from the C major, G major, and D major collections in turn, before returning to the C major collection at the end of the passage). Again in this example, Ives expands his basic technique in a later composition, using it as a part of his natural musical language. The passage concludes by using the same technique as the glissandos described earlier from this baseball sketch, where the *divisi* glissandos descend to arrive on a single note.

Open Cluster

Clusters are a common device for Ives, but sometimes he opens the voicing of clusters such that each note of the pitch-class cluster is approximately an octave away from the next. For example, in *Mike Donlin—Johnny Evers*, Ives places a three-note pitch-class cluster in the brass to support the written-out accelerandos in the woodwinds and upper strings, as shown in example 5.2 (p. 95), m. 6. However, this open cluster is spaced so that the bottom of the three adjacent pitch classes (E) is the highest pitch (E4) and the other notes of the cluster are arranged below it, approximately in octaves (with a G♭3 below and an F♮2 below that). Open clusters are a very common device in Ives's music, and examples abound in the literature. This technique owes very little to the baseball sketches in particular, since this arrangement of notes does not seem to bear any obvious programmatic references to baseball; nevertheless, Ives employed this technique in a prominent place in the *Mike Donlin—Johnny Evers* sketch, as a part of his depiction of the baseball scene, and thereby gained experience that could be applied in later pieces.

For example, some of the flutes' attempts to answer *The Unanswered Question* feature open clusters. Their third and fourth attempts to respond to the evocative trumpet line begin with open clusters, and the fourth attempt ends with another open cluster, as shown in example 6.3. In the first of these two examples, the lower flutes present a four-note open cluster, with the outer instruments and inner instruments paired. The first and fourth flutes present a half step an octave apart, G♯4-A5, while the second and third flutes offer an immediate half step, B4-C5. The overall effect, however, is a four-note open cluster, G♯-A-B-C, with two chromatic pairs

Example 6.3. *The Unanswered Question,* mm. 34–35, 41–42 (measure numbers are taken from the strings for reference, because measures are shown for the flute parts only while they are playing).
© Peer International Corporation.

separated by a whole step. However, the octave displacement and the late entrance of the third flute provide a more consonant sounding effect, with its minor third initially exposed on the bottom of the chord. At the beginning of the second of these two passages, these same notes have been redistributed to form thirds in the top and bottom registers of the texture, retaining the consonant flavor of this otherwise very dissonant sonority. This passage ends with all voices transposed up a perfect fifth from the sonority with which the passage began.

Additional examples of this technique occur, for example, in the first and second movements of the Second String Quartet. In the first movement, each of the strings plays double-stops, and the violins alternate with the lower strings in four-note whole-tone open clusters (mm. 70–71). The pairs of instruments are isolated from each other in terms of register (low-high), texture (by playing in alternation), and pitch (with each pair presenting a *different* whole-tone collection). Also, each pair transposes its initial chord up by a whole tone, thus saturating the whole-tone collection in each pair of voices and saturating the chromatic universe as an ensemble. The violins play B3-E♭4-F4-D♭5, while the viola and cello play G♯2-C3-D3-B♭3. Accordingly, the violin chord is an exact transposition of the chord first played by the lower voices, transposed up a minor tenth. The open cluster in the second movement will be discussed in conjunction with cluster scales shortly.

Cluster Scale

Mike Donlin—Johnny Evers and *Willy Keeler at the Bat* both feature cluster scales—incompletely notated clusters in the strings that move together rapidly in the same direction through scales.[25] The *Mike Donlin—Johnny*

Evers sketch begins with clusters descending through the chromatic scale in the upper strings in sixteenth notes, as shown in example 5.2 (on p. 94), mm. 1–3. Although the notation of the exact pitches is ambiguous, as discussed in chapter 5, the overall effect of the passage is clear. A five-note chord, or cluster, is maintained in parallel motion in a rapid scalar formation. Similarly, *Willy Keeler at the Bat* begins with a repeated descending chromatic scale with additional textual directions to indicate clusters in the strings—"Violins all take ½ ton[e] lower as many as possible" and below the viola, cello, and bass part, "4 wholeton[e] Down"—as shown in example 5.4 (on p. 116), m. 1. Thus both pieces feature clusters in *divisi* strings moving together through the descending chromatic scale.

The Fourth of July, one of Ives's completed baseball-related pieces discussed in chapter 4, also presents cluster scales, but these massive clusters seem to have more to do with fireworks than baseball. These seven-note clusters, *divisi* in the first and second violins and the violas, encompass three different diatonic collections in a polytonal outburst of sound near the end of the movement (mm. 97–115). Following this cacophonic passage, the scales from the previous section in the upper strings become glissandos, and the movement begins to draw to a close (mm. 116–120).

Ives used a similar short ascending cluster scale in the piano accompaniment to "General William Booth Enters into Heaven." This sudden sixteenth-note ascent (mm. 24–27) reaches up "from the ditches dank" in search of more needy souls to be assembled by Booth. The diatonic cluster scale begins in the right hand alone, but it is immediately joined by the left hand, with five notes in the right hand and four notes in the left, separated by an octave and forming massive clusters in a rapid, staccato crescendo, approaching the "Drabs from the alleyways and drug fiends" with a flouish.

The same technique also appears in the second movement of the Fourth Symphony. As shown in example 6.4, the first violins and violas present ascending chromatic scales using whole-tone clusters, a similar pitch configuration to the comparable passages in the baseball sketches. Here each chromatic scale ascends and encompasses an octave, and the clusters consist of five *divisi* voices, each separated by a whole step. The violas begin their chromatic scales, *divisi a 3*, from A4-B4-C♯5, and the first violins continue the whole-tone cluster, *divisi a 2*, from D♯5-F♮5. The solo piano (not shown in the example) joins the upper first violin line, adding strength and punctuation to this voice, suggesting its primacy in the passage. This accentuation of this upper voice of the clusters seems to be directly related to the similar cluster scales in the two baseball sketches, where Ives only bothered to write the upper voice, confining the other voices to written directions.

The second movement of Ives's Second String Quartet concludes with cluster scales involving open clusters, as mentioned earlier. In this passage the second violin and viola begin with ascending diatonic scales,

Example 6.4.   Fourth Symphony, mvmt. 2, Reh. 41, m. 3, first violins and violas.
© Associated Music Publishers.

soon joined by the cello. The three voices together form three-note diatonic open clusters as they all ascend through the "C major" diatonic collection. For example, when the cello enters (m. 106), the open cluster
formed by these three instruments is E2-G3-F4, an open cluster with each
voice separated by an octave, as in the stationary open cluster from this
piece mentioned earlier. However, when the first violin enters, about a
beat later, it dramatically alters the pattern by presenting a downward
sweeping scale, in opposition to the ascending cluster scales in the other
voices. The influence of the higher voice is very strong, because the second violin almost immediately joins it in its descent, in parallel fifths,
abandoning the other instruments (m. 107, b. 2). Soon the lower strings
also join in the descent, presenting cluster scales together with the first
violin—again with open diatonic clusters, beginning with F3-G4-E5—
while the second violin turns back to an ascending pattern. The rapid
scalar passage ends with the violins presenting a dramatic descent in
thirds against the viola and cello, who provide an equally dramatic two-
octave ascent in sevenths. This combination forms a wedge with the upper voices, another favorite Ives technique, deriving from his sketch,
Yale-Princeton Football Game, as mentioned in the introduction to this
book. The movement concludes with open fifths "con scratchy" in the violins, "as tuning up," and finally two forceful, "knockout" chords—a description Ives used for the "baseball bat" chord in his sketch for Study no.
23, as described in chapter 3. These final chords appear in the upper and
lower strings using double-stops and in pairs—indicated "as a K.O." and
"con fisti swatto"—using the same kind of "faux-Italian" directions
found in *Some South-Paw Pitching!* as discussed in chapter 4.

Sudden Textural Reduction

The climactic moment in Ives's baseball sketch *Willy Keeler at the Bat* occurs at the end of the piece where a held chord in all of the other instruments gives way to a single trumpet holding a B♮, as shown in example 5.4
(on p. 117), mm. 7–8. This sudden textural reduction creates a dramatic
and memorable effect, dropping from a massive cluster immediately to a
single note—to depict Keeler's ability to "hit 'em where they ain't."

A similar textural reduction occurs in the "gun-shot" of *The Fourth of July*, shown in example 4.6 (on p. 82), but the effect obtained is less about the drama of the textural reduction than the drama of the sudden crescendo and the accented and staccato articulation of the gunshot itself. But the fact that the three "extra" solo violins continue to play as the remainder of the orchestra suddenly drops out suggests that these two baseball-related pieces also share this compositional technique of a sudden textural reduction.

In *The Unanswered Question*, Ives uses a similar instrumental configuration as in *Willy Keeler at the Bat*. In both pieces Ives assigns definite and recognizable roles to different instrument groups. Both pieces feature a background consisting of the string section, a prominent part in the high woodwinds, and a trumpet exposed in the foreground of the texture. While the trumpet plays the role of the umpire in the baseball sketch through sporadic outbursts of "Ball" and "Strike" calls, Ives uses the same instrument to pose the questions in his more famous composition. Whereas an unidentified upper woodwind instrument plays the role of Keeler swinging the bat in anticipation, a choir of solo flutes futilely attempts to answer the trumpet's questions. In addition to these incidental associations, a sudden textural reduction also occurs near the close of *The Unanswered Question* (m. 55). The flutes have just taken over the texture through a sustained, rapid, and intricate contrapuntal outburst that continues for a longer period of time than any of their other statements earlier in the movement. At the end of this passage—which begins with a special rhythmic device that is also found in one of the baseball sketches, to be discussed later—the flutes reach a climax on an open cluster. This highly dissonant chord, at a dynamic marking of *ffff* and with a sforzando accent, immediately gives way to the quiet and simple tonally oriented strings that have been lurking in the background. Finally, these soft harmonious sonorities in the strings slowly die away as the trumpet poses the "perennial question of existence" one last time. In the baseball sketch, Ives uses this compositional device of textural reduction to reveal the place where Willie Keeler "hit 'em"; in *The Unanswered Question*, Ives uses this same device to reveal the "'The Silences' . . . heard in 'Undisturbed Solitude.'"[26]

Ives uses a similar technique in the middle of the second movement of the Fourth Symphony, occurring at the break between two subsections of the piece (Reh. 35, which consists of a single measure). The entire orchestra sustains a cluster chord that gives way to a single first violin, a single second violin, and a single viola playing a held C♯, with limited harmonic support from the solo piano and another single viola (playing A♯). Unlike the baseball sketch, however, the cluster chord in the symphony is not a chromatic cluster: It wavers in the strings, with each note ornamented by its quarter-tone upper neighbor; and it ends with more than a single pitch in a single instrument. But the basic technique is just an expanded version of the one used in the baseball sketch to depict Keeler's distinctive baseball skill.

Nonsynchronized Accelerando

Mike Donlin—Johnny Evers includes a written-out accelerando with two lines that are out of synchronization with each other.[27] To depict "Mike running in cf after ball," Ives uses chromatic scales that gradually increase in speed due to increasing numbers of notes per beat in the woodwinds and the upper strings, as shown in example 5.2 (on p. 95), mm. 6–7. On consecutive beats, the woodwinds use four sixteenth notes, a quintuplet, a sextuplet, and a septuplet. Meanwhile the strings join the woodwinds in their chromatic ascent, but the strings begin with a quintuplet and gradually work their way up to an octuplet. Also, the strings begin just after and a major sixth above the woodwinds, and because the strings move one note per beat faster than the woodwinds, the interval between the strings increases from a major sixth apart on their first simultaneity (m. 6, b. 3), to a minor seventh (m. 7, b. 1), and finally to a perfect octave (m. 7, b. 2), when the two parts begin their fastest rhythmic pattern. Ives uses this same device in *All the Way Around and Back*, also to depict the acceleration of a baseball player running, as discussed in chapter 4.

A nonsynchronized accelerando also appears in *The Unanswered Question* where the flutes begin to ridicule the question by means of a faster and louder imitation of the trumpet material, in a contrapuntal passage occurring near the end of the piece during their last statement, as shown in example 6.5. After a long-held chromatic cluster in the lowest register of the flutes, the first and second flutes begin with a triplet-oriented version of the question, soon joined by the other two flutes in eighth notes. As in the baseball sketch, the instruments gradually accelerate in rhythmic activity (assisted by an increase in tempo) by moving to sixteenth notes in the upper two flutes and triplets in the lower two flutes before reaching the first of two consecutive climaxes in register and volume.

The first movement of the Second String Quartet also contains two brief examples of nonsynchronized accelerandos. Early in the movement, the viola and cello begin to accelerate by moving from eighth notes to triplets and finally to sixteenth notes (mm. 14–16). Against these gradually accelerating patterns, the first violin presents steady sixteenth notes before the second violin enters with a triplet, creating a metric dissonance against the lower strings. The result is less regular and considerably less dramatic than in the baseball sketch, and the passage ends abruptly with only the

Example 6.5.   *The Unanswered Question*, mm. 51–53, flutes.
© Peer International Corporation.

second violin continuing for a quarter note before being joined by the other voices in a held chord.

A similar passage occurs later in the same movement, but this accelerando concludes with a homorhythmic written-out deceleration in the upper three strings (m. 101). Leading up to this dramatic, synchronized event, the strings combine to form a composite nonsynchronized accelerando. The first violin gradually accelerates from triplets (m. 99), to sixteenth notes, to quintuplets and sextuplets (m. 100), gradually picking up speed just like the center fielder in the baseball sketch. Against this consistent pattern, the other voices sporadically participate in the general acceleration by placing conflicting rhythmic patterns against the violins one beat behind the pace of the leading voice. The nonsynchronized polyrhythmic nature of the first violin against the other voices is in keeping with the comparable pattern from the baseball pieces, where the level of excitement increases as Mike Donlin runs after the ball in center field in the sketch and where the baserunner rounds second and heads toward third in *All the Way Around and Back*.

Metric Displacement

In his sketch of *Willy Keeler at the Bat*, Ives uses a repetitive melodic line that is gradually displaced against the notated meter by one eighth note each measure, to depict Willie Keeler waiting at home plate casually swinging the bat to warm up for the next pitch, as shown in example 5.4 (on p. 116), mm. 1–5. The displaced three-note motivic idea produces a polymetric effect with the notated meter, since each repetition of the motive takes four-and-a-half beats, rather than adhering to the notated meter of four beats per measure.

A stunning example of metric displacement also occurs in "General William Booth Enters into Heaven." The passage in which this compositional device appears is the emotional and spiritual climax of the song, when "Jesus came from the court house door, Stretched his hands above the passing poor," as shown in example 6.6.[28] This text is set with an effortless A♭ major (primarily) diatonic melody in a written simple quadruple meter. This melody essentially consists of only three pitches (C-B♭-A♭, or *mi-re-do*) presented one beat at a time in a circular fashion, as Booth's throng marches "round and round and round" the courthouse square. The combination of four-four meter and a three-beat motive creates a metric

Example 6.6.   "General William Booth Enters into Heaven," mm. 82–92.
© Mercury Music Corporation, used by permission of the publisher.

displacement, where the repeated melodic line is one beat shorter than the measure. Ives uses this compositional technique in *Willy Keeler at the Bat* to depict the circling of the bat in Keeler's swings, and in a similar fashion Ives uses this same technique to depict the marchers circling round and round the courthouse square. Ives uses this technique to picture the effect of Wee Willie's lazy practice swings by falling more and more out of synchronization with the meter, and Ives uses the same lack of synchronization to illustrate the fact that "Booth saw not" when Jesus suddenly appeared in the courthouse door. The lack of synchronization between the meter and the melody in this song seems to depict the idea that these two spiritual figures did not meet in the scene, in the same way that Keeler's initial swings did not meet the ball. Thus, in both the baseball sketch and the song, Ives uses metric displacement as an essential means of telling the story through music. While other metric displacements are added in the accompaniment of the song, the voice ends with an elongated version of the pattern, as Ives employs an inconsistent written-out ritard, using the repetitive melodic motive to compound the effect of the metric displacement, seemingly to depict the circling crowd tiring and slowing down. The linking of music and text through the use of this compositional device in this passage is spectacular.

Ives also employs metric displacement in several passages of the second movement of the Fourth Symphony. In one such passage (Reh. 17, mm. 1–3), Ives displaces the meter by holding the last note of a five-note melodic idea—played in unison by the clarinets, trumpets, trombone, and second violins—into the next measure for an additional eighth-note value, extending the length of the last note in the pattern by the value of one eighth note each time. In the same way as in the baseball sketch, this melodic displacement creates a polymetric effect against the notated meter. Rather than a constant five eighth notes per measure, as indicated in the meter signature, Ives begins the next utterance of the melodic line on the second eighth note of the third measure in the passage. However, following this metric disruption, Ives then begins to alter the meter of the melody entirely—here by extending the length of other notes, rather than continuing to shift the meter in a regular pattern as in *Willy Keeler at the Bat*.

Polymetric Hemiola

The principal compositional technique explored in *Rube Trying to Walk 2 to 3!!* is the simultaneous juxtaposition of duple and triple meters. For example, as shown in example 5.5 (on p. 120), mm. 1–4, the opening of this baseball sketch begins with the notated triple meter articulated in the clarinet, while the bassoon presents an implied duple meter, indicated by means of accents, slurs, beams, and register. Although Ives undoubtedly employed polymetric hemiolas earlier than this baseball sketch, his attempts to portray the antics of Rube Waddell through music gave him an exciting vehicle for exploring this compositional idea full scale.

A very similar example of a polymetric hemiola occurs in "General William Booth Enters into Heaven." When the "big voiced lassies made their banjos bang, bang, bang," Ives uses a relatively straightforward articulation of the written four-four meter in both the voice and the accompaniment, as shown in example 6.7. But when "tranced, fanatical

Example 6.7. "General William Booth Enters into Heaven," mm. 52–58.
© Mercury Music Corporation, used by permission of the publisher.

they shrieked and sang," the rhythmic complexity increases dramatically. Here, at first, the accompaniment presents three eighth-note groupings—shown by beams, accents, and note lengths—against the regular two eighth-note groupings of the written meter articulated in the voice (m. 56). But although Ives retains the three-note groupings in the accompaniment, he inserts a four-and-a-half-beat measure (m. 57), totally disrupting the regular meter of the voice, as the lassies continue shrieking and singing. This two-against-three passage is an isolated though important moment in the song, and Ives's familiarity with this compositional technique, developed in *Rube Trying to Walk 2 to 3!!* as well as in other pieces, may have provided him with a firm comfort level with the technique that allowed him to incorporate it into this later song in this way.

Each movement of the Second String Quartet features a polymetric hemiola involving patterns of three against two, as in the *Rube* sketch. In a particularly striking passage from the first movement, the viola presents the borrowed tune *Dixie*, set on off-beats in common time, with the downbeat of the borrowed tune relocated to the second half of beat two, as shown in example 6.8. Meanwhile, the other strings present sextuplets against this familiar tune, but the sextuplets are themselves divided into groups of four. On one hand, each half beat of the meter presents two against three—two sixteenth notes in the borrowed melody against three notes of a sextuplet in the accompaniment—but on the other hand each pair of beats presents an alternate two-against-three reading, where every two beats of the borrowed tune interact with three accented four-note groupings of the accompanimental sextuplets. The multifaceted nature of this passage seems to reflect the diversity of viewpoints brought forth in the "Discussions" mentioned in the movement's programmatic title.

Example 6.8.   Second String Quartet, mvmt. 1, mm. 60-61.
© Peer International Corporation.

In the second movement of this quartet, Ives also depicts the "Arguments" mentioned in the title of this movement through conflicting patterns of two against three (mm. 15–18). In this passage, the second violin argues by presenting duple groupings in the context of a three-eight meter that is clearly articulated by the other instruments—the same combination of meters employed in *Rube Trying to Walk 2 to 3!!* Unlike the baseball sketch, however, Ives renotates the duple patterns into simple time almost immediately, rather than only at the end of the piece, and later the other instruments join into the argument through similar metric schemes. The third movement of this quartet reverses the procedure by presenting three-unit groupings (strings of dotted eighth notes) in a clearly articulated simple-quadruple meter (mm. 45–54), raising the intensity of the "Call to the Mountains."

This section of the chapter has given a few representative examples of how Ives reused and sometimes developed and expanded compositional techniques that he earlier employed to depict baseball scenes and ballplayers in some of his sketches. The following section will detail how a single sketch influenced several later compositions, not just in terms of isolated techniques but also in a more extensive and sometimes more direct manner.

RUBE AS A MODEL

Although Rube Waddell certainly was not an ideal *role model*, as discussed in connection with his bizarre and unpredictable behavior in chapter 5, Ives's sketch *Take-off #3: Rube Trying to Walk 2 to 3!!* served as an important *compositional model* for several of Ives's other pieces. Moreover, although the inscription at the end of the sketch declares that it was "written as a Joke + sounds like one!" Ives evidently saw this sketch as much more than a mere "joke." At least five pieces are related to this earlier sketch, including the song called "1, 2, 3"; both Piano Sonatas; Study no. 23; and *Scherzo: Over the Pavements*. The nature of the relationship between the sketch and some of these pieces seems to have been overstated in the literature, and this section of this chapter seeks to rectify some of these errors by providing a detailed comparison of each of these pieces with the earlier sketch. In addition, this section will provide more evidence that suggests that *Rube Trying to Walk 2 to 3!!* is about baseball, as argued in chapter 5, not just about some "rube" from the country.

"1, 2, 3"

Ives's song, "1, 2, 3," like the *Rube* sketch, seems to refer to the primary rhythmic and metric features of the piece suggested by its title. The conflict

Example 6.9. "1, 2, 3," mm. 19–22.
© Mercury Music Corporation, used by permission of the publisher.

between duple and triple meter, which is the most prominent feature of the sketch and of the song, is embodied in Ives's title and text. This song was composed or assembled in 1921 and was included as no. 41 in Ives's self-publication, *114 Songs*. Ives's comment written in ink at the bottom of the first page of the *Rube* sketch [f3051] identifies this publication and the page (p. 88) on which this song appears. Ives obviously added this comment to the sketch after 1921 when his *114 Songs* was published.

The song begins with a piano introduction that lasts for over half of the entire length of the song, which is very short in the first place, a total of only thirty-one measures. The main material drawn from *Take-off #3: Rube Trying to Walk 2 to 3!!* begins when the voice enters (m. 19), as shown in example 6.9. The voice presents a new melody featuring syncopation, while the accompaniment begins with the same material that starts the *Rube* sketch, with an added alto voice to fill out the texture in the piano. The intricate syncopation offset by a sixteenth note found throughout the earlier sketch is absent from the song, but it is replaced by eighth-note syncopation, using the same notes and dropping down an octave or more on nonaccented notes, as in the original sketch.

After the first three measures of this accompaniment to the vocal entrance, Ives departs from his model. Instead of just quoting the exact material from the *Rube* sketch, Ives begins to develop the material from the first three measures in new ways, still presenting similar motives but employing different notes. Later in the song, material from the sketch returns relatively intact from time to time (for example, in m. 25), but for the most part this part of the song explores new ground. Finally, as shown in example 6.10, the end of the song features a sudden shift from triple to duple meter for only the last measure, to support the closing words of the text, "one, two!" These last three measures of the song, the measure of du-

Example 6.10.   "1, 2, 3," mm. 29–31.
© Mercury Music Corporation, used by permission of the publisher.

ple meter and the two measures of triple meter that lead up to it, are very closely related to the last four measures of the sketch, which ends with two duple meter measures rather than one. The piano melodies are the same, but down an octave in the song, and the harmony projected is an augmented triad in both sketch and song. The only significant differences are the added vocal line, which sustains a D5 until the last measure, and the left-hand-over notes added in the piano accompaniment to the song, which are B♭ in the song but a sounding B♮ in the trumpet part of the sketch. The last beat of the song also features a shift to a C major triad to conclude with a surprisingly simple sonority, and this move to C major is lacking in *Take-off #3: Rube Trying to Walk 2 to 3!!* However, another piece based on this sketch, *Scherzo: Over the Pavements*, ends with a similar shift to C major, as discussed later.

Concord Sonata

Ives's Second Piano Sonata, the *Concord Sonata*, contains a passage in its second movement, subtitled "Hawthorne," that derives from the *Rube* sketch.[29] This passage, shown in example 6.11, features conflicting duple and triple meters, with the duple meter projected by octave leaps in the lower register and the triple meter projected by four sixteenth notes followed by an eighth note in a turn figure, as in the sketch. The pitches of both voices and the contour of the upper voice are entirely different than in the earlier sketch, but the relationship is clear due to the conflicting meter and the distinctive motivic figure in the right hand. In the sonata, Ives develops the motivic material rather than sticking close

Example 6.11.   *Concord Sonata*, mvmt. 2, p. 28, end of system 3 and system 4. Because of the lack of consistent bar lines in this piece, specific locations are located by page and system number in the second edition.
© Associated Music Publishers.

to the model. First he moves the figure up an octave, then the figure continues to rise slowly and in syncopation with both the triple meter and the implied duple meter. Meanwhile, the left hand abandons the straight octave leaps, instead pausing for the equivalent of a quarter note on every third eighth note. The resulting pattern retains its duple implications, but Ives notates it with beams that reflect the main triple groupings implied in the upper voice. Finally, the left hand, occupying the registral space immediately below (C♯4) and above (D♯5) that of the right hand (between E4 and D5), takes over the abandoned triple meter previously seen in the right hand, while Ives shifts the meter in the other voices inconsistently away from both duple and triple, as mentioned previously. After repeating this passage directly, using the only repeat signs found in the entire sonata, Ives quickly but gradually moves away from the motivic material derived from *Rube Trying to Walk 2 to 3!!* Ives's use of this whimsical material in the "Hawthorne" movement may reflect his attempt "to suggest the wilder, fantastical adventures into the half-childlike, half-fairylike phantasmal realms" mentioned in the preface.[30]

First Piano Sonata

Ives's First Piano Sonata, profiled in chapter 4 in connection with its programmatic reference to baseball and specifically to Fred's home run, also includes material related to *Take-off #3: Rube Trying to Walk 2 to 3!!* in its fourth and fifth movements.[31] It appears that the baseball reference in the program and the use of material from a baseball-related sketch are not interrelated, however. The program of this sonata, discussed in chapter 4, has nothing to do with Rube Waddell. Nevertheless, the use of material from the *Rube* sketch links this piece to baseball in another way, in addition to its programmatic content.

Example 6.12.   First Piano Sonata, mvmt. 4, mm. 36–41.

The fourth movement, an intricate ragtime movement, begins with an extensive section featuring syncopated quintuplet clusters in the right hand against an active eighth-note-oriented left hand featuring diminished octaves and minor sevenths (mm. 1–35). As the section continues the left hand becomes more active rhythmically, exploring other rhythmic configurations in metric opposition to the quintuplets maintained in the right hand. Immediately following this extensive section, the texture, rhythm, and dynamics change drastically as material indirectly related to the *Rube* sketch is introduced, as shown in example 6.12.

Syncopated patterns in the right hand produce an implied triple meter in sixteenth notes (mm. 36–41), while the left hand presents slower-moving tertian chords in parallel motion. This hand resembles the parallel triads contained in the middle of *Rube Trying to Walk 2 to 3!!* shown in example 5.5 (on pp. 120–121, mm.12–15). Although the relationship between the sketch and this movement is not as immediately evident as in some other pieces to be discussed in this section, the general orientation of the metric opposition, as well as the harmonic implications, strongly suggest that this passage and the earlier sketch are related. However, this relationship is best described in connection with another piece that derives from the *Rube* sketch, *Scherzo: Over the Pavements*.

Compare example 6.12 (First Piano Sonata, mvmt. 4, mm. 36–41) with example 6.17 (*Scherzo: Over the Pavements*, mm. 32–35, on p. 160). Although the meter is different between the two excerpts, the right hand of the piano in the two pieces is nearly identical—they both use the same pitches, and only the first rhythmic value is different: a sixteenth note in the First Piano Sonata and an eighth note in *Scherzo: Over the Pavements*. In addition, both Sonata and *Scherzo* feature parallel triads, mentioned earlier in connection with the *Rube* sketch, but the notes and rhythmic

Example 6.13.   First Piano Sonata, mvmt. 5, mm. 54–59.

orientation have been altered significantly in comparison to the sketch. The close relationship between the two passages, especially in the right hand, suggests that the passage from the First Piano Sonata, like the similar passages in Study no. 23 to be discussed later, derives from the *middle* section of *Scherzo: Over the Pavements*, rather than directly from the baseball-related sketch. James Sinclair stated that "mm. 36–47 [of the First Piano Sonata, fourth movement] resemble material in *Take-Off No. 3: Rube Trying to Walk 2 to 3!!*"[32] However, it would be more accurate to say that mm. 36–47 of the sonata movement resemble material in *Scherzo: Over the Pavements* and that *Scherzo: Over the Pavements* includes material derived from the *Rube* sketch.[33]

A closer relationship between this sonata and the *Rube* sketch, not identified by Sinclair or elsewhere, occurs in the fifth movement (mm. 54–59). As shown in example 6.13, pairs of quarter notes project a simple-triple meter, matching the three-two written meter, by employing octave leaps in the bass line, as in the beginning of the *Rube* sketch. Meanwhile the right hand presents parallel triads, as in the middle of the earlier sketch, in syncopation against the steady quarter notes in the left hand. Although this passage, too, is remarkably different from *Rube Trying to Walk 2 to 3!!* at least on the surface, the passage from the First Piano Sonata strongly resembles aspects of the earlier sketch in terms of both pitch and rhythmic configuration. The passage from the fourth movement cited by Sinclair and others, on the contrary, does not closely resemble any of the pitch or rhythmic material in the sketch. The relationship cited by these scholars is only loosely motivic and to a large extent circumstantial, seemingly based on the erroneous assumption that *all* of the material in *Scherzo: Over the Pavements* also appears in *Take-off #3: Rube Trying to Walk 2 to 3!!*

Study No. 23

Study no. 23 is another piece that is cited as derived from the *Rube* sketch. This study was composed primarily between 1912 and 1914, though some patches were added in the 1920s.[34] A relationship between this piece and baseball was established previously in chapter 3 based on a sketch of this piece with its "Knock Out Chord play with BASE Ball BAT." The numbering of this study was supplied by John Kirkpatrick, who "gave it this number since it follows Study no. 22 in the bound set of photostat repro[ductions] given to him by Ives around 1938."[35]

According to Burkholder,

> *Study no. 23* . . . also includes ragtime sections, partly new, partly paraphrasing the chorus of Joseph E. Howard's ragtime song "Hello! Ma Baby" . . . and partly based on a ragtime-derived ostinato figure Ives had earlier used in *Take-Off No. 3 ("Rube trying to Walk 2 to 3!!").*[36]

The passage to which Burkholder referred (mm. 32–36) is directly and almost literally taken from the middle section of *Scherzo: Over the Pavements,* which is only indirectly based on the *Rube* sketch, as mentioned previously and as discussed in more detail later in this chapter. The passage in question does not appear in the original baseball-related sketch. This passage seems to have been composed expressly for *Scherzo: Over the Pavements* rather than for *Take-off #3: Rube Trying to Walk 2 to 3!!* Nevertheless, some motivic similarities between the original sketch and this passage from Study no. 23 may be observed. The passage, marked "Prestoto con blasta *ffff*" in Ives's usual faux-Italian, also extends the parallel triads, found in the corresponding passages from *Scherzo: Over the Pavements* and the fourth movement of the First Piano Sonata, as noted earlier. In the study, instead of retaining triads throughout the passage, as in the earlier works, Ives fills out some of the harmonies with diatonic clusters, as shown in example 6.14. This passage is repeated toward the end of the

Example 6.14.   Study no. 23, mm. 32–37.
© Merion Music, Inc., used by permission of the publisher.

study (mm. 90–94). Sinclair noted that "for Ives, these piano studies were exercises, often merely sketches, in working out new compositional ideas."[37] However, in this case the *sonata* served as a sort of "study" for Study no. 23, which was composed later (1912–1914).[38] Furthermore, both the sonata and this study derive not from the *Rube* sketch but from the *Scherzo*.

Scherzo: Over the Pavements

Of the five pieces cited as derived from the *Rube* sketch, Ives's *Scherzo: Over the Pavements* bears the closest resemblance to the original sketch. Like *Take-off #3: Rube Trying to Walk 2 to 3!!*, *Scherzo: Over the Pavements* is also for a small chamber ensemble (piccolo, clarinet, bassoon, trumpet, three trombones, percussion, and piano).[39] Sinclair's commentary on dating this piece is a fine example of the fallout from the difficulties faced when dating Ives's music: "composed possibly in 1907 based on material composed possibly in 1906; revised probably in 1913."[40]

The opening of *Scherzo: Over the Pavements*, shown in example 6.15, is almost identical to the *Rube* sketch. The chamber work features the same instruments playing the same notes as in the earlier sketch. The only dif-

Example 6.15. *Scherzo: Over the Pavements, mm. 1–5.*

ferences seen in the later piece in the first six measures are that the trumpet is down an octave, the clarinet (rather than the trumpet) switches octaves periodically, and the bassoon part has been completed (rather than left incomplete as in the sketch). As *Scherzo: Over the Pavements* continues, the close correspondences between model and piece continue. Ives changed a few notes or chords here and there, but for the most part he simply added voices that were missing from the incomplete sketch. For example, the parallel chords in the piano that begin on a D minor triad in the sketch (example 5.5, on p. 120, m.   12) begin instead on an F major triad in the later piece, and the continuation of that line—moving into the left hand to a tied sixteenth-note dyad, F♯-A♯—moves instead to a dyad a third higher, A♯-C♯, remaining in the right hand in the *Scherzo* (m. 13). On the other hand, some individual parts are changed more profoundly. For example the melody that begins in the trumpet, but is written in the bassoon part (as mentioned in chapter 5), thirteen measures into the sketch is replaced by different music in the trumpet *and* bassoon in the later *Scherzo*. Notably, however, the clarinet part—with its distinctive, syncopated, augmented-fifth leaps—is retained from the original model (mm. 12–18).

The ensuing passage of *Scherzo: Over the Pavements* continues to remain close to the music sketched in *Take-off #3: Rube Trying to Walk 2 to 3!!* The conclusion of the syncopated pattern in the clarinet, where a sixteenth-note pattern has some lightly crossed-out notes in the sketch, is retained and slightly

Example 6.16. *Scherzo: Over the Pavements*, **mm. 29–31.**

Example 6.17. *Scherzo: Over the Pavements*, mm. 32–35.

expanded by an additional note in the later piece (m. 22). Ives seems to have decided to stick with his initial impulse, despite his earlier misgivings suggested by the crossed-out notes. Meanwhile, Ives divided the piano part, which appears in the right hand only in the sketch, into both hands in the finished piece, but he retained the close, dissonant harmonies. Later, he reorchestrated the sixteenth-note wedge that appears in the piano in the sketch, placing the lower voice in the bassoon in the later piece and changing the rhythm slightly while retaining the chromatic pitches (m. 25).

The first section of *Scherzo: Over the Pavements* concludes with the same material as in the original sketch, with a few changes in the accompanimental patterns in the winds and with only a single measure of duple time, as shown in example 6.16. The same single-measure metric modulation (m. 31) also concludes the song "1, 2, 3," as noted previously. In addition, the last measure of this section in the *Scherzo* contains a couple of revisions to both rhythm and pitch in the right hand of the piano. Instead of a three-note scalar descent in thirds, as in the sketch, the first beat of this measure in the *Scherzo* seems to extract from the notes of the model— taking only the first note of the top line and the second note of the lower line, to present only a C-F♯ tritone after a sixteenth rest. Then Ives repeats this basic rhythmic configuration on the last beat, which similarly presents a sixteenth note followed by a longer note, as in the first beat and unlike the straight eighth notes of the *Rube* sketch.

After this sudden shift from triple to duple meter, *Scherzo: Over the Pavements* continues with a lengthy section of new material (mm. 32–80),

Example 6.18. *Scherzo: Over the Pavements,* **mm. 125–129.**

some of which is motivically related to material from this first section, such as the parallel triads that open the middle section in the piano, joined by the trombones on the repeat of the section, as shown in example 6.17. This new large section goes on to explore more intricate polyrhythmic complexities than the largely two-against-three metric structure of the first section and of the sketch—or polymetric hemiolas, as discussed earlier in this chapter in terms of isolated compositional techniques.[41] This middle section of the *Scherzo* is the section from which material found in the fourth movement of the First Piano Sonata and Study no. 23 are derived, rather than the *Rube* sketch, as noted earlier.

At the center of the formally palindromic *Scherzo* is a cadenza, marked "to play or not to play," which is broader in feel, despite the tempo marking of "*Allegro molto* (or as fast as possible)" (mm. 81–95). This middle section of intricate counting and radically sweeping piano arpeggios, set with serialized pitch and rhythmic materials, is followed by a direct repeat of the second large section, and finally a return to the opening material derived from the *Rube* sketch.[42] The written-out da capo (mm. 97–129) of this material was inherent in Ives's compositional conception from the beginning, as the original sketch includes the indication "D.C." immediately before the shift to duple meter that ends the sketch.

The written-out repeat in the *Scherzo* includes a few changes from the first presentation of the *Rube*-related material, mostly in terms of filled-out orchestration, especially the introduction of three trombones and some added percussion. However, the most significant change occurs at the conclusion of the piece, shown in example 6.18. Here Ives retains the idea of ending with two measures of duple meter, as in the sketch, but the tonal orientation—like that of "1, 2, 3"—shifts dramatically to a simple C-major orientation, to heighten the surprise effect of the end of the piece—a "jack-in-the box," as John Rinehart described it.[43]

Chapter 5 presented the claim that *Take-off #3: Rube Trying to Walk 2 to 3!!* is about the baseball pitcher Rube Waddell, not just the irregular walking pattern of some country bumpkin. Unlike his ambiguous title of the *Rube* sketch, Ives offered a clear description of the inspiration for *Scherzo: Over the Pavements*, the sights and sounds of the pavements of New York:

> *Over the Pavements* was started one morning, when George Lewis and I had the front bedroom in Poverty Flat, 65 Central Park West. In the early morning, the sounds of people going to and fro, all different steps, and sometimes all the same—the horses, fast trot, canter, sometimes slowing up into a walk (few if any autos in those days)—an occasional trolley throwing all rhythm out (footsteps, horse and man)—then back again. I was struck with how many different and changing kinds of beats, time rhythms, etc. went on together— but quite naturally, or at least not unnaturally when you got used to it—and it struck me often [how] limited, static, and unnatural, almost weak-headed (at least in the one-syllable mental state), the time and rhythm (so called) in music had been: —1-2-, or 1-2-3, and if a 5 or 7 is played, the old ladies . . . divide it up nice into a 2 and 3, or 3 and 4, missing the whole point of a 5 or 7.[44]

Because the parts of *Scherzo: Over the Pavements* that come directly from the *Rube* sketch are about 2 against 3, while the new material in the middle of the *Scherzo* explores more complex rhythmic structures, it seems clear that Ives is referring mainly to this middle section of the chamber work in this remembrance. He is complaining about the interpretation of 5 and 7 patterns, which often are dissected into simpler and more familiar components, not about how duple patterns interact and intersect with triple patterns. And quintuplets and septuplets play a substantial role in the middle section of the *Scherzo*, but do not appear at all in the sections that derive from the *Rube* sketch at the beginning and end of the piece.

Moreover, Ives's addendum at the bottom of the *Rube* sketch unambiguously names this sketch as the source of his later song "1, 2, 3," as discussed earlier. Alternatively, he could have named *Scherzo: Over the Pavements*, the completed work rather than the earlier sketch, as the source of the song. The fact that Ives linked "1, 2, 3" to *Rube Trying to Walk 2 to 3!!* instead of to the *Scherzo* suggests that Ives viewed the *Rube* sketch as distinct from *Scherzo: Over the Pavements*, not just a sketch of material that forms a part of this larger work.

Based on these factors, Ives must have tacked the *Rube* materials onto the middle section of the *Scherzo*, to form the beginning and ending sections of the complete piece. If the *Rube* sketch is about a rube walking, then why not include this specific image at the beginning of his story about *Scherzo: Over the Pavements*, in addition to the horses, men (in general), and trolleys he describes? He seems to be referring instead to a cacophony of sounds, not to the distinct walking pattern of an unrefined individual.

Finally, if Ives's sketch is about the unrefined walking pattern of a country bumpkin, it seems clear that Ives would be making fun of a person from the country in this sketch. However, Ives's *reverence* for simple country folk suggests that Ives would not want to deride a rube in this way: Ives wrote, regarding parts of his *Holidays* Symphony, that he attempted "to make pictures in music of common events in the lives of common people (that is, fine people), mostly of the rural communities."[45] Because Ives singled out common people of the rural communities as "fine people," it seems unlikely that he would characterize such a fine individual as a rube to be stumbling down the street in this sketch.

On the other hand, if the *Rube* sketch is about baseball—a pitcher walking batters rather than a person walking, as suggested in chapter 5—then the story of the origin of *Scherzo: Over the Pavements* would be separate from the story of the sketch. Ives's account of his inspiration for the middle section of the *Scherzo* strongly suggests that he had an entirely different inspiration than a city street for the material taken from the *Rube* sketch. Furthermore, he mentions George Lewis in his account of the origin of *Scherzo: Over the Pavements*, rather than Wally McCormack and Harry Farrar, listed as the *only ones* to see his sketch of *Rube*. It seems more likely that Ives's sketch was about the outrageous antics of Rube Waddell on the pitcher's mound where he tried to walk 2 to 3 batters on purpose!!—and therefore the story about the inspiration for *Scherzo: Over the Pavements* appropriately focuses entirely on the middle section, the only part of the *Scherzo* that was composed specifically for that piece.

Finally, Stuart Feder proposed another image to go along with Ives's story of the general meaning of *Scherzo: Over the Pavements*:

> The scoring conjures the image of a miniature marching band with the three trombones leading the way—not down the cobbled Main Street of Ives's boyhood memory or the dirt-packed country road of George's time, but down Central Park West. A note in the margin of the score contains a reminiscence: "2 Bands! C.P.W. 'D.D.' May 1906."[46]

And Rube Waddell's outlandish antics may be linked to *this* image as well. Admittedly, I may be stretching the point, but if Ives strongly associated marching bands with *Scherzo: Over the Pavements* and associated *Scherzo: Over the Pavements* with Rube Waddell (based on the sketch from which the later piece draws), then the following anecdote would bring us full circle: Rube Waddell's manager Connie Mack recounted that one "time when he was missing during a training trip, he returned to us as the drum major of a band marching up the main street, a look of ineffable bliss on his face."[47]

BALLGROUNDS AND PROVING GROUNDS

As this book has shown, in addition to the importance of baseball as a framework through which to explore new compositional ideas, baseball occupied a primary position in Ives's life as a whole. Ives treated baseball as a *proving ground* by playing "One old cat" with the other boys in Danbury, by playing shortstop for the Alerts and recording his experiences in his diary, by pitching Hopkins Grammar School to victory over the Yale Freshmen, by watching major league baseball in New York while idolizing the ballplayers who were in many ways most like himself, by preserving his baseball memories into his later years, and finally by transferring compositional techniques developed in connection with baseball into his later pieces.[48] Baseball gave Ives a way to establish male associations in his interactions with other boys by excelling in a "manly" sport and a means for Ives to prove himself as a man and as a composer to his friends in Poverty Flat by linking his love of music directly with his love of baseball.

Notes

INTRODUCTION

1. Charles Ives, postface, *114 Songs* (Redding, Conn.: Author, 1922; reprint, New York: Peer International, Associated Music Publishers, and Theodore Presser, 1975), [261].

2. John Kirkpatrick, s.v. "Ives, Charles (Edward)," in *New Grove Dictionary of American Music*, ed. H. Wiley Hitchcock and Stanley Sadie (New York: Macmillan Press, 1986).

3. Henry Cowell and Sidney Cowell, *Charles Ives and His Music* (New York: Oxford University Press, 1955; reprint, 1969), 27.

4. Frank R. Rossiter, *Charles Ives and His America* (New York: Liveright, 1975), 31–33.

5. Jan Swafford, *Charles Ives: A Life with Music* (New York: W. W. Norton, 1996), 55–59.

6. Swafford, *Charles Ives: A Life with Music*, 150, 455 n. 31; and John Bowman and Joel Zoss, *Diamonds in the Rough: The Untold History of Baseball* (New York: Macmillan Publishing Company, 1989), 375.

7. Stuart Feder, *Charles Ives: "My Father's Song": A Psychoanalytic Biography* (New Haven, Conn.: Yale University Press, 1992), 96, 118–20. Feder's later, more general biography also mentions the importance of sports in Ives's life but does not delve into the matter very deeply; see Stuart Feder, *The Life of Charles Ives* (Cambridge: Cambridge University Press, 1999).

8. Thomas Giebisch, *Take-off als Kompositionsprinzip bei Charles Ives*, vol. 181 of *Kölner Beiträge zur Musikforschung*, ed. Klaus Wolfgang Niemöller (Kassel, Germany: Gustav Bosse, 1993).

9. Jay Feldman, "Sports Were Music to His Ears," *Sports Illustrated* 75, no. 15 (Oct. 7, 1991): 106. I would like to thank James Sinclair for calling my attention to this article.

10. J. Peter Burkholder gives the composition date as 1899, depicting a game played in 1897. Stuart Feder placed both game and composition date in 1899 and identified Twichell as Ives's companion at the game; see J. Peter Burkholder, "Ives and Yale: The Enduring Influence of a College Experience," *College Music Symposium* 39 (1999): 32; and Feder, *Charles Ives: "My Father's Song,"* 170.

11. Burkholder's essay includes considerable descriptive details about programmatic aspects of this piece and the borrowed tunes Ives employed, while a section of Giebisch's book provides detailed analytical observations, featuring the special techniques employed in this sketch; see Burkholder, "Ives and Yale," 32; and Giebisch, *Take-off als Kompositionsprinzip,* 151–64). Also see J. Peter Burkholder, "Ives and the Four Musical Traditions," in *Charles Ives and His World,* ed. J. Peter Burkholder (Princeton, N.J.: Princeton University Press, 1996), 18–19.

12. Donald Hall, quoted in Geoffrey C. Ward, *Baseball: An Illustrated History,* based on a documentary film script by Geoffrey C. Ward and Ken Burns (New York: Alfred A. Knopf, 1994), xviii.

13. Charles Wilson Ward, "Charles Ives: The Relationship between Aesthetic Theories and Compositional Processes" (Ph.D. diss., University of Texas at Austin, 1974), 149.

CHAPTER 1: AN AMERICAN SPORT—
AN AMERICAN COMPOSER

1. Walt Whitman, "Baseball Is Our Game," in *Baseball as America: Seeing Ourselves through Our National Game,* ed. John Odell (Washington, D.C.: National Geographic, 2002), 37.

2. Tom Brokaw, "The Front Lines to the Backyard," in *Baseball as America: Seeing Ourselves through Our National Game,* ed. John Odell (Washington, D.C.: National Geographic, 2002), 63.

3. Henry Cowell and Sidney Cowell, *Charles Ives and His Music* (New York: Oxford University Press, 1955; reprint, 1969), 4.

4. Frank R. Rossiter, *Charles Ives and His America* (New York: Liveright, 1975), xi–xii.

5. Jan Swafford, *Charles Ives: A Life with Music* (New York: W. W. Norton, 1996), 3.

6. Swafford, *Charles Ives: A Life with Music,* 2.

7. Stuart Feder, *The Life of Charles Ives* (Cambridge: Cambridge University Press, 1999), 91–92.

8. "Charles E. Ives' Concert and New Cantata, 'The Celestial Country,'" *Musical Courier* 44, no. 17 (April 23, 1902): 34; reprint, "Selected Reviews 1888–1951," in *Charles Ives and His World,* comp. Geoffrey Block and ed. J. Peter Burkholder (Princeton, N.J.: Princeton University Press, 1996), 277.

9. Charles Wilson Ward, "Charles Ives: The Relationship between Aesthetic Theories and Compositional Processes" (Ph.D. diss., University of Texas at Austin, 1974), 125.

10. Leon Botstein, "Innovation and Nostalgia: Ives, Mahler, and the Origins of Twentieth-Century Modernism," in J. Peter Burkholder, ed., *Charles Ives and His World* (Princeton, N.J.: Princeton University Press, 1996), 35.

11. Stuart Feder, *Charles Ives: "My Father's Song": A Psychoanalytic Biography* (New Haven, Conn.: Yale University Press, 1992), 174.

12. Swafford, *Charles Ives: A Life with Music*, 143.

13. Swafford, *Charles Ives: A Life with Music*, 196–97; and Feder, *The Life of Charles Ives*, 99, 119.

14. Swafford, *Charles Ives: A Life with Music*, 194.

15. Feder, *The Life of Charles Ives*, 138.

16. Feder, *The Life of Charles Ives*, 126.

17. Swafford, *Charles Ives: A Life with Music*, 148–49.

18. Swafford, *Charles Ives: A Life with Music*, 198.

19. Rossiter, *Charles Ives and His America*, 84–85.

20. J. Peter Burkholder, "Ives and the Nineteenth-Century European Tradition," in *Charles Ives and the Classical Tradition*, ed. Geoffrey Block and J. Peter Burkholder (New Haven, Conn.: Yale University Press, 1996), 14.

21. Charles Ward treats the impact, importance, and characteristics of Ives's program music in detail; see Charles Ward, "Charles Ives: The Relationship between Aesthetic Theories," 127–54.

22. Charles Ives, *Essays before a Sonata, The Majority, and Other Writings*, ed. Howard Boatwright (New York: W. W. Norton, 1970), 4.

23. Feder, *Charles Ives: "My Father's Song,"* 244.

24. Feder, *Charles Ives: "My Father's Song,"* 246.

25. Rosalie Sandra Perry, *Charles Ives and the American Mind* (Kent, Ohio: Kent State University Press, 1974), 57.

26. Rossiter, *Charles Ives and His America*, xii–xiii.

27. Rossiter, *Charles Ives and His America*, 89–90.

28. J. Peter Burkholder, *Charles Ives: The Ideas behind the Music* (New Haven, Conn.: Yale University Press, 1985), 14.

29. Lawrence Gilman, "Music: A Masterpiece of American Music Heard Here for the First Time," *New York Herald Tribune* (January 21, 1939), 9; reprint, "Selected Reviews 1888–1951," 320.

30. J. Peter Burkholder, *All Made of Tunes: Charles Ives and the Uses of Musical Borrowing* (New Haven, Conn.: Yale University Press, 1995), 424.

31. Burkholder, *Charles Ives: The Ideas behind the Music*, 101–2.

32. Rossiter, *Charles Ives and His America*, 43.

33. The work of uncovering the origins of baseball is still in progress by a number of scholars, and the game is in all likelihood much older than previously believed; see Tom Altherr and Dave Block, "More Nails in Old Abner's Coffin: New Discoveries of Pre-1839 Baseball," paper presented at the Fifteenth Cooperstown Symposium on Baseball and American Culture, Cooperstown, N.Y., June 11–13, 2003. For more information on early forerunners and variants of baseball, see Thomas L. Altherr, "'A Place Leavel Enough to Play Ball': Baseball and Baseball-Type Games in the Colonial Era, Revolutionary War, and Early American Republic," *Nine* 8, no. 2 (2000): 15–49; and David Block, *Baseball before We Knew It: A Search for the Roots of the Game* (Lincoln: University of Nebraska Press, 2005).

34. Tom Shieber and Ted Spencer, "Spalding's Commission," in *Baseball as America: Seeing Ourselves through Our National Game*, ed. John Odell (Washington, D.C.: National Geographic, 2002), 41–43.

35. Burkholder, "Ives and the Nineteenth-Century European Tradition," 11.
36. Burkholder, "Ives and the Nineteenth-Century European Tradition," 12–13.
37. Burkholder, *Charles Ives: The Ideas behind the Music*, 65.
38. Burkholder, "Ives and the Nineteenth-Century European Tradition," 14.
39. Cowell and Cowell, *Charles Ives and His Music*, 147.
40. Burkholder, *All Made of Tunes*, 3–4.
41. Cowell and Cowell, *Charles Ives and His Music*, 164.
42. Stuart Feder, "The Nostalgia of Charles Ives: An Essay in Affects and Music," in *Psychoanalytic Explorations in Music*, ed. Stuart Feder, Richard L. Karmel, and George H. Pollock (Madison, Conn.: International Universities Press, 1990), 260.
43. David Metzer also linked Ives's nostalgia and use of borrowing with his depictions of childhood activities; see David Metzer, "'We Boys': Childhood in the Music of Charles Ives," *19th Century Music* 21 (1997): 77–95.
44. Feder, *Charles Ives: "My Father's Song,"* 253.
45. Cowell and Cowell, *Charles Ives and His Music*, 4.
46. Burkholder, "Ives and the Four Musical Traditions," 3.
47. Burkholder, *Charles Ives: The Ideas behind the Music*, 3.
48. Burkholder, *Charles Ives: The Ideas behind the Music*, 3.
49. Burkholder, *Charles Ives: The Ideas behind the Music*, 3.
50. Burkholder, *Charles Ives: The Ideas behind the Music*, 3–4.
51. Cowell and Cowell, *Charles Ives and His Music*, 207.
52. Swafford, *Charles Ives: A Life with Music*, 366.
53. Cowell and Cowell, *Charles Ives and His Music*, 143.
54. Swafford, *Charles Ives: A Life with Music*, ix.

CHAPTER 2: CONSTANT CHANGE—THE GROWTH
OF MAJOR LEAGUE BASEBALL

1. Dates and facts about events in Ives's life in this chapter are drawn from the "Chronological Index of Dates" in Ives's autobiographical *Memos* unless otherwise noted; see Charles E. Ives, *Memos*, ed. John Kirkpatrick (New York: W. W. Norton & Company, 1972), 325–37.
2. Bill James, *The New Bill James Historical Baseball Abstract* (New York: The Free Press, 2001), 8.
3. James, *Historical Baseball Abstract*, 10.
4. The baseball-related statistics, dates, and facts in this chapter are drawn from the seventh edition of *Total Baseball*, unless otherwise noted; see John Thorn, Peter Palmer, and Michael Gershman, eds., with Matthew Silverman, Sean Lahman, and Greg Spira, *Total Baseball: The Official Encyclopedia of Major League Baseball*, 7th ed. (Kingston, N.Y.: Total Sports Publishing, 2001).
5. Rule changes cited in this chapter are taken from the fifth edition of *Total Baseball*, unless otherwise noted; see John Thorn, Peter Palmer, Michael Gershman, and David Pietrusza, eds., *Total Baseball: The Official Encyclopedia of Major League Baseball*, 5th ed. (New York: Viking Penguin, 1997), 2376–413.

6. The Philadelphia Athletics (who later became known simply as the A's and moved to Oakland) were unrelated to the Athletic of Philadelphia. The Philadelphia Athletics was an American League team added later, whereas the Athletic of Philadelphia was an early National League team that soon folded.

7. Thorn et al., *Total Baseball*, 7th ed., 19.

8. James, *Historical Baseball Abstract*, 37.

9. James, *Historical Baseball Abstract*, 44.

10. James, *Historical Baseball Abstract*, 43.

11. James, *Historical Baseball Abstract*, 52.

12. James, *Historical Baseball Abstract*, 71.

13. Leonard Koppett, *Koppett's Concise History of Major League Baseball* (Philadelphia: Temple University Press, 1998), 106–7.

14. 223 wins for a two-year span (1906–1907), 322 wins over three years (1906–1908), 426 wins over four years (1906–1909), 530 wins over five years (1906–1910), and 622 wins over six years (1905–1910); see James, *Historical Baseball Abstract*, 81.

15. Lawrence Ritter and Donald Honig, *The Image of Their Greatness: An Illustrated History of Baseball from 1900 to the Present* (New York: Crown Publishers, 1979), 30–31.

16. James, *Historical Baseball Abstract*, 94.

17. James, *Historical Baseball Abstract*, 94.

18. James, *Historical Baseball Abstract*, 105.

19. Stuart Feder, *The Life of Charles Ives* (Cambridge: Cambridge University Press, 1999), 136.

20. Koppett, *Koppett's Concise History of Major League Baseball*, 129.

21. James, *Historical Baseball Abstract*, 120.

22. Jan Swafford, *Charles Ives: A Life with Music* (New York: W. W. Norton, 1996), 205–6.

23. Koppett, *Koppett's Concise History of Major League Baseball*, 168.

24. Koppett, *Koppett's Concise History of Major League Baseball*, 168.

25. Julian Myrick, "What the Business Owes to Charles E. Ives," *Eastern Underwriter* (September 19, 1930); reprint, Ives, *Memos*, 272–73.

26. G. Edward White, *Creating the National Pastime: Baseball Transforms Itself 1903–1953* (Princeton, N.J.: Princeton University Press, 1996), 175–79.

27. Lawrence Gilman, "Music: A Masterpiece of American Music Heard Here for the First Time," *New York Herald Tribune*, January 21, 1939, 9.

28. Koppett, *Koppett's Concise History of Major League Baseball*, 202.

29. Franklin Delano Roosevelt, letter to Commissioner Landis, January 15, 1942; original held in archives of The National Baseball Library and Hall of Fame; reprint, Geoffrey C. Ward, *Baseball: An Illustrated History*, based on a documentary film script by Geoffrey C. Ward and Ken Burns (New York: Alfred A. Knopf, 1994), 276–78.

30. James, *Historical Baseball Abstract*, 197.

31. Swafford, *Charles Ives: A Life with Music*, 419.

32. J. Peter Burkholder, *Charles Ives: The Ideas Behind the Music* (New Haven, Conn.: Yale University Press, 1985), 34–35.

33. Swafford, *Charles Ives: A Life with Music*, 9.

34. Burkholder, *Charles Ives: The Ideas Behind the Music*, 35.

35. Swafford, *Charles Ives: A Life with Music*, 219.

36. Charles Ives, quoted in Henry Cowell and Sidney Cowell, *Charles Ives and His Music* (New York: Oxford University Press, 1955; reprint, 1969), 115.

37. Swafford, *Charles Ives: A Life with Music*, 422.

38. Grantland Rice, "Setting the Pace: The Duffer Speaks Again—Choosing the Best Combination Pitcher—Connie Mack Casts Vote for Waddell," in "Rube Waddell" Biography File, National Baseball Library and Archive, Cooperstown, New York.

39. James, *Historical Baseball Abstract*, 220.

40. Joshua Prager has called into question the integrity of this moment and this pennant race by exposing the secret that the Giants had been stealing signs using a telescope and an elaborate electronic buzzer system; see Joshua Harris Prager, "Inside Baseball: Giants' 1951 Comeback, the Sport's Greatest, Wasn't All It Seemed—Miracle Ended with 'The Shot Heard Round the World'; It Began with a Buzzer—'Papa's' Collapsible Legacy," *Wall Street Journal* (January 31, 2001), A1.

41. Koppett, *Koppett's Concise History of Major League Baseball*, 247–48.

CHAPTER 3: A LIFE OF BASEBALL—A "MANLY" GAME

1. Jacques Barzun, *God's Country and Mine: A Declaration of Love Spiced with a Few Harsh Words* (Boston: Little, Brown and Company, 1954), 159.

2. Barzun, *God's Country and Mine*, 161–62.

3. *The Danbury News*, 21, no. 7 (Wednesday, May 21, 1890), 1.

4. *Danbury Evening News*, Monday, May 18, 1891, 1.

5. *Danbury Evening News*, Monday, July 28, 1890, 8.

6. *Danbury Evening News*, Monday, April 21, 1890, 8.

7. For example, see *The Dime Base-Ball Player for 1881: Containing the Revised Code of Playing Rules Applicable to the Professional, Amateur and College Clubs of the Country for 1881, Together with Review of the Season's Work in the Professional, College and Amateur Arenas, with the Batting and Pitching Averages and the College Club Statistics, also the League Club Records for 1880* (New York: Beadle and Adams, 1881).

8. *Danbury Evening News*, Monday, May 13, 1895, 4. The two-word phrase "base ball" was a more common early spelling than the present-day compound word.

9. *Danbury Evening News*, Monday, May 13, 1895, 4.

10. *The Danbury News*, 16, no. 23 (Wednesday, July 22, 1885), 3.

11. *The Danbury News*, 21, no. 7 (Wednesday, May 21, 1890), 1.

12. I would like to thank Brigid Durkin, executive director of the Danbury Museum and Historical Society, for this suggestion.

13. I would like to thank Tom Altherr, professor of history, Metropolitan State College of Denver, for this observation. The early history of the Danbury Fire Department is contained in James Montgomery Bailey, *History of Danbury, Conn. 1684–1896*, from notes and manuscript left by the author, compiled with additions by Susan Benedict Hill (New York: Burr Printing House, 1896), 485–90. Unfortunately, however, unlike some other towns such as Adams, Massachusetts, whose

fire company is still called The Alerts, none of the Danbury fire companies listed had this as their official name. According to Denny Randall, curator of the American Museum of Firefighting, Hudson, New York, "It is supposed that the term originally derived from the necessity of having to be alert for the sound of the watchman's rattle, a device not unlike a child's party noisemaker, which when spun created a loud buzzing rattle. Eventually the alarms were raised by bells, similar to church bells, for which one would not have to be quite so 'alert'." (Denny Randall, E-mail communication to author, August 25, 2003).

14. Stuart Feder, *Charles Ives: "My Father's Song": A Psychoanalytic Biography* (New Haven, Conn.: Yale University Press, 1992), 96.

15. Charles Ives, Papers, New Haven, Yale University Music Library Archival Collection, Box 45, D2, entries for May 30–31, 1889.

16. Ives, Papers, Box 45, D2, entries for May 11, 1888, and April 27, 1889.

17. Ives, Papers, Box 45, D2, entries for May 18, June 22, and July 6, 1889.

18. John Kirkpatrick, "Appendix 13: George Edward Ives (1845–1894) and His Family," in Charles E. Ives, *Memos,* ed. John Kirkpatrick (New York: W. W. Norton & Company, 1972), 248.

19. Ives, Papers, Box 45, D2, unlabeled clipping of June 8, 1889.

20. Ives, Papers, Box 45, D2, entry for April 16, 1889, unlabeled clipping, hand-marked "Apr. 19."

21. Ives, Papers, Box 45, D2, unlabeled clipping from the *New Street Monthly* on November page with no date listed.

22. Ives, Papers, Box 45, D2.

23. Ives, Papers, Box 33, folder 1, letter to Sarah Amelia Ives ("Auntie"), September 14, 1886.

24. Ives, Papers, Box 33, folder 1, letter to George Ives ("Papa"), August 14, 1889.

25. Ives, Papers, Box 33, folder 1, letter to George Ives ("Papa"), August 15, 1889.

26. Feder, *Charles Ives: "My Father's Song,"* 119.

27. William E. Devlin, *We Crown Them All: An Illustrated History of Danbury,* sponsored by the Danbury Scott-Fanton Museum and Historical Society (Woodland Hills, Calif.: Windsor Publications, 1984), 64.

28. Devlin, *We Crown Them All,* 47.

29. Stuart Feder, *The Life of Charles Ives* (Cambridge: Cambridge University Press, 1999), 36.

30. For detailed information about this sculpture and Ives's piece, see Feder, *The Life of Charles Ives,* 29–33.

31. For example, see Feder, *Charles Ives: "My Father's Song,"* 37–46; and Jan Swafford, *Charles Ives: A Life with Music* (New York: W. W. Norton, 1996), 19–26.

32. Feder, *Charles Ives: "My Father's Song,"* 230.

33. Patricia Millen, *From Pastime to Passion: Baseball and the Civil War* (Bowie, Md.: Heritage Books, 2001), ix.

34. Millen, *From Pastime to Passion,* xiii.

35. Millen, *From Pastime to Passion,* x–xi.

36. Albert G. Spalding, *America's National Game: Historic Facts Concerning the Beginning, Evolution, Development and Popularity of Base Ball, with Personal Reminiscences of Its Vicissitudes, Its Victories and Its Votaries* (New York: American Sports Publishing Company, 1911), 92–93.

37. Feder, *Charles Ives: "My Father's Song,"* 39.

38. Millen, *From Pastime to Passion,* xiii.

39. Judith Tick presents a thoughtful assessment of the literature on Ives and issues of masculinity, and she offers social and cultural perspectives on Ives's frequent tirades about music and gender in his writings; see Judith Tick, "Charles Ives and Gender Ideology," in *Musicology and Difference: Gender and Sexuality in Music Scholarship,* ed. Ruth A. Solie (Berkeley: University of California Press, 1993), 83–106.

40. Feder, *The Life of Charles Ives,* 53.

41. Ives, *Memos,* 130–31 (Kirkpatrick's bracketed insertion).

42. Swafford, *Charles Ives: A Life with Music,* 55.

43. Feder, *Charles Ives: "My Father's Song,"* 119.

44. Donald J. Mrozek, *Sport and American Mentality, 1880–1910* (Knoxville: University of Tennessee Press, 1983), 232.

45. *The Dime Base-Ball Player for 1881,* 10.

46. *The Dime Base-Ball Player for 1881,* 9.

47. Colin D. Howell, *Northern Sandlots: A Social History of Maritime Baseball* (Toronto: University of Toronto Press, 1995), 14.

48. Howell, *Northern Sandlots,* 227–28.

49. Michael S. Kimmel, "Baseball and the Reconstitution of American Masculinity, 1880–1920," in *Cooperstown Symposium on Baseball and the American Culture (1989),* ed. Alvin L. Hall (Westport, CT: Meckler in association with the State University of New York College at Oneonta, 1991), 281.

50. Steven A. Riess, "Sport and Middle-Class Masculinity," in *The New American Sport History: Recent Approaches and Perspectives,* ed. S. W. Pope (Urbana: University of Illinois Press, 1997), 191.

51. Harold Seymour, *Baseball: The People's Game* (New York: Oxford University Press, 1990), 46.

52. Howell, *Northern Sandlots,* 105.

53. Frank R. Rossiter, *Charles Ives and His America* (New York: Liveright, 1975), 31–32.

54. Feder, *Charles Ives: "My Father's Song,"* 120.

55. Stuart Feder, "Charles and George Ives: The Veneration of Boyhood," in *Psychoanalytic Explorations in Music,* ed. Stuart Feder, Richard L. Karmel, and George H. Pollock, Applied Psychoanalysis Series, Monograph 3, edited by Chicago Institute for Psychoanalysis, George H. Pollock, president (Madison, Conn.: International Universities Press, 1990), 138.

56. James Isham Gardner and William Butler Tyler, ed., *The Hopkinsonian,* vol. 2 (New Haven, Conn.: James Isham Gardner and William Butler Tyler, 1897), 50.

57. John Kirkpatrick, s.v. "Ives, Charles (Edward)," in *New Grove Dictionary of American Music,* ed. H. Wiley Hitchcock and Stanley Sadie (New York: Macmillan Press, 1986), 504.

58. Swafford, *Charles Ives: A Life with Music,* 78–80.

59. Henry Cowell and Sidney Cowell, *Charles Ives and His Music* (New York: Oxford University Press, 1955; reprint, 1969), 28.

60. Swafford, *Charles Ives: A Life with Music,* 73. Walter Camp later attended Yale and then remained at Yale as a coach, where he became legendary as a founding fa-

ther of American football and collegiate athletics; he codified and totally transformed the rules and strategies of football; see Mark F. Bernstein, *Football: The Ivy League Origins of an American Obsession* (Philadelphia: University of Pennsylvania Press, 2001): 12–14. The football field at Yale is named in Camp's honor. For further information on Camp, see Kathleen D. Valenzi and Michael W. Hopps, *Champion of Sport: The Life of Walter Camp, 1859–1925* (Charlottesville, Va.: Howell Press, 1990).

61. Letter from Charles Ives to his family, March 29, 1894, quoted in Feder, *Charles Ives: "My Father's Song,"* 126.

62. Feder, *Charles Ives: "My Father's Song,"* 126.

63. Ives, Papers, Box 33, folder 1, letter to George Ives ("Father"), May 8, Evening, [1894].

64. Ives, Papers, Box 33, folder 1, letter to George Ives ("Father"), Sunday, May 13, 1894.

65. *Yale Daily News*, February 16, 1895, [1]; February 28, 1895, [1]; March 15, 1895, [1]; cited in Rossiter, *Charles Ives and His America*, 335, n. 84.

66. Kirkpatrick, "Ives," in *New Grove Dictionary of American Music*, 504.

67. Ronald Story, "The Country of the Young: The Meaning of Baseball in Early American Culture," in *Cooperstown Symposium on Baseball and the American Culture (1989)*, ed. Alvin L. Hall (Westport, CT: Meckler in association with the State University of New York College at Oneonta, 1991), 324.

68. Feder, *The Life of Charles Ives*, 77.

69. Feder, *Charles Ives: "My Father's Song,"* 151.

70. Feder, *Charles Ives: "My Father's Song,"* 155. Details of Ives's fraternal involvement and his election as a senior to the "secret-society system, the ultimate honor" appear in Feder, *Charles Ives: "My Father's Song,"* 151–65.

71. Rossiter, *Charles Ives and His America*, 32; Swafford, *Charles Ives: A Life with Music*, 144; and Julian Southall Myrick, quoted in Ives, *Memos*, 269.

72. Vivian Perlis, *Charles Ives Remembered: An Oral History* (New Haven, Conn.: Yale University Press, 1974), 84.

73. Barzun, *God's Country and Mine*, 160.

74. Perlis, *Charles Ives Remembered*, 84–85.

75. Barzun, *God's Country and Mine*, 160.

76. Perlis, *Charles Ives Remembered*, 81.

77. Swafford, *Charles Ives: A Life with Music*, 288.

78. Ives, Papers, Box 45, D8, diary of Charles and Harmony Ives, entry for "Wednesday, Jan. 1, 1919."

79. Ives, Papers, Box 37, folder 3, letter to Editor, *New York Times*, May 7, 1922.

80. Perlis, *Charles Ives Remembered*, 112.

81. Photographs of these doors also appear in Perlis, *Charles Ives Remembered*, 90; and in Rossiter, *Charles Ives and His America*, following 211. However, the baseball teams are difficult to see in book-size reproductions. A large print of this photograph is displayed at the Ives Homestead of the Danbury Museum and Historical Society, where the details of the items displayed on the doors are quite visible.

82. Ives's manuscript materials are identified by their microfilm numbers, preceded by the letter "f" and enclosed in brackets. Alan Mandel recorded a version of this sketch that includes the baseball bat chord, but he made an unfortunate choice, as far as baseball fans are concerned: "In this instance the pianist refrained

from following the composer's directions" (Mandel did not use a baseball bat to play the chord); Alan Mandel, Liner notes, *Charles Ives: The Complete Works for Piano*, Alan Mandel, Piano (Desto Records DST-6458-6461), [8].

83. Feder, *The Life of Charles Ives*, 78.

84. Feder, *Charles Ives: "My Father's Song*," 241, 255.

85. Maggi E. Sokolik, "Out of Left Field: Baseball and American Idiom," in *Cooperstown Symposium on Baseball and the American Culture (1989)*, ed. Alvin L. Hall (Westport, Conn.: Meckler, in association with The State University of New York College at Oneonta, 1991), 85.

86. Rossiter, *Charles Ives and His America*, 32.

87. Charles Ives, Postface, *114 Songs* (Redding, Conn.: Author, 1922; reprint, New York: Peer International, Associated Music Publishers, and Theodore Presser, 1975), [261].

88. Spalding, *America's National Game*, 406–7 (Spalding's emphasis).

89. Spalding, *America's National Game*, 405.

90. Ives, *Memos*, 26.

91. Ives, *Memos*, 243.

92. Ives, *Memos*, 132. Kirkpatrick identified the professor as most likely Horatio Parker, Ives's teacher at Yale (n. 1).

93. John Kirkpatrick, ed., *Memos*, by Charles E. Ives (New York: W. W. Norton, 1972) 132, n. 2.

94. Charles Ives, *Essays before a Sonata, The Majority, and Other Writings*, ed. Howard Boatwright (New York: W. W. Norton, 1970), 97.

95. Ives, *Essays before a Sonata*, 23 (Ives's emphasis).

96. Ives, *Memos*, 120–21 (Kirkpatrick's bracketed insertions).

97. J. Peter Burkholder, "The Critique of Tonality in the Early Experimental Music of Charles Ives," *Music Theory Spectrum* 12 (1990): 205, 207.

98. Ives, *Essays before a Sonata*, 116.

99. Feder, *Charles Ives: "My Father's Song*," 118–19.

100. Some additional baseball references in Ives's writings include "forty thousand souls at a ball game does not, necessarily, make baseball the highest expression of spiritual emotion," suggesting that popularity does not equal quality; and "the value or success of but one precept [of Emerson] is dependent, like that of a ballgame, as much on the batting-eye as on the pitching-arm," though in the margin of the manuscript he seemed unsatisfied with this latter comparison, where he wrote "get better simile?" (Ives, *Essays before a Sonata*, 56; 16; 16, n. j).

101. Ives, *Memos*, 57.

102. Ives, *Memos*, 135.

103. Rossiter, *Charles Ives and His America*, 33.

CHAPTER 4: PLAYING THE GAME—BASEBALL IN COMPLETED COMPOSITIONS

1. Charles Wilson Ward, "Charles Ives: The Relationship between Aesthetic Theories and Compositional Processes" (Ph.D. diss., University of Texas at Austin, 1974), 94.

2. Charles E. Ives, *Memos*, ed. John Kirkpatrick (New York: W. W. Norton & Company, 1972), 61 (Kirkpatrick's bracketed insertion).

3. Carol K. Baron, "Meaning in the Music of Charles Ives," in *Metaphor: A Musical Dimension*, ed. Jamie C. Kassler, Australian Studies in the History, Philosophy and Social Studies of Music, vol. 1, gen. ed. Margaret J. Kartomi (Sydney, Australia: Currency Press, 1991), 38.

4. J. Peter Burkholder, *Charles Ives: The Ideas behind the Music* (New Haven, Conn.: Yale University Press, 1985), 52.

5. Frank R. Rossiter, *Charles Ives and His America* (New York: Liveright, 1975), 122.

6. Philip Lambert, "Ives and Berg: 'Normative' Procedures and Post-Tonal Alternatives," in *Charles Ives and the Classical Tradition*, ed. Geoffrey Block and J. Peter Burkholder (New Haven and London: Yale University Press, 1996), 113.

7. Ives, *Memos*, 61–62.

8. Rossiter, *Charles Ives and His America*, 242.

9. Ives, *Memos*, 63.

10. Ulrich Maske was one of the first people to present a detailed analysis of this piece, including its polymetric, palindromic, and programmatic aspects; see Ulrich Maske, "Charles Ives in seiner Kammermusik für drei bis sechs Instrumente" (Regensburg, Germany: Gustav Bosse Verlag, 1971), 15, 60, 62, 105, 134. J. Peter Burkholder also discussed this piece in some detail; see Burkholder, *Charles Ives: The Ideas behind the Music*, 87.

11. John Thorn and Peter Palmer with Michael Gershman, eds., and David Pietrusza, managing ed., *Total Baseball: The Official Encyclopedia of Major League Baseball*, 4th ed. (New York: Viking, 1995), 2438.

12. Thorn et al., *Total Baseball*, 4th ed., 2439.

13. It is also possible that the event depicted occurred later in Ives's childhood, because the boys in Danbury probably were unaware of the precise rules of baseball while these rules were gradually evolving in the major leagues, especially with the limited coverage of the professional game in Danbury. The boys may have retained outdated rules long after new rules were adopted by the professional leagues.

14. Thorn et al., *Total Baseball*, 4th ed., 2429.

15. Christine Ammer, *Southpaws & Sunday Punches and Other Sporting Expressions* (New York: Plume/Penguin Books, 1993), 206. In Pittsfield, Massachusetts, at single-A level minor league games, I spent many evenings squinting into the setting sun, along with the batter, because Wahconah Park, unfortunately, does not exhibit this optimum layout.

16. For some of these other theories, see Paul Dickson, *The New Dickson Baseball Dictionary: A Cyclopedic Reference to More Than 7,000 Words, Names, Phrases, and Slang Expressions That Define the Game, Its Heritage, Culture, and Variation* (San Diego: Harcourt Brace & Company, 1999), s.v. "Southpaw."

17. *Sporting Life*, January 14, 1885; also cited in Dickson, *The New Dickson Baseball Dictionary*, s.v. "Southpaw."

18. Dickson, *The New Dickson Baseball Dictionary*, s.v. "Southpaw."

19. John Kirkpatrick, "Editor's Notes," in Charles E. Ives, *Study No. 21: Some South-Paw Pitching! for Piano* (Bryn Mawr, Pa.: Mercury Music Corporation, 1975), 7.

20. Kirkpatrick, "Editor's Notes," in Ives, *Study No. 21*, 7.

21. Noel H. Magee, "The Short Piano Works of Charles Ives" (M.M. thesis, Indiana University, 1966), 61.

22. Keith Ward, "Musical Idealism: A Study of the Aesthetics of Arnold Schoenberg and Charles Ives" (D.M. diss., Northwestern University, 1985), 215.

23. Charles E. Ives, *Some South-Paw Pitching*, ed. Henry Cowell, in Charles E. Ives, *Five Piano Pieces* (Bryn Mawr, Pa.: Mercury Music Corporation, 1949), 28.

24. Keith Ward interprets the sectional layout of this piece as a modified sonata form. Although his reading of the form of this piece is difficult to accept (his preliminary conjecture, a ternary design, seems more plausible), his fairly thorough analytical comments provide valuable insights on rhythmic, melodic, metric, and especially textural aspects of this piece; see Ward, "Musical Idealism," 135–46.

25. Noel Magee also recognized the importance of interval cycles in his brief analysis of this study; see Magee, "The Short Piano Works of Charles Ives," 62. For a systematic treatment of interval cycles in Ives's music in general, see J. Philip Lambert, "Interval Cycles as Compositional Resources in the Music of Charles Ives," *Music Theory Spectrum* 12 (1990): 43–82.

26. For more information on the borrowed material in this piece, see Clayton W. Henderson, *The Charles Ives Tunebook*, Bibliographies in American Music, no. 14, ed. James R. Heintze, published for The College Music Society (Warren, Mich.: Harmonie Park Press, 1990), 204.

27. These markings appear only in the Kirkpatrick edition and not in the earlier edition by Cowell.

28. Stuart Feder, "Charles and George Ives: The Veneration of Boyhood," in *Psychoanalytic Explorations in Music*, edited by Stuart Feder, Richard L. Karmel, and George H. Pollock, Applied Psychoanalysis Series, Monograph 3, edited by Chicago Institute for Psychoanalysis, George H. Pollock, president (Madison, Conn.: International Universities Press, 1990), 133.

29. Dickson, *The New Dickson Baseball Dictionary*, s.v. "One Old Cat."

30. Dickson, *The New Dickson Baseball Dictionary*, s.v. "Catball."

31. Tristram Potter Coffin, *The Old Ball Game: Baseball in Folklore and Fiction* (New York: Herder and Herder, 1971), 6–7. With a great deal of pleasure, I played in a game of town ball myself at the Fifteenth Cooperstown Symposium on Baseball and American Culture, using the Massachusetts rules of 1858. Town ball is a highly anticipated annual event at this academic symposium, and "base hits filled the air" that evening as well.

32. Harold Seymour, *Baseball: The Early Years* (New York: Oxford University Press 1960), 7.

33. For the names of the other seven borrowed tunes that have been identified in this song, see Henderson, *The Charles Ives Tunebook*, 209.

34. For more details on this point, see Timothy A. Johnson, "Chromatic Quotations of Diatonic Tunes in Songs of Charles Ives," *Music Theory Spectrum* 18 (1996): 257–58.

35. Ives, *Memos*, 96.

36. Ives, *Memos*, 104.

37. Charles Ives, "Ives's Program Note," quoted in *The Fourth of July: Third Movement of A Symphony: New England Holidays*, ed. Wayne D. Shirley, Charles Ives Society Critical Edition (Milwaukee, Wis.: Associated Music Publishers, 1992), vii.

38. Ives, "Ives's Program Note," in *The Fourth of July*, vii.

39. Ives, *Memos*, 104. Editor John Kirkpatrick identified Ives's quotation as "from Mark Twain's *Huckleberry Finn*, end of Chap. 28" (n. 3).

40. Bill James, *The New Bill James Historical Baseball Abstract* (New York: The Free Press, 2001), 53.

41. Wayne D. Shirley, preface, in Charles E. Ives, *The Fourth of July: Third Movement of A Symphony: New England Holidays*, Charles Ives Society Critical Edition (Milwaukee, Wis.: Associated Music Publishers, 1992), iv.

42. Ives, "Ives's Program Note," in *The Fourth of July*, vii.

43. Ives, *Memos*, 104.

44. Another aspect of the relationship between this piece and baseball is the fact that Ives based part of the fourth movement on material from one of his baseball-related sketches: This derivation will be addressed in chapter 6.

45. Ives, *Memos*, 74 (Kirkpatrick's bracketed insertion).

46. Paul C. Echols, "Editorial Note: 1979," in Charles E. Ives, Sonata no. 1 for Piano (New York: Peer International, 1954; reprint, 1990), [iv].

47. J. Peter Burkholder, *All Made of Tunes: Charles Ives and the Uses of Musical Borrowing* (New Haven, Conn.: Yale University Press, 1995), 243. For detailed analytical commentary on this piece, also see 187–93, 212–14, and 243–44.

48. Jan Swafford, *Charles Ives: A Life with Music* (New York: W. W. Norton, 1996), 166.

49. [f3723]. Kirkpatrick's transcription presents a different interpretation of a few words; see Ives, *Memos*, 75.

50. The borrowed tune appears in Henderson, *The Charles Ives Tunebook*, 59.

51. John Kirkpatrick also suggested this interpretation of this reference; see Ives, *Memos*, 75.

CHAPTER 5: MUSICAL SKETCHES OF BALLPLAYERS— A BASEBALL FAN'S RECORD

1. Stuart Feder, *Charles Ives: "My Father's Song": A Psychoanalytic Biography* (New Haven, Conn.: Yale University Press, 1992), 187. Elsewhere, Feder specifically identified "slump" as a baseball term Ives employed to describe his "depressed mood"; see Stuart Feder, *The Life of Charles Ives* (Cambridge: Cambridge University Press, 1999), 95.

2. J. Peter Burkholder, "Ives and the Four Musical Traditions," in *Charles Ives and His World*, ed J. Peter Burkholder (Princeton, N.J.: Princeton University Press, 1996), 16.

3. Charles E. Ives, *Memos*, ed. John Kirkpatrick (New York: W. W. Norton & Company, 1972), 61.

4. Burkholder, "Ives and the Four Musical Traditions," 17.

5. David Nasaw, *Going Out: The Rise and Fall of Public Amusements* (New York: Basic Books, 1993), 96–97.

6. Nasaw, *Going Out*, 99.

7. Jan Swafford, *Charles Ives: A Life with Music* (New York: W. W. Norton, 1996), 457, n. 75.

8. Swafford, *Charles Ives: A Life with Music*, 151.

9. The locations of each of these old ballparks are mapped in Marc Okkonen, *Baseball Memories: 1900–1909* (New York: Sterling Publishing, 1992), 58.

10. Swafford, *Charles Ives: A Life with Music*, 150.

11. Michael Benson, *Ballparks of North America: A Comprehensive Historical Reference to Baseball Grounds, Yards and Stadiums, 1845 to Present* (Jefferson, N.C.: McFarland & Company, 1989), 252–63.

12. Benson, *Ballparks of North America*, 263–66.

13. Benson, *Ballparks of North America*, 265.

14. James Sinclair listed the title of the Keeler sketch without the definite article. The handwriting on the sketch is difficult to decipher, but the title appears to be "Willy Keeler at *the* Bat," not just at bat, and Sinclair acknowledged this interpretation in his "Comment"; see James B. Sinclair, *A Descriptive Catalogue of the Music of Charles Ives* (New Haven, Conn.: Yale University Press, 1999), 124-25.

15. Ives, *Memos*, 149.

16. Ives, *Memos*, 160.

17. Sinclair, *A Descriptive Catalogue*, 596–97. *All the Way Around and Back* is also numbered "3" in Ives's planned set of "athletic" take-offs. The ambiguity of this duplicate number as a possible part of the collection of take-offs has not been resolved. Presumably one or the other is misnumbered. For more information on the set, see Sinclair, *A Descriptive Catalogue*, 176–77, 182–83.

18. J. Peter Burkholder described the use of borrowed tunes in this piece in detail and also provided some descriptive commentary on the music and its baseball program. He did not discuss the baseball characters mentioned in the piece; see J. Peter Burkholder, *All Made of Tunes: Charles Ives and the Uses of Musical Borrowing* (New Haven, Conn.: Yale University Press, 1995), 347.

19. Ward noted that "quoted tunes . . . acquire some kind of symbolism through association with specific texts"; see Charles Wilson Ward, "Charles Ives: The Relationship between Aesthetic Theories and Compositional Processes" (Ph.D. diss., University of Texas at Austin, 1974), 166. Thus, the assertion that this tune symbolizes a link between this baseball-related piece and the Civil War is in keeping with Ward's findings.

20. Ward, "Charles Ives: The Relationship between Aesthetic Theories," 347.

21. In his incipit of this sketch, James Sinclair editorially suggests sextuplets for this line to make it fit into the meter; see Sinclair, *Descriptive Catalogue*, 123.

22. A. D. Suehsdorf, s.v. "Donlin, Michael Joseph 'Mike,' 'Turkey Mike,'" in *Biographical Dictionary of American Sports: Baseball*, ed. David L. Porter (New York: Greenwood Press, 1987).

23. Both of these items are exhibited at the Baseball Hall of Fame Museum, Cooperstown, New York.

24. "Donlin a Colorful Figure," hand-stamped "*NY Sun* Sept 25, 1933," in "Mike Donlin" Biography File, National Baseball Library and Archive, Cooperstown, New York.

25. "Mike Donlin, 55, Dies: Quit Giants to Be an Actor," special to the *Herald Tribune* (hand-marked 9/24/33), in "Mike Donlin" Biography File, National Baseball Library and Archive, Cooperstown, New York.

26. "Mike Donlin, 55, Dies," in "Mike Donlin" Biography File, National Baseball Library and Archive, Cooperstown, New York.

27. Lawrence S. Ritter, "Ladies and Gentlemen, Presenting Marty McHale," in *The Armchair Book of Baseball,* ed. John Thorn, illus. James Stevenson, foreword by Peter V. Ueberroth (New York: Scribner's Sons, 1985), 254.

28. James K. Skipper, Jr., s.v. "Donlin, Michael Joseph," in *Baseball Nicknames: A Dictionary of Origins and Meanings* (Jefferson, N.C.: McFarland & Company, 1992).

29. Marty McHale, "A Closeup of Mike Donlin," in "Mike Donlin" Biography File, National Baseball Library and Archive, Cooperstown, New York.

30. "Donlin a Colorful Figure," in "Mike Donlin" Biography File, National Baseball Library and Archive, Cooperstown, New York.

31. Newspaper clipping, hand-marked 1-5-1907, in "Mike Donlin" Biography File, National Baseball Library and Archive, Cooperstown, New York.

32. *Sporting Life,* March 16, 1907, 2.

33. *Sporting Life,* March 30, 1907, 6.

34. *Sporting Life,* April 6, 1907, 6.

35. *Sporting Life,* April 13, 1907, 8.

36. *Sporting Life,* April 20, 1907, 9.

37. *Sporting Life,* April 20, 1907, 9.

38. *Sporting Life,* April 27, 1907, 6.

39. John Thorn, Peter Palmer, and Michael Gershman, eds., with Matthew Silverman, Sean Lahman, and Greg Spira, *Total Baseball: The Official Encyclopedia of Major League Baseball,* 7th ed. (Kingston, N.Y.: Total Sports Publishing, 2001), 733; and Skipper, s.v. "Donlin," in *Baseball Nicknames.*

40. John Kirkpatrick with Paul C. Echols, Work List, s.v. "Ives, Charles (Edward)," in *New Grove Dictionary of American Music,* ed. H. Wiley Hitchcock and Stanley Sadie (New York: Macmillan Press, 1986).

41. Letter from Gayle Sherwood to J. Peter Burkholder of 1 June 1994, cited in Burkholder, *All Made of Tunes,* 487, n. 22.

42. Maynard Solomon, "Charles Ives: Some Questions of Veracity," *Journal of the American Musicological Society* 40 (1987): 443–50.

43. Feder, *Charles Ives: "My Father's Song,"* 352–53.

44. Swafford, *Charles Ives: A Life with Music,* xiii. Carol Baron also presents a far less suspicious view than Solomon of Ives's dating practices; see Carol K. Baron, "Dating Charles Ives's Music: Facts and Fictions," *Perspectives of New Music* 28 (1990): 20–56.

45. "'In Days of Old, When Knights,' etc.," hand-marked 12-18-1930, in "Johnny Evers" Biography File, National Baseball Library and Archive, Cooperstown, New York.

46. Franklin P. Adams, "Baseball's Sad Lexicon," *New York Evening Mail,* July 1910; reprint, Franklin P. Adams, *In Other Words* (Garden City, N.Y.: Doubleday, Page & Company, 1912), 62; modern reprint, Nicholas Dawidoff, ed., *Baseball: A Literary Anthology* (New York: Library of America, 2002), 20.

47. Bill James, *The New Bill James Historical Baseball Abstract* (New York: The Free Press, 2001), 80.

48. Skipper, s.v. "Evers, John Joseph," in *Baseball Nicknames*.

49. Donald Honig, *Baseball's 10 Greatest Teams* (New York: Macmillan Publishing, 1982), 5.

50. Unlabelled clipping, "Johnny Evers" Biography File, National Baseball Library and Archive, Cooperstown, New York.

51. John Thorn and Peter Palmer with Michael Gershman, eds., and David Pietrusza, managing ed., *Total Baseball: The Official Encyclopedia of Major League Baseball*, 4th ed. (New York: Viking, 1995), 865.

52. Ernest Thayer, *Casey at the Bat* (1888; reprint, illustrated by Barry Moser, afterword by Donald Hall, Boston: D.R. Godine, 1988).

53. Thorn et al., *Total Baseball*, 4th ed., 1011–12.

54. Skipper, s.v. "Keeler, William Henry," in *Baseball Nicknames*.

55. Unlabelled clipping, "Willie Keeler" Biography File, National Baseball Library and Archive, Cooperstown, New York.

56. Ronald L. Gabriel, s.v. "Keeler, William Henry 'Willie,' 'Wee Willie,'" in *Biographical Dictionary of American Sports: Baseball*, ed. David L. Porter (New York: Greenwood Press, 1987).

57. Gabriel, s.v. "Keeler," in *Biographical Dictionary*.

58. Gabriel, s.v. "Keeler," in *Biographical Dictionary*.

59. Unlabelled clipping, hand-marked December 1913, in "Willie Keeler" Biography File, National Baseball Library and Archive, Cooperstown, New York.

60. Gabriel, s.v. "Keeler," in *Biographical Dictionary*.

61. Frederick G. Lieb, "McGraw Calls Willie Keeler Baseball's Smartest Batsman," in "Willie Keeler" Biography File, National Baseball Library and Archive, Cooperstown, New York.

62. "Keeler's Feat of Not Fanning in 700 Times Never Been Equaled," in "Willie Keeler" Biography File, National Baseball Library and Archive, Cooperstown, New York.

63. Thomas S. Rice, "Willie Keeler, Greatest of Place Hitters, Leaves behind a Brilliant Record," in "Willie Keeler" Biography File, National Baseball Library and Archive, Cooperstown, New York.

64. "Oldtimer Remembers Wee Willie," hand-marked 8-2-78, in "Willie Keeler" Biography File, National Baseball Library and Archive, Cooperstown, New York.

65. "Keeler's Feat of Not Fanning," in "Willie Keeler" Biography File, National Baseball Library and Archive, Cooperstown, New York. *Total Baseball* lists nine strikeouts for that year in 544 at bats, still a remarkably low number of strikeouts; Thorn et al., *Total Baseball*, 7th ed., 906.

66. "Keeler's Feat of Not Fanning," in "Willie Keeler" Biography File, National Baseball Library and Archive, Cooperstown, New York.

67. "Keeler Great Personality as Well as Wonderful Player," hand-marked 1923, in "Willie Keeler" Biography File, National Baseball Library and Archive, Cooperstown, New York.

68. Vivian Perlis, *Charles Ives Remembered: An Oral History* (New Haven, Conn.: Yale University Press, 1974), 150.

69. Perlis, *Charles Ives Remembered*, 221.

70. "Keeler's Feat of Not Fanning," in "Willie Keeler" Biography File, National Baseball Library and Archive, Cooperstown, New York.

71. A photostat of the first of these pages, with Ives's added date of 1906, appears in the Ives Collection as [f3053]; see Charles E. Ives, Papers (New Haven, Yale University Music Library Archival Collection).

72. David Wooldridge, *From the Steeples and Mountains: A Study of Charles Ives* (New York: Alfred A. Knopf, 1974), 126.

73. Feder, *Charles Ives: "My Father's Song,"* 190; and John Bowman and Joel Zoss, *Diamonds in the Rough: The Untold History of Baseball* (New York: Macmillan, 1989), 375.

74. James K. Skipper, Jr., profiles exactly thirty "Rubes" in his index; see Skipper, *Baseball Nicknames*, 370.

75. Dickson, s.v. "Rube," *The New Dickson Baseball Dictionary*.

76. Bowman and Zoss, *Diamonds in the Rough*, 375. Jan Swafford repeats this attribution; see Swafford, *Charles Ives: A Life with Music*, 455, n. 31.

77. Thorn et al., *Total Baseball*, 4th ed., 1698.

78. John Kirkpatrick, comp., *A Temporary Mimeographed Catalogue of the Music Manuscripts and Related Materials of Charles Edward Ives, 1874–1954* (New Haven, Conn.: Library of the Yale School of Music, 1960), 64; and Sinclair, *Descriptive Catalogue*, 183.

79. John Kirkpatrick, "Appendix 17: Poverty Flat, 1898–1908," in Charles E. Ives, *Memos*, ed. John Kirkpatrick (New York: W. W. Norton & Company, 1972), 265.

80. Fred Stein, s.v. "Marquard, Richard William 'Rube,'" in *Biographical Dictionary of American Sports: Baseball*, ed. David L. Porter (New York: Greenwood Press, 1987).

81. Letters from Gayle Sherwood to J. Peter Burkholder of 15 July and 31 May 1994, cited in Burkholder, *All Made of Tunes*, 473, n. 27.

82. Gerald E. Brennan, s.v. "Foster, Andrew 'Rube,'" in *Biographical Dictionary of American Sports: Baseball*, ed. David L. Porter (New York: Greenwood Press, 1987).

83. Skipper, s.v. "Foster, Andrew," in *Baseball Nicknames*.

84. Mike Shatzkin, ed., *The Ballplayers: Baseball's Ultimate Biographical Reference* (New York: William Morrow and Company, 1990), 670.

85. Unlabelled clipping, hand-marked 11-4-26, in "Rube Waddell" Biography File, National Baseball Library and Archive, Cooperstown, New York.

86. Connie Mack, "The One and Only Rube," *The Saturday Evening Post* (March 14, 1936): 12. Waddell's skills as a pitcher, his interest in sportsmanship in general, and perhaps his eccentricity are also reflected by an exhibit, at the Baseball Hall of Fame Museum in Cooperstown, New York, that displays two items of his memorabilia: the glove "worn by Waddell on July 4, 1905 when he defeated Cy Young, 4-2, in 20 innings at Boston" and Waddell's double-barrel shotgun.

87. Bowman and Zoss, *Diamonds in the Rough*, 336–37.

88. Harold Helfer, "The Rube and the Slicker," *American Legion Magazine* (October 1947): 69.

89. (Philadelphia) *Public Ledger*, May 9, 1915, 4, in "Rube Waddell" Biography File, National Baseball Library and Archive, Cooperstown, New York.

90. Thorn et al., *Total Baseball*, 7th ed., 281.

91. Charles E. Whitehead, *A Man and His Diamonds* (New York: Vantage Press, 1980).

92. Grantland Rice, "Setting the Pace," in "Rube Waddell" Biography File, National Baseball Library and Archive, Cooperstown, New York.

93. Thorn et al., *Total Baseball*, 4th ed., 1885.

94. Victor Lauriston, "Archie Has Own Plaque for Rube," in "Rube Waddell" Biography File, National Baseball Library and Archive, Cooperstown, New York.

95. George F. Will, "The First Michael Jordan," *Newsweek*, March 22, 1999, 61.

96. Will, "The First Michael Jordan," 61.

97. Skipper, *Baseball Nicknames*, xxi.

98. Skipper, *Baseball Nicknames*, xxi.

99. Skipper, *Baseball Nicknames*, xvi–xvii.

100. Burkholder discusses the importance of humor for connecting Ives's friends with his music in Burkholder, *Charles Ives: The Ideas behind the Music*, 90–91. Using baseball to forge the same kind of relationship with his friends is an extension of the motivation that Burkholder describes.

101. Burkholder, "Ives and the Four Musical Traditions," 18.

102. Rossiter, *Charles Ives and His America*, 172–73.

103. Rossiter, *Charles Ives and His America*, 173.

CHAPTER 6: BASEBALL TECHNIQUES—FROM SKETCH TO COMPOSITIONAL LANGUAGE

1. J. Peter Burkholder, *Charles Ives: The Ideas behind the Music* (New Haven, Conn.: Yale University Press, 1985), 90.

2. Charles Wilson Ward, "Charles Ives: The Relationship between Aesthetic Theories and Compositional Processes" (Ph.D. diss., University of Texas at Austin, 1974).

3. Charles E. Ives, *Memos*, ed. John Kirkpatrick (New York: W. W. Norton & Company, 1972), 64.

4. Ives, *Memos*, 61.

5. Jan Swafford, *Charles Ives: A Life with Music* (New York: W. W. Norton, 1996), 128.

6. James B. Sinclair, *A Descriptive Catalogue of the Music of Charles Ives* (New Haven, Conn.: Yale University Press, 1999).

7. The primary resource for information on Ives's "self-borrowing" is J. Peter Burkholder, *All Made of Tunes: Charles Ives and the Uses of Musical Borrowing* (New Haven, Conn.: Yale University Press, 1995).

8. Swafford, *Charles Ives: A Life with Music*, 178.

9. John Rinehart, "Ives' Compositional Idioms: An Investigation of Selected Short Compositions as Microcosms of His Musical Language" (Ph.D. diss., The Ohio State University, 1970).

10. Philip Lambert, *The Music of Charles Ives* (New Haven, Conn.: Yale University Press, 1997).

11. Thomas Dyer Winters, "Additive and Repetitive Techniques in the Experimental Works of Charles Ives" (Ph.D. diss., University of Pennsylvania, 1986).

12. Stuart Feder, *The Life of Charles Ives* (Cambridge: Cambridge University Press, 1999), 96.

13. John Rinehart discussed the spatial orientation of this piece in some detail; see Rinehart, "Ives' Compositional Idioms," 154–58.

14. Charles E. Ives, foreword, *The Unanswered Question* (New York: Southern Music Publishing, 1953), [2].

15. Stuart Feder likened the shape of the notes on paper to a question mark; see Stuart Feder, *Charles Ives: "My Father's Song": A Psychoanalytic Biography* (New Haven, Conn.: Yale University Press, 1992), 196.

16. Swafford, *Charles Ives: A Life with Music*, 268.

17. Swafford, *Charles Ives: A Life with Music*, 269.

18. [f2950]. Quoted in Sinclair, *A Descriptive Catalogue*, 143.

19. Swafford, *Charles Ives: A Life with Music*, 239–40.

20. H. Wiley Hitchcock, *Ives*, Oxford Studies of Composers, no. 14 (London: Oxford University Press, 1977), 61.

21. Swafford, *Charles Ives: A Life with Music*, 241. Swafford also presented a valuable analysis of this piece (pp. 349–65).

22. Thomas M. Brodhead, "Ives's *Celestial Railroad* and His Fourth Symphony," *American Music* 12 (1994): 395–407. The conventional view was that *The Celestial Railroad* derives from the Fourth Symphony, rather than the other way around; however, Brodhead convincingly established the opposite order for these pieces.

23. Brodhead, "Ives's *Celestial Railroad*," 389–94.

24. Feder, *The Life of Charles Ives*, 124.

25. This technique is related to Rinehart's "Scalar Athematicism"; see Rinehart, "Ives' Compositional Idioms," 116–24.

26. Ives, foreword, *The Unanswered Question*, [2].

27. The nonsynchronized accelerando technique is a more specific form of Rinehart's "numerical ordering of duration"; see Rinehart, "Ives' Compositional Idioms," 34–61.

28. Ward presents a beautiful interpretation of the music immediately following this passage; see Ward, "Charles Ives: The Relationship between Aesthetic Theories," 166–68.

29. Geoffrey Block listed this material as deriving from "1, 2, 3" and *Scherzo: Over the Pavements*, but all three of these pieces derive from the earlier sketch, as discussed in this chapter; see Geoffrey Block, *Ives: Concord Sonata: Piano Sonata No. 2 ("Concord, Mass., 1840–1860)*, Cambridge Music Handbooks, gen. ed. Julian Rushton (Cambridge: Cambridge University Press, 1996), 62.

30. Charles Ives, preface, "Hawthorne," Piano Sonata No. 2: *"Concord, Mass., 1840–1860,"* 2nd ed. (New York: Associated Music Publishers, 1947), 20.

31. The dating of this piece, like most of Ives's works, is problematic due to the condition of the manuscript sources. James Sinclair claimed that this five-movement sonata "was assembled or revised perhaps as late as 1919; [it] incorporates music composed 1901-09, according to Ives. Mvt iv [which contains the material derived from the baseball sketch] was probably the last new music to be added"; see Sinclair, *A Descriptive Catalogue*, 189. On the other hand, Ives listed the date of the fourth movement as 1903–1904 in a work list, which would date it before the *Rube* sketch; however, the actual date of this movement likely is 1909 or even later, well after the probable date of *Take-off #3: Rube Trying to Walk 2 to 3!!* (1906). John Kirkpatrick and Paul Echols posited a tentative date of 1909 for the first part of the fourth movement, where the material derived from the *Rube* sketch is located— and earlier for the second part; see John Kirkpatrick with Paul C. Echols, Work List, s.v. "Ives, Charles (Edward)," in *New Grove Dictionary of American Music*, ed.

H. Wiley Hitchcock and Stanley Sadie (New York: Macmillan Press, 1986). However, Burkholder reported that the first movement was sketched in 1907–1914, based on Gayle Sherwood's assessment of the handwriting, and if this fourth movement contains the last music to be added, as claimed by Sinclair, then it may have been composed even later; see Burkholder, *All Made of Tunes*, 187, 457, n. 59. Likewise, the fifth movement may have been composed later than the 1905–1908 dates offered by Kirkpatrick and Echols; see Kirkpatrick and Echols, Work List, s.v., "Ives, Charles (Edward)," in *New Grove Dictionary of American Music*. Finally, according to Sinclair, "mvmt v caused particular problems and was revised in 1914"; see Sinclair, *A Descriptive Catalogue*, 189.

32. Sinclair, *A Descriptive Catalogue*, 190.

33. Judith Tick earlier established the link between this material in the First Piano Sonata and the similar passage in *Over the Pavements*. She also proposed that this material stems from Ives's ragtime pieces composed between 1902 and 1904; see Judith Tick, "Ragtime and the Music of Charles Ives," *Current Musicology* 18 (1974): 106–7.

34. Sinclair, *A Descriptive Catalogue*, 213.

35. Sinclair, *A Descriptive Catalogue*, 214.

36. Burkholder, *All Made of Tunes*, 277.

37. James Sinclair, preface, *Study no. 23 for Piano* (Bryn Mawr, Pa.: Merion Music, 1990), [i].

38. Sinclair's listed date "(by the paper)"; see Sinclair, *A Descriptive Catalogue*, 213.

39. Larry Starr presented an interesting and fairly detailed analysis of this piece; see Larry Starr, *A Union of Diversities: Style in the Music of Charles Ives* (New York: Schirmer Books, 1992), 43–48.

40. Sinclair, *A Descriptive Catalogue*, 178.

41. This second section probably should be divided into two different sections based on tempo (mm. 32–65, 66–80). For the purposes of this discussion, these two sections will be considered as a single unit due to the repetition scheme inherent in the piece. For more information on the intricate rhythmic relationships explored in this section, see Rinehart, "Ives' Compositional Idioms," 99–106.

42. For a full discussion of the serial aspects of this piece, see Rinehart, "Ives' Compositional Idioms," 44–48, 91–93.

43. Rinehart, "Ives' Compositional Idioms," 211.

44. Ives, *Memos*, 62 (Kirkpatrick's bracketed insertion).

45. Ives, *Memos*, 97.

46. Feder, *Charles Ives: "My Father's Song,"* 189. C.P.W. stands for Central Park West; D.D. for Decoration Day.

47. Connie Mack, "The One and Only Rube," *The Saturday Evening Post* (March 14, 1936): 106.

48. According to Burkholder, even Ives's monumental but unfinished *Universe Symphony* draws compositional techniques from *All the Way Around and Back* and other pieces; see J. Peter Burkholder, "Ives Today," in *Ives Studies*, ed. Philip Lambert (Cambridge: Cambridge University Press, 1997), 272.

Bibliography

Adams, Franklin P. "Baseball's Sad Lexicon." *New York Evening Mail*, July 1910. Reprint, *In Other Words* by Franklin P. Adams, 62. Garden City, N.Y.: Doubleday, Page & Company, 1912. Modern reprint, *Baseball: A Literary Anthology*, edited by Nicholas Dawidoff, 20. New York: Library of America, 2002.

Altherr, Thomas L. "'A Place Leavel Enough to Play Ball': Baseball and Baseball-Type Games in the Colonial Era, Revolutionary War, and Early American Republic." *Nine* 8, no. 2 (2000): 15–49.

Altherr, Tom, and Dave Block. "More Nails in Old Abner's Coffin: New Discoveries of Pre-1839 Baseball." Paper presented at the Fifteenth Cooperstown Symposium on Baseball and American Culture, Cooperstown, New York, June 11–13, 2003.

Ammer, Christine. *Southpaws & Sunday Punches and Other Sporting Expressions*. New York: Plume/Penguin Books, 1993.

Bailey, James Montgomery. *History of Danbury, Conn.: 1684–1896*. From notes and manuscript left by the author, compiled with additions by Susan Benedict Hill. New York: Burr Printing House, 1896.

Baron, Carol K. "Dating Charles Ives's Music: Facts and Fictions." *Perspectives of New Music* 28 (1990): 20–56.

———. "Meaning in the Music of Charles Ives." In *Metaphor: A Musical Dimension*, edited by Jamie C. Kassler, general editor Margaret J. Kartomi, 37–50. Australian Studies in the History, Philosophy and Social Studies of Music, vol. 1. Sydney: Currency Press, 1991.

Barzun, Jacques. *God's Country and Mine: A Declaration of Love Spiced with a Few Harsh Words*. Boston: Little, Brown and Company, 1954.

Benson, Michael. *Ballparks of North America: A Comprehensive Historical Reference to Baseball Grounds, Yards and Stadiums, 1845 to Present*. Jefferson, N.C.: McFarland & Company, 1989.

Bernstein, Mark F. *Football: The Ivy League Origins of an American Obsession.* Philadelphia: University of Pennsylvania Press, 2001.

Block, David. *Baseball before We Knew It: A Search for the Roots of the Game.* Lincoln: University of Nebraska Press, 2005.

Block, Geoffrey. *Ives: Concord Sonata: Piano Sonata No. 2 ("Concord, Mass., 1840–1860).* Cambridge Music Handbooks, general editor Julian Rushton. Cambridge: Cambridge University Press, 1996.

Botstein, Leon. "Innovation and Nostalgia: Ives, Mahler, and the Origins of Twentieth-Century Modernism." In *Charles Ives and His World*, edited by J. Peter Burkholder, 35–74. Princeton, N.J.: Princeton University Press, 1996.

Bowman, John, and Joel Zoss. *Diamonds in the Rough: The Untold History of Baseball.* New York: Macmillan, 1989.

Brennan, Gerald E. s.v. "Foster, Andrew 'Rube.'" In *Biographical Dictionary of American Sports: Baseball*, edited by David L. Porter. New York: Greenwood Press, 1987.

Brodhead, Thomas M. "Ives's *Celestial Railroad* and His Fourth Symphony." *American Music* 12 (1994): 389–424.

Brokaw, Tom. "The Front Lines to the Backyard." In *Baseball as America: Seeing Ourselves through Our National Game*, edited by John Odell, 63. Washington, D.C.: National Geographic, 2002.

Burkholder, J. Peter. *All Made of Tunes: Charles Ives and the Uses of Musical Borrowing.* New Haven, Conn.: Yale University Press, 1995.

———. *Charles Ives: The Ideas behind the Music.* New Haven, Conn.: Yale University Press, 1985.

———. "The Critique of Tonality in the Early Experimental Music of Charles Ives." *Music Theory Spectrum* 12 (1990): 203–23.

———. "Ives and the Four Musical Traditions." In *Charles Ives and His World*, edited by J. Peter Burkholder, 3–34. Princeton, N.J.: Princeton University Press, 1996.

———. "Ives and the Nineteenth-Century European Tradition." In *Charles Ives and the Classical Tradition*, edited by Geoffrey Block and J. Peter Burkholder, 11–33. New Haven, Conn.: Yale University Press, 1996.

———. "Ives and Yale: The Enduring Influence of a College Experience." *College Music Symposium* 39 (1999): 27–42.

———. "Ives Today." In *Ives Studies*, edited by Philip Lambert, 263–90. Cambridge: Cambridge University Press, 1997.

"Charles E. Ives' Concert and New Cantata, 'The Celestial Country.'" *Musical Courier* 44, no. 17 (April 23, 1902): 34. Reprint, "Selected Reviews 1888–1951," in *Charles Ives and His World*, compiled by Geoffrey Block and edited by J. Peter Burkholder, 276–77. Princeton, N.J.: Princeton University Press, 1996.

Coffin, Tristram Potter. *The Old Ball Game: Baseball in Folklore and Fiction.* New York: Herder and Herder, 1971.

Cowell, Henry, and Sidney Cowell. *Charles Ives and His Music.* New York: Oxford University Press, 1955. Reprint, 1969.

Danbury Evening News. April 21, 1890–May 13, 1895.

The Danbury News. July 22, 1885–May 21, 1890.

Devlin, William E. *We Crown Them All: An Illustrated History of Danbury.* Sponsored by the Danbury Scott-Fanton Museum and Historical Society. Woodland Hills, Calif.: Windsor Publications, 1984.

Dickson, Paul. *The New Dickson Baseball Dictionary: A Cyclopedic Reference to More Than 7,000 Words, Names, Phrases, and Slang Expressions That Define the Game, Its Heritage, Culture, and Variation.* San Diego, Calif.: Harcourt Brace & Company, 1999.

The Dime Base-Ball Player For 1881: Containing the Revised Code of Playing Rules Applicable to the Professional, Amateur and College Clubs of the Country for 1881, Together with Review of the Season's Work in the Professional, College and Amateur Arenas, with the Batting and Pitching Averages and the College Club Statistics, also the League Club Records for 1880. New York: Beadle and Adams, 1881.

"Donlin, Mike." Biography File, National Baseball Library and Archive, Cooperstown, New York. (Individual items from this file are not cited separately in this bibliography except when the author is known.)

Echols, Paul C. "Editorial Note: 1979." In Charles E. Ives, *Sonata No. 1 for Piano,* [iv]. New York: Peer International, 1954. Reprint, 1990.

"Evers, Johnny." Biography File, National Baseball Library and Archive, Cooperstown, New York. (Individual items from this file are not cited separately in this bibliography except when the author is known.)

Feder, Stuart. "Charles and George Ives: The Veneration of Boyhood." In *Psychoanalytic Explorations in Music,* edited by Stuart Feder, Richard L. Karmel, and George H. Pollock, 115–76. Applied Psychoanalysis Series, Monograph 3, edited by Chicago Institute for Psychoanalysis, George H. Pollock, president. Madison, Conn.: International Universities Press, 1990.

———. *Charles Ives: "My Father's Song": A Psychoanalytic Biography.* New Haven, Conn.: Yale University Press, 1992.

———. *The Life of Charles Ives.* Cambridge: Cambridge University Press, 1999.

———. "The Nostalgia of Charles Ives: An Essay in Affects and Music." In *Psychoanalytic Explorations in Music,* edited by Stuart Feder, Richard L. Karmel, and George H. Pollock, 233–66. Applied Psychoanalysis Series, Monograph 3, edited by Chicago Institute for Psychoanalysis, George H. Pollock, president. Madison, Conn.: International Universities Press, 1990.

Feldman, Jay. "Sports Were Music to His Ears." *Sports Illustrated* 75, no. 15 (Oct. 7, 1991): 106.

Gabriel, Ronald L. s.v. "Keeler, William Henry 'Willie,' 'Wee Willie.'" In *Biographical Dictionary of American Sports: Baseball,* edited by David L. Porter. New York: Greenwood Press, 1987.

Gardner, James Isham, and William Butler Tyler, eds. *The Hopkinsonian,* vol. 2. New Haven Conn.: James Isham Gardner and William Butler Tyler, 1897.

Giebisch, Thomas. *Take-off als Kompositionsprinzip bei Charles Ives.* Volume 181 of *Kölner Beiträge zur Musikforschung,* edited by Klaus Wolfgang Niemöller. Kassel, Germany: Gustav Bosse, 1993.

Gilman, Lawrence. "Music: A Masterpiece of American Music Heard Here for the First Time," *New York Herald Tribune,* January 21, 1939, 9. Reprint, "Selected Reviews 1888–1951," in *Charles Ives and His World,* compiled by Geoffrey Block and edited by J. Peter Burkholder, 316–21. Princeton, N.J.: Princeton University Press, 1996.

Goodwin, Doris Kearns. *Wait Till Next Year: A Memoir.* New York: Simon & Schuster, 1997.

Hall, Donald. Quoted in Geoffrey C. Ward, *Baseball: An Illustrated History*, based on a documentary film script by Geoffrey C. Ward and Ken Burns, xviii. New York: Alfred A. Knopf, 1994.

Helfer, Harold. "The Rube and the Slicker." *American Legion Magazine* (October 1947): 69.

Henderson, Clayton W. *The Charles Ives Tunebook*. Bibliographies in American Music, no. 14, edited by James R. Heintze. Published for the College Music Society. Warren, Mich.: Harmonie Park Press, 1990.

Hitchcock, H. Wiley. *Ives*. Oxford Studies of Composers, no. 14. London: Oxford University Press, 1977.

Honig, Donald. *Baseball's 10 Greatest Teams*. New York: Macmillan Publishing, 1982.

Howell, Colin D. *Northern Sandlots: A Social History of Maritime Baseball*. Toronto: University of Toronto Press, 1995.

Ives, Charles E. *Essays before a Sonata, The Majority, and Other Writings*, edited by Howard Boatwright. New York: W. W. Norton, 1970.

———. Foreword. *The Unanswered Question*, [2]. New York: Southern Music Publishing, 1953.

———. "Ives's Program Note." Quoted in *The Fourth of July: Third Movement of A Symphony: New England Holidays*, edited by Wayne D. Shirley, vii. Charles Ives Society Critical Edition. Milwaukee, Wis.: Associated Music Publishers, 1992.

———. *Memos*, edited by John Kirkpatrick. New York: W. W. Norton & Company, 1972.

———. Papers. New Haven, Yale University Music Library Archival Collection.

———. Postface. *114 Songs*. Redding, Conn.: Author, 1922. Reprint, New York: Peer International, Associated Music Publishers, and Theodore Presser, 1975, [261–62].

———. Preface to "Hawthorne," Piano Sonata no. 2: *"Concord, Mass., 1840–1860,"* 2nd ed. New York: Associated Music Publishers, 1947.

———. *Some South-Paw Pitching*, edited by Henry Cowell. In Charles E. Ives, *Five Piano Pieces*, 28–32. Bryn Mawr, Pa.: Mercury Music Corporation, 1949.

James, Bill. *The New Bill James Historical Baseball Abstract*. New York: The Free Press, 2001.

Johnson, Timothy A. "Chromatic Quotations of Diatonic Tunes in Songs of Charles Ives." *Music Theory Spectrum* 18 (1996): 236–61.

"Keeler, Willie." Biography File, National Baseball Library and Archive, Cooperstown, New York. (Individual items from this file are not cited separately in this bibliography except when the author is known.)

Kimmel, Michael S. "Baseball and the Reconstitution of American Masculinity, 1880–1920." In *Cooperstown Symposium on Baseball and the American Culture (1989)*, edited by Alvin L. Hall, 281–97. Westport, Conn.: Meckler in association with the State University of New York College at Oneonta, 1991.

Kirkpatrick, John. "Appendix 13: George Edward Ives (1845–1894) and His Family." In Charles E. Ives, *Memos*, edited by John Kirkpatrick, 245–49. New York: W. W. Norton & Company, 1972.

———. "Appendix 17: Poverty Flat, 1898–1908." In Charles E. Ives, *Memos*, edited by John Kirkpatrick, 262–67. New York: W. W. Norton & Company, 1972.

————. s.v. "Ives, Charles (Edward)." In *New Grove Dictionary of American Music,* edited by H. Wiley Hitchcock and Stanley Sadie. New York: Macmillan Press, 1986.

————. "Editor's Notes." In Charles Ives, *Study No. 21: Some South-Paw Pitching! for Piano,* 7-12. Bryn Mawr, Pa.: Mercury Music Corporation, 1975.

Kirkpatrick, John, comp. *A Temporary Mimeographed Catalogue of the Music Manuscripts and Related Materials of Charles Edward Ives, 1874–1954.* New Haven, Conn.: Library of the Yale School of Music, 1960.

Kirkpatrick, John, ed. *Memos,* by Charles E. Ives. New York: W. W. Norton & Company, 1972.

Kirkpatrick, John, with Paul C. Echols. Work List, s.v. "Ives, Charles (Edward)." In *New Grove Dictionary of American Music,* edited by H. Wiley Hitchcock and Stanley Sadie. New York: Macmillan Press, 1986.

Koppett, Leonard. *Koppett's Concise History of Major League Baseball.* Philadelphia: Temple University Press, 1998.

Lambert, J. Philip. "Interval Cycles as Compositional Resources in the Music of Charles Ives." *Music Theory Spectrum* 12 (1990): 43–82.

————. "Ives and Berg: 'Normative' Procedures and Post-Tonal Alternatives." In *Charles Ives and the Classical Tradition,* edited by Geoffrey Block and J. Peter Burkholder, 105–30. New Haven, Conn.: Yale University Press, 1996.

————. *The Music of Charles Ives.* New Haven, Conn.: Yale University Press, 1997.

Lauriston, Victor. "Archie Has Own Plaque for Rube." In "Rube Waddell." Biography File, National Baseball Library and Archive, Cooperstown, New York.

Lieb, Frederick G. "McGraw Calls Willie Keeler Baseball's Smartest Batsman." In "Willie Keeler." Biography File, National Baseball Library and Archive, Cooperstown, New York.

Mack, Connie. "The One and Only Rube." *The Saturday Evening Post* 208 (March 14, 1936): 12–13, 106.

Magee, Noel H. "The Short Piano Works of Charles Ives." M.M. thesis, Indiana University, 1966.

Mandel, Alan. Liner notes. *Charles Ives: The Complete Works for Piano.* Alan Mandel, Piano. Desto Records DST-6458-6461.

Maske, Ulrich. "Charles Ives in seiner Kammermusik für drei bis sechs Instrumente." Regensburg, Germany: Gustav Bosse Verlag, 1971.

McHale, Marty. "A Closeup of Mike Donlin." In "Mike Donlin." Biography File, National Baseball Library and Archive, Cooperstown, New York.

Metzer, David. "'We Boys': Childhood in the Music of Charles Ives." *19th Century Music* 21 (1997): 77–95.

Millen, Patricia. *From Pastime to Passion: Baseball and the Civil War.* Bowie, Md.: Heritage Books, 2001.

Mrozek, Donald J. *Sport and American Mentality, 1880–1910.* Knoxville: University of Tennessee Press, 1983.

Myrick, Julian. "What the Business Owes to Charles E. Ives." *Eastern Underwriter,* September 19, 1930. Reprint, Charles E. Ives, *Memos,* edited by John Kirkpatrick, 272–73. New York: W. W. Norton & Company, 1972.

Nasaw, David. *Going Out: The Rise and Fall of Public Amusements.* New York: Basic Books, 1993.

Okkonen, Marc. *Baseball Memories: 1900–1909.* New York: Sterling Publishing, 1992.

Perlis, Vivian. *Charles Ives Remembered: An Oral History.* New Haven, Conn.: Yale University Press, 1974.

Perry, Rosalie Sandra. *Charles Ives and the American Mind.* Kent, Ohio: Kent State University Press, 1974.

Prager, Joshua Harris. "Inside Baseball: Giants' 1951 Comeback, the Sport's Greatest, Wasn't All It Seemed—Miracle Ended with 'The Shot Heard Round the World'; It Began with a Buzzer—'Papa's' Collapsible Legacy," *Wall Street Journal* (January 31, 2001), A1.

Randall, Denny. E-mail communication to author, August 25, 2003.

Rice, Grantland. "Game Called" *New York Sun,* August 17, 1948. Reprint, "Babe Ruth Dies (1948)," In *Middle Innings: A Documentary History of Baseball, 1900–1948,* compiled and edited by Dean A. Sullivan, 218. Lincoln: University of Nebraska Press, 1998.

———. "Setting the Pace: The Duffer Speaks Again—Choosing the Best Combination Pitcher—Connie Mack Casts Vote for Waddell." In "Rude Waddell." Biography File, National Baseball Library and Archive, Cooperstown, New York.

Rice, Thomas S. "Willie Keeler, Greatest of Place Hitters, Leaves behind a Brilliant Record." In "Willie Keeler." Biography File, National Baseball Library and Archive, Cooperstown, New York.

Riess, Steven A. "Sport and Middle-Class Masculinity." In *The New American Sport History: Recent Approaches and Perspectives,* edited by S. W. Pope, 173–97. Urbana: University of Illinois Press, 1997.

Rinehart, John. "Ives' Compositional Idioms: An Investigation of Selected Short Compositions as Microcosms of His Musical Language." Ph.D. diss., The Ohio State University, 1970.

Ritter, Lawrence S. "Ladies and Gentlemen, Presenting Marty McHale." In *The Armchair Book of Baseball,* edited by John Thorn, illustrations by James Stevenson, foreword by Peter V. Ueberroth, 253–61. New York: Scribner's Sons, 1985.

Ritter, Lawrence, and Donald Honig. *The Image of Their Greatness: An Illustrated History of Baseball from 1900 to the Present.* New York: Crown Publishers, 1979.

Roosevelt, Franklin Delano. Letter to Commissioner Landis, January 15, 1942. Original held in archives of The National Baseball Library and Hall of Fame. Reprint, Geoffrey C. Ward, *Baseball: An Illustrated History,* based on a documentary film script by Geoffrey C. Ward and Ken Burns, 276–78. New York: Alfred A. Knopf, 1994.

Rossiter, Frank R. *Charles Ives and His America.* New York: Liveright, 1975.

Seymour, Harold. *Baseball: The Early Years.* New York: Oxford University Press 1960.

———. *Baseball: The People's Game.* New York: Oxford University Press, 1990.

Shatzkin, Mike, ed. *The Ballplayers: Baseball's Ultimate Biographical Reference.* New York: William Morrow and Company, 1990.

Shieber, Tom, and Ted Spencer. "Spalding's Commission." In *Baseball as America: Seeing Ourselves through Our National Game,* edited by John Odell, 41–43. Washington, D.C.: National Geographic, 2002.

Shirley, Wayne D. Preface. In Charles E. Ives, *The Fourth of July: Third Movement of A Symphony: New England Holidays,* iii–vii. Charles Ives Society Critical Edition. Milwaukee, Wis.: Associated Music Publishers, 1992.

Sinclair, James B. *A Descriptive Catalogue of the Music of Charles Ives*. New Haven, Conn.: Yale University Press, 1999.

———. Preface. *Study no. 23 for Piano*, [3]. Bryn Mawr, Pa.: Merion Music, 1990.

Skipper, Jr., James K. *Baseball Nicknames: A Dictionary of Origins and Meanings*. Jefferson, N.C.: McFarland & Company, 1992.

Sokolik, Maggi E. "Out of Left Field: Baseball and American Idiom." In *Cooperstown Symposium on Baseball and the American Culture (1989)*, edited by Alvin L. Hall, 85–99. Westport, Conn.: Meckler, in association with The State University of New York College at Oneonta, 1991.

Solomon, Maynard. "Charles Ives: Some Questions of Veracity." *Journal of the American Musicological Society* 40 (1987): 443–50.

Spalding, Albert G. *America's National Game: Historic Facts Concerning the Beginning, Evolution, Development and Popularity of Base Ball, with Personal Reminiscences of Its Vicissitudes, Its Victories and Its Votaries*. New York: American Sports Publishing Company, 1911.

Sporting Life. January 14, 1885. Cited in Paul Dickson, *The New Dickson Baseball Dictionary: A Cyclopedic Reference to More Than 7,000 Words, Names, Phrases, and Slang Expressions That Define the Game, Its Heritage, Culture, and Variation* (San Diego: Harcourt Brace & Company, 1999), s.v. "Southpaw."

Sporting Life. March 16–April 27, 1907.

Starr, Larry. *A Union of Diversities: Style in the Music of Charles Ives*. New York: Schirmer Books, 1992.

Stein, Fred. s.v. "Marquard, Richard William 'Rube.'" In *Biographical Dictionary of American Sports: Baseball*, edited by David L. Porter. New York: Greenwood Press, 1987.

Story, Ronald. "The Country of the Young: The Meaning of Baseball in Early American Culture." In *Cooperstown Symposium on Baseball and the American Culture (1989)*, edited by Alvin L. Hall, 324–42. Westport, Conn.: Meckler in association with the State University of New York College at Oneonta, 1991.

Suehsdorf, A. D. s.v. "Donlin, Michael Joseph 'Mike,' 'Turkey Mike.'" In *Biographical Dictionary of American Sports: Baseball*, edited by David L. Porter. New York: Greenwood Press, 1987.

Swafford, Jan. *Charles Ives: A Life with Music*. New York: W. W. Norton, 1996.

Thayer, Ernest. *Casey at the Bat*. 1888. Reprint, illustrated by Barry Moser, afterword by Donald Hall. Boston: D. R. Godine, 1988.

Thorn, John, and Peter Palmer with Michael Gershman, eds., and David Pietrusza, managing ed. *Total Baseball: The Official Encyclopedia of Major League Baseball*, 4th ed. New York: Viking, 1995.

Thorn, John, Pete Palmer, Michael Gershman, and David Pietrusza, eds. *Total Baseball: The Official Encyclopedia of Major League Baseball*, 5th ed. New York: Viking Penguin, 1997.

Thorn, John, Peter Palmer, and Michael Gershman, eds., with Matthew Silverman, Sean Lahman, and Greg Spira. *Total Baseball: The Official Encyclopedia of Major League Baseball*, 7th ed. Kingston, N.Y.: Total Sports Publishing, 2001.

Tick, Judith. "Charles Ives and Gender Ideology." In *Musicology and Difference: Gender and Sexuality in Music Scholarship*, edited by Ruth A. Solie, 83–106. Berkeley: University of California Press, 1993.

———. "Ragtime and the Music of Charles Ives." *Current Musicology* 18 (1974): 105–13.

Valenzi, Kathleen D., and Michael W. Hopps. *Champion of Sport: The Life of Walter Camp, 1859–1925*. Charlottesville, Va.: Howell Press, 1990.

"Waddell, Rube." Biography File, National Baseball Library and Archive, Cooperstown, New York. (Individual items from this file are not cited separately in this bibliography except when the author is known.)

Ward, Charles Wilson. "Charles Ives: The Relationship between Aesthetic Theories and Compositional Processes." Ph.D. diss., University of Texas at Austin, 1974.

Ward, Geoffrey C. *Baseball: An Illustrated History*. Based on a documentary film script by Geoffrey C. Ward and Ken Burns. New York: Alfred A. Knopf, 1994.

Ward, Keith. "Musical Idealism: A Study of the Aesthetics of Arnold Schoenberg and Charles Ives." D.M. diss., Northwestern University, 1985.

White, G. Edward. *Creating the National Pastime: Baseball Transforms Itself 1903–1953*. Princeton, N.J.: Princeton University Press, 1996.

Whitehead, Charles E. *A Man and His Diamonds*. New York: Vantage Press, 1980.

Whitman, Walt. "Baseball Is Our Game." In *Baseball as America: Seeing Ourselves through Our National Game*, edited by John Odell, 37. Washington, D.C.: National Geographic, 2002.

Will, George F. "The First Michael Jordan." *Newsweek* (March 22, 1999): 61.

Winters, Thomas Dyer. "Additive and Repetitive Techniques in the Experimental Works of Charles Ives." Ph.D. diss., University of Pennsylvania, 1986.

Wooldridge, David. *From the Steeples and Mountains: A Study of Charles Ives*. New York: Alfred A. Knopf, 1974.

Yale Daily News. February 16–March 15, 1895. Cited in Frank R. Rossiter, *Charles Ives and His America*, 335, n. 84. New York: Liveright, 1975.

Index

Works by Charles Ives are indexed alphabetically by title under the composer's name.

About the Author

Timothy A. Johnson teaches music theory at Ithaca College in Ithaca, New York. He received the Ph.D. in music theory from the University at Buffalo in 1991. He also holds the M.M. in music composition (University of Connecticut) and the B.M. in theory-composition (University of Massachusetts—Lowell). His research has focused on the songs of Charles Ives, minimalist music, diatonic theory, and the music of John Adams (including the first dissertation written about this enormously successful contemporary composer). In addition, Johnson has published articles or presented papers in the areas of the history of music theory, twelve-tone theory, music technology, and theory pedagogy. His articles have appeared in the *Journal of Music Theory*, *Musical Quarterly*, *Music Theory Spectrum*, *Theoria*, and *Music Theory Online*. He has given numerous presentations at a variety of conferences, including the Society for Music Theory, the Society for American Music, the American Mathematical Association, and the Cooperstown Symposium on Baseball and American Culture at the National Baseball Hall of Fame. A previous book of his, *Foundations of Diatonic Theory: A Mathematically Based Approach to Music Fundamentals* (Emeryville, Calif.: Key College Publishing, 2003), provides an introductory-level approach to diatonic set theory and is suitable for classroom use or self-study by musicians and non-musicians alike.